Contemporary Ju

M000306335

The Society of Analytical Psychology was founded in London in 1946 with the support of Jung himself. With its distinctive pluralistic approach to the key issues in analytical and psychotherapeutic practice the SAP has made a significant contribution to the history of psychotherapy.

Contemporary Jungian Analysis brings together essays by leading practitioners in the SAP today. Students and teachers of analysis and psychotherapy will find within it a stimulating and fresh approach to many of the issues they face in training. The different perspectives offered on topics such as gender, infancy, transference, popular culture, dreams and active imagination, spiritual issues and training, constitute not only a rich resource but also a catalyst for ongoing debate in many centres round the world.

Ian Alister is a Jungian analyst in full-time private practice in Cambridge and London. He supervises widely and teaches at the Society of Analytical Psychology and at the University of Cork.

Christopher Hauke is a Jungian analyst in private practice in Greenwich. He is also Lecturer for the MA in Applied Psychoanalytic Theory at Goldsmiths College, University of London, at the Laban Centre for Movement and Dance and at the Centre for Psychoanalytic Studies, University of Kent at Canterbury.

The members of the Publications Committee of the SAP who contributed to the preliminary editing and production of this book are: Mary Addenbrooke, Ian Alister, Rosemary Gordon, Christopher Hauke, Jane Haynes, Peggy Jones, Catherine Kaplinsky, Veronika Marlow, Hazel Robinson, Fiona Ross, Andrew Samuels, Jean Thomson, Bob Withers and Marcus West.

Contemporary Jungian Analysis

Post-Jungian Perspectives from the
Society of Analytical Psychology

Edited by Ian Alister and
Christopher Hauke

London and New York

First published 1998
by Routledge
11 New Fetter Lane, London EC4P 4EE

Simultaneously published in the USA and Canada
by Routledge
29 West 35th Street, New York, NY 10001

Typeset in Times by
J&L Composition Ltd, Filey, North Yorkshire
Printed and bound in Great Britain by
T.J. International Ltd, Padstow, Cornwall

British Library Cataloguing in Publication Data
A catalogue record for this book is available
from the British Library

Library of Congress Cataloguing in Publication Data
Contemporary Jungian analysis: post-Jungian perspectives from the
   Society of Analytical Psychology/edited by Ian Alister and Christopher Hauke.
   Includes bibliographical references and index.
   1. Jungian psychology. 2. Psychoanalysis. 3. Jung, C. G. (Carl
   Gustav), 1875–1961. I. Alister, Ian. II. Hauke,
   Christopher. III. Society of Analytical Psychology.
   BF173.C568 1998
   150.19'54–dc21

ISBN 0 415 14165 6 (hbk)
ISBN 0 415 14166 4 (pbk)

Contents

Contributors

All writers are Jungian analysts trained at the Society of Analytical Psychology.

Mary Addenbrooke is in private practice in West Sussex and is the director of the Volunteer Alchohol Counsellors' Training Scheme for the Mid-Sussex NHS Trust. At the University of Essex she is researching psychological aspects of recovery from addiction to chemical substances and has published papers on substance abuse and on the creative potential of play and regression in analytic training.

Ian Alister is in full-time private practice in Cambridge and London. He teaches analytical psychology at the SAP and at the University of Cork, and is review editor of the *Journal of Analytical Psychology*. He also supervises widely and is a training supervisor in psychoanalytic psychotherapy for the Westminster Pastoral Foundation.

James Astor is a training analyst in private practice in West London and a member of the Association of Child Psychotherapists. His most recent publication is *Michael Fordham – Innovations in Analytical Psychology* (1995) published by Routledge.

Wendy Bratherton is an analytical psychologist working mainly in private practice in Cambridge. She also works as a therapist in a school, teaches an infant observation seminar and is actively involved in organising analytic workshops and talks. She manages a complementary medicine practice and is an accomplished ceramicist.

Clive Britten is an assistant director of the C.G. Jung Clinic. He is also a child psychiatrist and has written about children with pervasive refusal, group therapy for children with eating disorders and talking to children about death and dying.

Geoff Brown is Consultant Adolescent Psychiatrist at St Andrew's Hospital, Northampton, works with severely disturbed adolescents in inpatient settings and has an interest in the impact of child abuse on maturation. He is a director of the C.G. Jung Clinic and the author of a chapter in *Incest Fantasies and Self-Destructive Acts* edited by Mara Sidoli and G. Bovensiepen (1995).

Margaret Clark is a training therapist of the Institute of Psychotherapy and Counselling (WPF). She works in private practice in South London.

Warren Colman worked for fifteen years at the Tavistock Marital Studies Institute as a practitioner and trainer in marital psychotherapy. He has published numerous articles on couple relationships, sexuality and gender. He now works as an analyst in private practice in St Albans, Hertfordshire.

Catherine Crowther is a Professional Member in private practice in London. She also works in the Maudsley Hospital Psychotherapy Unit and has written papers on eating disorders and on a psychoanalytic perspective on family therapy.

Jenny Duckham qualified as a doctor specialising in hospital medicine and general practice. She is a group analytic psychotherapist and ex-Coordinator of Training at the Institute of Group Analysis (London). She is currently assistant to the Director of the C.G. Jung Clinic and works in private practice with individuals and groups.

Robert Fenton is a training analyst, a former Chair of the Professional Development Committee and former Director of Training at the SAP. He has previously published on the fear of ordinariness and on talionic responses in the countertransference.

Rosemary Gordon has a Ph.D. in psychology with anthropology, University of London, and is a training analyst of the SAP and the British Association of Psychotherapists. She has been the Chair of the SAP, the Editor of the *Journal of Analytical Psychology* and is the author of many papers on analytical psychology. Her books include *Dying and Creating: A Search for Meaning* and *Bridges: Metaphor for Psychic Processes* (1993). She is currently Consulting Editor for the *Journal of Analytical Psychology* and works in private practice in London.

Christopher Hauke is Lecturer at Goldsmiths College, University of London, in charge of the MA in Applied Psychoanalytic Theory. He also teaches Jungian studies and psychoanalytic psychotherapy at the University of Kent, Centre for Psychoanalytic Studies, the Laban Centre for Movement and Dance, and on various psychotherapy trainings. He has published in Britain and the United States and is writing a book on Jung and the Postmodern, also for Routledge. He is an analyst in private practice with adults and families in Greenwich, South London.

Jane Haynes is a Professional Member and works in London in full-time private practice. She is co-editor of *The Place of Dialogue in the Analytic Setting: The Selected Papers of Louis Zinkin*, to be published in Spring 1998.

Peggy Jones is a Professional Member in private practice. She has published in the *British Journal of Psychotherapy* and is interested in healing in its widest sense – including traditional practices amongst indigenous people.

Catherine Kaplinsky is a Professional Member in private practice in Sussex and also works in the Adolescent Centre at Ticehurst Hospital. She is an assistant editor of *The Journal of Analytical Psychology* in which she has published.

Jane Knight became a member in 1975 and is now a training analyst supervising trainees who take the course for the analysis of adults. From 1991–97 she was Director of Training.

Jean Knox trained as a medical doctor and is a Professional Member in private practice in Oxford. She is author of papers on alcohol misuse and internal objects and is currently involved in doctoral studies at the University of London, comparing psychodynamic and cognitive science models of the mind.

Veronika Marlow is a Supervisor/Consultant to the Student Counselling Services at the University of Warwick and works in private practice in West London.

Mel Marshak is a Professional Member of the SAP and a training analyst and supervisor at the Psychoanalytic Institute of Northern California. She is President of the Independent Society for Analytical Psychologists in the USA and an Emeritus Associate Professor, University of London. She is in private practice in California and is a writer, seminar leader, lecturer and supervisor to several American analytical training institutes.

Kathleen Newton is a training analyst in private practice in London. Her previous papers include 'Mediation of the image of infant–mother togetherness', 'Separation and pre-Oedipal guilt', 'The weapon and the wound, the archetypal and personal dimensions in "Answer to Job"'.

Roderick Peters is a Professional Member and a training therapist of the British Association of Psychotherapists. He is the author of *Living With Dreams* and a number of papers relating to the practice of analytical psychology.

Fred Plaut has been a training analyst of the Society and is now in private practice in Berlin. He is the author of many papers including 'What do you actually do?', 'Analysis: ritual without witnesses', 'Why people still want analysis' and the recent book *Analysis Analysed*. He co-authored the essential reference work *A Critical Dictionary of Jungian Analysis* (1986).

Sheila Powell is a past Chairman of SAP and training analyst. She is most interested in psychological development and the roots of creativity. Her major interests are in teaching and practice involving active imagination and she has also written on the subjects of Electra and Bluebeard.

Joseph Redfearn is a past Chairman and Director of Training of the SAP. He studied at Cambridge University and the Johns Hopkins Medical School and was analysed by Michael Fordham. Apart from numerous papers, his books include *My Self, My Many Selves* (1985) and *The Exploding Self* (1992).

Fiona Ross is a Professional Member working in private practice in South London and involved in teaching and research. She is a Chartered Psychologist and Associate Fellow of the British Psychological Society. She is concerned with developing an understanding of the psychological patterning associated with perverse states of mind. Another field of interest is textile art: she has studied and taught stitchery and design.

Andrew Samuels is Professor of Analytical Psychology at the University of Essex and a training analyst in private practice in London. He has published *Jung and the Post-Jungians* (1985), *A Critical Dictionary of Jungian Analysis* (1986), *The Father* (1986), *The Plural Psyche* (1989), *Psychopathology* (1989), and *The Political Psyche* (1993).

Jean Thomson is a Professional Member in private practice in London. She was formerly a member of the Senior Professional Staff, Tavistock Clinic Adolescent Department and Tutor in Student Counselling, London University Centre for Extra-Mural Studies. She is currently editor of *Saplink*, the newsletter of the SAP.

Jan Wiener is a Professional Member in private practice and in the National Health Service in London. She has published several papers on analytical psychology and is co-author of *Counselling and Psycho-therapy in Primary Health Care* to be published by Macmillan in 1998.

Preface

Andrew Samuels

The history of psychotherapy speaks of those places and times when relatively small groups of women and men created institutions that shifted the field. One thinks of the Vienna Psychoanalytic Society or the Psychology Club of Zürich or the Chicago Institute for Psychoanalysis in Kohut's heyday or the British Psycho-Analytical Society before, during and after the Controversial Discussions. These groupings, with all the advantages of cross-fertilisation and co-operation and all the stresses of internecine strife, have, perhaps, not been given their due in and of themselves.

The Society of Analytical Psychology in London, which was founded in 1946, deserves to be counted as a member of the list. Following Michael Fordham's pioneering work in marrying key psychoanalytic ideas with Jungian psychology, successive generations of members of the Society have produced a veritable wave of papers and books which have exerted an influence so far beyond the confines of London that geography (the 'London School') has had to be abandoned as an identification tag in favour of something much more general such as 'Developmental School' (Samuels, 1985).

The Developmental School attempted the linkage with contemporary psychoanalysis via a stress on the importance of early experience and on paying attention to the details of interaction in the analytical session ('transference–countertransference'). This is somewhat different from the approach of the Classical School which seeks on the whole to work in a way consistent with what is known about Jung's own methods of work. But this should not be understood as implying a static situation – there can be evolutions and movements within a broadly classical tradition as we find in many disciplines. A third school of Jungian psychology, the Archetypal School, is perhaps not now strictly a clinical group at all. Its principal writers valorise Jung's key concept of the archetype, using it as a base from which to explore the mythic and depth dimensions of the world via an engagement with its particular imagery.

There is a good deal of overlap between these schools and it is possible to utilise the categorisation in a more metaphorical way – to see the schools as co-existing in the mind of any post-Jungian analyst. We should bear in mind that there are now more than 2,000 Jungian analysts worldwide in twenty-eight countries and probably an additional 5,000 psychotherapists and counsellors either Jungian in orientation or heavily influenced by analytical psychology. And the debates between the schools have been going on explicitly for fifty years and implicitly for perhaps seventy-five. Many practitioners will have by now internalised the debates themselves and could feel perfectly capable of functioning as either a Developmental or a Classical or an Archetypal analytical psychologist according to the needs of the individual patient. Or the analyst may regard himself as primarily Developmental, for example, but with a flourishing Classical component.

Returning to the Society of Analytical Psychology, this institution has commanded the respect of many individuals and organisations who do not usually take Jungian psychology too seriously. However, there has been an inevitable corresponding tendency to overlook the rich, pluralistic diversity of viewpoints within it. This book, by being organised so that more than one voice may be heard addressing many of the key issues in analytical and psychotherapeutic theory and practice, makes express and conscious use of the idea that there are different viewpoints and practices to be found in the Society.

The authors were asked to write chapters that indicated where they stood today. The book was not intended as a comprehensive or encyclopaedic offering but rather as something that many teachers of analysis and psychotherapy often say they would like to have in their possession: to start off a multi-layered and rewarding discussion within the training programme about the key issues with which the candidates are confronted.

But the book is more than a progressive aid to teaching. It sets out a stall on behalf of the SAP, demonstrating the creative energy in the Society today, and offering something from the world of Jungian analysis to the world of psychotherapy generally. For Jungian analysis and Jungian psychology are needed by those who would not want to fly under the exclusive banner 'Jungian'. Rather, as we have seen in countries such as Britain and the United States, Jungian 'tracks' have arisen in many generic or eclectic training programmes. Sometimes, a candidate will want to have exposure to Jungian supervision only for a part of her or his supervised caseload. Such candidates, and the growing number of practitioners (analysts, psychotherapists, counsellors) who fit this description, need a book of this kind.

Jungian analysis and psychotherapy are proving increasingly popular all over the world. There are many reasons for this and I would like to single out one. What clients and patients want, it seems to me, is something that combines the clinical rigour and groundedness of psychoanalysis and psychoanalytic psychotherapy with a world view that radiates Jung's wide culture and profound and compassionate humanity. The range of styles of working and thinking encompassed by the Society of Analytical Psychology all have such combinations in common: rigour *and* respect for imagination, honouring the body's drives *and* respect for spiritual experience, understanding the meaning of the past *and* decoding one's material for signs of how to live productively in the future.

So, without pretending that the book speaks for all of the Society's members, I believe that it captures the remarkable essence of what the Society stands for. It is going to become an indispensable resource and a stimulus to debate in many centres all over the world – and, in its diversity, I think readers will be able to discover a kind of underlying unity.

Reference

Samuels, A. (1985) *Jung and the Post-Jungians*, London and Boston: Routledge and Kegan Paul.

Introduction

Ian Alister and Christopher Hauke

Analytical psychology has never been a frozen or rigid body of theory and practice. It has always been developing as new insights and formulations become integrated with, or replace, the old. C.G. Jung himself revised and supplemented his own ideas throughout his life. Since his death in 1961, analytical psychology as a body of knowledge has extended beyond the Jungian analytic training institutions into the wider culture and, more recently, into university and college departments.

The Society of Analytical Psychology, the first Jungian training institution in Great Britain, has just celebrated its fiftieth anniversary (June 1996). The Society was founded, with Jung's encouragement, by Michael Fordham and Gerhard Adler. Fordham brought to Jung's psychology an element that had, by Jung's own admission, been poorly developed or absent – the investigation and modelling of the development of the human psyche from birth. Fordham introduced a way of theorising about psychological growth, which starts with the development of the ego and object relations in the earliest years, using a Jungian model of the psyche. In this way, an important aspect of analytical psychology was brought into relation with the parallel developments in psychoanalysis – especially those of Klein and other post-Freudians.

The influence of Fordham's ideas led to disagreements and in 1976, after much consternation and meetings aimed at preventing it, the Adler group broke away to form the Association of Jungian Analysts (Alternative Training). London holds three separate Jungian training organisations – AJA, the Independent Group of Analytical Psychologists (IGAP) and the Jungian section of the British Association of Psychotherapists. All belong to an umbrella group – the International Association of Analytical Psychology (IAAP), which holds a world congress every three years. The joint Chairs of Analytical Psychology at the University of Essex, England, are presently senior members of the SAP and IGAP. These painful splits and developments over the last twenty years reflect a tolerance for difference and plurality that is also fully represented in the Jungian attitude to the psyche.

A question often asked is: how 'Jungian' is the SAP since the split with Adler and the forming of the AJA? To what extent might Freudian and Kleinian ideas be outweighing Jungian ideas and practice in the modern SAP? There is both a political answer and a psychological answer to these questions and a brief comment will have to suffice here – the rest of the essays provide the fullest expression of the answer required. The present book shows twenty-eight individuals holding a range of ideas, rather like twenty-eight complexes in an individual staying in full *communication*. Although the elements are different, and sometimes even opposed, there feels no need to split but, on the contrary, the centre can hold a dynamic state that avoids equally an over-rational rigidity, on the one hand, or a private, over-subjective fluidity on the other. It demonstrates a quality that may be found in the modern SAP – that of the triumph of fluidity over rigidity – that both exemplifies the Jungian attitude to the psyche and the difference between the SAP in the early 1970s and now.

To take an example of this, attention to the transference relationship has been of central importance to the SAP since the 1960s. The difference, however, might be that whereas at the time of the split with Adler transference was seen as a *distinguishing factor* that brought the SAP more in line with psychoanalytic practice in the UK as opposed to a symbolic-mythological emphasis on interpretation stemming from the classical Zürich style, nowadays the emphasis on transference is regarded more flexibly as part of a range of clinical techniques. The essence of the Jungian spirit is the development of a capacity to hold the fullest range of different, even contradictory, positions within oneself without the need to split or deny these parts of the personality. So in analytic treatment, Jungian analysts feel enabled to work out of their own personalities, personal positions that also grow and change through interaction with the other, rather than using their professional positions to interpret from and apply views from any particular theoretical canon. Hence, Jungian emphasis on individual difference and individuation means that in the modern SAP transference issues may be more or less important in the work according to each analyst–patient pair. In other words, transference is clearly still conceived as an important element in the work but not necessarily as an *alternative* to other elements which may have been regarded as more 'Jungian'. It seems to be more a matter of the degree of emphasis rather than a positivistic inclusion or exclusion of Jung's and psychoanalytic ideas that characterises the modern SAP.

Equally, although modern SAP practice as illustrated in this book places a firm emphasis on images and symbols, most of the analysts do not embrace Hillman's Archetypal School position which emphasises the imaginal in all psychological phenomena. But this should not eclipse the fact that there are some SAP analysts who bring a strongly imaginal focus to their work. The difference seems to be the way this may be found *in combination* with more psychoanalytic views in the individual SAP analyst.

In this book it is our purpose to demonstrate the rich diversity of ideas within the SAP. As editors we encouraged all writers to speak from a personal position so that this collection of papers would convey a range of views at the SAP however divergent or homogeneous these turned out to be. What we received was far more diverse than we expected. Any suggestion of an SAP party line would have to be discarded. We also believe that the pluralistic capacity to understand and to use different 'psychologies' is essential in contemporary culture – a culture which has to come to terms with its own plurality and and diversity and engage with the difficult task of integrating difference without damaging it via hegemony.

The phenomena of a plurality of ideas and the individuality of writers in this volume can also be understood in terms of the Jungian concept of individuation. This is a life-long process of psychological differentiation that makes every human psyche unique. Within the SAP, ideas around 'development' of the ego are articulated together with fundamental Jungian theories of individuation involving the relationship of the ego and the self – and the relationship of both of these with environmental conditions encountered from birth and throughout life. Each of these papers is not only an expression that is individual, but an expression of each writer's *individuation* – a statement of where each analyst is on his or her personal journey.

This range of ideas reflects a further important aspect of Jungian thinking – the creative potential of *opposition*. Analytical psychology places an emphasis on seemingly irresolvable tensions in the psyche, such as that between the conscious and the unconscious mind itself. Out of the tension comes a third element that has the capacity to move development on. Jung called this the transcendent function because the usual hard-and-fast line between conscious and unconscious can be transcended. We hope that the reader's dialogue with some of these papers may encourage a similar process.

It is these three emphases – diverse development, individuation and the benefits of conflicting positions – that distinguish the contribution of the SAP to the field. They provide a quality that is pivotal to the creative life of the SAP and have found expression in the range of approaches presented in this book – they are the very energy that produced these pages.

At the start of this introduction, we emphasised the diversity of views held by the analysts at the SAP. However, as you read the book it will be clear how many things we all have in common. The most important of these is the individual and collective passion that we all have for the clinical and cultural work that is Jungian analysis.

Chapter I

Infancy and Childhood, Research and Therapy

Veronika Marlow describes two infant observations in great detail paying special attention to the emotions and fantasies which were stirred up in her. This living experience complements and illustrates James Astor's paper which provides a thorough description of Michael Fordham's researches into childhood and infancy. Before Fordham, Jungian psychology did not have a sound genetic base. The classical Jungian view saw the self as an organising centre of the personality which came into prominence in the second half of life, when the tasks of the ego had been accomplished. By contrast, Astor writes, Fordham showed how Jung's developmental concept of individuation was, in fact, a lifetime task made possible by the dynamic of the self, deintegration and reintegration. The practice of psychotherapy is illustrated by Astor with reference to mandala symbolism and to the children whose behaviour first suggested to Fordham a new way of viewing the child and individuation. Fordham's model was both structural and dynamic and kept a distinction between pathological development and normal development. It has underpinned the London School's integration of the clinical discoveries of psychoanalysis and analytical psychology. Marlow uses Fordham's paper 'On Not Knowing Beforehand' as the theoretical background for her infant observation, while Astor emphasises how the infant should be viewed as significantly influencing the environment in which he or she develops.

Fordham's Developments of Jung in the Context of Infancy and Childhood

The self in infancy and childhood

James Astor

Introduction

A number of doctors, psychiatrists, social workers and psychologists in the 1930s became interested in the ideas of Jung as they applied to children. Prominent among them was Michael Fordham, a Jungian psychiatrist and analyst who was to become the key figure in the establishment of analytical psychology in Great Britain (see Astor, 1995). Central to Jung's model of the mind is the idea that there is an individual self which is the totality of psyche and soma. Jung studied the symbols of the self but not primarily in childhood. He was interested in development, in what he called individuation and he worked most often with patients who came to him in the second half of their lives. Jung's view of child development, however, was that 'the things which have the most powerful effect upon children do not come from the conscious state of the parents but from their [the parents'] unconscious background' (1954: para. 84). Coupled with this forthright attribution of children's difficulties to their parents' unlived lives was his assertion based on the dreams of three- and four-year-old children that, 'The unconscious psyche of the child is truly limitless in extent and of incalculable age' (1954: para. 95).

Jung's ideas about the influence of the parents' unconscious and the limitlessness of the child's unconscious (primitive identity) held up the development of Jungian child analysis because they denied the existence of the child's own individual life. Further, Jung contrasted the tasks of the first half of life with the tasks of the second. In the first half of life the child had to adapt to the collective values of the society in which he or she lived. He wrote, 'before individuation can be taken for a goal, the educational aim of adaptation to the necessary minimum of collective standards must first be attained' (1960: para. 760).

Jung thought of the child as leaving parts of the psyche projected into the world. Later he saw the second half of life as being a gradual process of withdrawing these projections so that individuation became a sort of intense introversion. Jung's psychology was a purposeful one with aims and goals. The aim of childhood therefore seemed to be different from the aims of the mature adult. Fordham summarised the difference as follows:

> Individuation is conceived to involve a goal opposite to that of child-hood, when strengthening the ego is all important; the goal of indi-viduation appears, on the contrary, only when 'a suspension of the will results'.
>
> (Fordham, 1969: 24–5)

Fordham, who was working in child guidance and who was basing his research on Jung's theory of the archetypes, was discovering that there were processes active in childhood which were not describable exclusively in terms of ego development. He was encouraged in this view by another statement of Jung's that 'individuation is practically the same as the development of consciousness out of the original state of identity' (1960: para. 762).

Early researches

In the early stages of his researches Fordham did not dare to think that individuation occurred in childhood, although it was implied in his studies. The significant data which led to a change in his thinking began with observations of a one-year-old boy who was allowed by his parents to scribble on the walls of his nursery. He noticed that the scribbles became more and more circle-like and, as they did, the boy discovered 'as if by revelation' the word 'I'. The circles then stopped.

> The relation in time between the discovery of the circle and the discovery of 'I' suggests that the circle represented the matrix of the self out of which the ego arose. The self seemed to prepare the ground for its emergence, to create a temenos in which the event could occur.
>
> (Fordham, 1957: 134)

The circle seemed both to express the feeling of 'I', of completeness, of momentary recognition of his individual status, and a feeling of a bound-ary between himself and others, thus bringing together the ego and the self. This is because, according to Jung's discussions of mandala symbolism, there is always a centre to a developed mandala and this centre and its circumference represents the self. Its particular significance to Fordham was that the presence of the boundary to the self suggested that the infant and young child's world was not one of 'participation mystique', in which the environment and psyche were one. Fordham's observation of this child's 'action of the self' challenged Jung's idea that the child's uncon-scious psyche was limitless in extent.

The significance of Mandala symbolism

Jung discovered that mandalas were 'cryptograms concerning the state of the self'. The discovery was gradual. It began with him sketching in a notebook. He noticed the form of his drawings, which were circles, with a centre, framed by a square and with the whole area loosely divided into four. He saw that the variations in these drawings corresponded to the state of his self, 'In them I saw the self – that is my whole being actively at work' (Jung, 1963: 187). Later he was to discover that the mandala was an important Taoist symbol of wholeness. Combining these experiences with his work with patients, who in dreams produced a series of mandalas, Jung began to work out their significance, not just as a symbol of the self, but also as a way of understanding how his fragmented patients sought and found containment.

What then was the purpose of the boundary to the circle? Jung had implied that the function of the mandala was protective. Fordham had noticed in his work with children that they used the circles they drew, both as containers which could even include bad experiences, *and* as protective barriers against intra-psychic dangers. In Jung's examinations of mandala symbolism the centre, the contents which surrounded it, and the boundary circumference represented the self, which Jung differentiated from the ego. Fordham noticed with young children a relationship between this boundary, often a circle, and the beginnings of ego development. The boundary could therefore represent, he thought, a circumference to the ego (not the self) but also refer to the self, because of having emerged from it. This was because his investigations indicated that the danger to the child's ego came from within the psyche (for instance nightmares) and the purpose of the boundary was to protect the ego from these dangers. But the self had to have a boundary too, for without it differentiation of consciousness from unconsciousness could not occur since the ego emerged from and existed outside of the self.

The two-year-old with 'fits'

A case which made a deep impression on him was one in which a two-year-old girl was brought to him suffering from fits during which she became completely unconscious. She was clingy and would hardly let go of her mother – separating from her to come into the consulting room was at first too difficult. Gradually this changed, then one day she drew a circle and said 'me'. 'Almost at once her whole manner changed and she got down off her chair and played with some toys for several minutes' (Fordham, 1957: 149). She became more confident and Fordham started making mothers and babies under her direction, in plasticine, which she tore up and then ran out of the room to see if her actual mother was all right. Her mother reported to Fordham at this time that her daughter had a tremendous curiosity about babies. Whenever she saw a pram she had to investigate it. More and more she wanted to repair the plasticine mummies and babies and with this came greater independence from her mother. The fits stopped. Fordham understood this experience of anxiety, followed by the emergence of 'me' and the subsequent working through of the destruction and then reparation of mummy as being her way of working out the difficulty. This had arisen from her not being able to separate her attacks on her internal mummy from herself (expressed in her fits which indicated the absence of the protective function of the boundary to the self and her consequent regression into unconsciousness). Checking on mummy during sessions and on babies in prams was part of the process of separating fantasy and reality. For Fordham the gradual psychotherapeutic resolution guided by him but resolved by her was another instance of an ego development arising from actions of the self: the scribble became a circle, and she integrated the realisation that there was a boundary between fantasy and reality.

At about this time Kellogg, in San Francisco, published some of her research into the scribbles and drawings of nursery-age children. She noted that the children's pictures seemed to begin with rhythmic activities producing scribbles, out of which were abstracted definite shapes that were then combined to form pictures. Fordham thought of these pictures as examples of how, out of basic scribbles, emerged definite shapes and forms, as if the process was similar to how the ego developed out of the self.

The self

From these and numerous other observations Fordham was beginning to work out a theory of development which, while deriving from Jung's work, was very different from it. In particular Fordham was evolving a theory of the self which extended Jung's use of the concept to include eventually a primary state somewhat analogous to DNA but probably without its hereditary constituents, which gave rise to structures from interaction with the environment. This self, whose manifestations had archetypal form, existed outside of time and space and had mystical qualities similar to those described by William James (1902). Some of these manifestations would in time contribute to ego development. This original integrate, this primary self, combined the totality of conscious and unconscious systems and was an organising principle within the psyche. Fordham thought of it as continuous with the self Jung had described as significant for the integration of experience in the second half of life. The most important quality of Fordham's self was its dynamic.

Deintegration and reintegration

For this integrated self to come into relation to the environment it needed to deintegrate; he therefore called the dynamic of the self deintegration and reintegration. Parts of the self which deintegrated were called deintegrates. The most important deintegrate of the self was the ego. A deintegrate of the self would retain characteristics of wholeness. A deintegrative activity could be an instinctual act, such as the hungry baby's cry, that is, it would be contributing to the organism's biological adaptation, or it could be the creation of an image with potentially symbolic meaning. This primary self was an agency of the psyche which transcended opposites. Fordham, however, in imagining how the infant self would come into relation to the environment, described the process as follows:

> In essence, deintegration and reintegration describe a fluctuating state of learning in which the infant opens itself to new experiences and then withdraws in order to reintegrate and consolidate those experiences. During a deintegrative activity, the infant maintains continuity with the main body of the self (or its centre), while venturing into the external world to accumulate experience in motor action and sensory stimulation. . . .
>
> (Fordham, 1988: 64)

Ego development

When does deintegration begin? This is difficult to say. Fordham thought the behaviour of neonates such as kicking, thumb-sucking, responding to sounds and tastes, even swallowing amniotic fluid, observed *in utero* with new scanning techniques, were instances of deintegrative activity. Towards the end of his life he suggested (Fordham, 1993) that birth can be understood as a massive deintegrative experience. If, as usually happens, the baby is immediately given to the mother after birth, then reintegration would occur. As normal development proceeds subject and object become more distinct. It is frequently stimulated by the infant encountering difficulties in adapting to aspects of the environment – for instance, the shape of the nipple or teat. The discomfort which arises from these experiences Fordham thought of as constructive anxiety, since the infant's pain is in the service of its own development. This is the beginning of the individuation process and leads to what, in my view, is one of the most significant discoveries Fordham has made. This is that *the infant's self helps create the environment in which the infant develops,* whether by evocative actions which elicit an empathic response from its mother or by its own sensitivity to what its mother can bear. *Following on from this and inherent in Fordham's idea is that the reintegrative experiences lead to changes in the infant's way of experiencing 'the world' and consequently modifying his or her expectations of it.*

A major difference here from Jung's theorising was that Fordham did not think that the infant was mainly in touch with the collective unconscious, but that he or she was engaged in a dynamic interaction with another person. Important in this process was the mother's capacity to receive and make sense of the baby's communications in such a way that the baby took in from its mother's attention an experience of the world, usually that it was safe and could be understood.

By observing infants and mothers, one can perceive sequences of deintegration and reintegration – the feeding/sleeping sequence being the most obvious one. Infant observations are full of instances where the baby stirs, the mother responds, a feed is initiated, more or less successfully negotiated, then the baby dozes off. Originally Fordham thought that the fit between mother and baby had to be perfect. Later he realised that by not being perfect it set in motion actions of the self, arising from constructive anxiety, which stimulated ego development. Later he summarised his theory:

> According to the theory of the self that I was working on, deintegration leads to the formation of ego-nuclei round the oral, anal and genital zones especially. In the course of maturation they become linked to form a body image by a complex of processes. Though anatomically the zones are separated and serve distinct and different functions, this is not how a baby experiences them; the knowledge has to be acquired. At first it may be assumed experiences are registered in terms of pleasure and pain, very little located in space or time, and so similar experiences are treated as identical. Because of this, states of excitement in the zones are very much mixed up with each other; . . . The distinguishing of different kinds of excitement no doubt grows by repeated experience but they cannot be completely located and differentiated until a body image is formed; this involves perception and cathexis of the skin surface. . . .
>
> (Fordham, 1976: 218)

The self provided the underlying potential structure for the individual baby's response to the world. Later further structuring of the personality occurred with the development of the ego. Previously Jungians had thought of the self as an integrator of experience. Fordham has said that this is only half the story. The *self actively creates a dynamic system*. Babies do not react passively to their mothers, but engage in numerous actions of the self, eliciting from their mothers what they need. Fordham further understood the mother's function of containment as something the infant also in part created. There are two points here, the first that the baby is not passive but is active in the way it engages the mother's interest, and the second that its expectation that it will be met with an appropriate response contributes to that happening. Following on from this, as the infant takes in the experience of his mother, developments occur in his own internal world.

Self objects, splitting and deintegration

Additionally, what Fordham is proposing is that the baby, in its sensuous and physical being, has the capacity to generate the mental equivalent of physical experiences, rudimentary thoughts which can later be used for thinking as the ego develops. Thinking here becomes the equivalent of digestion. Out of this interaction, of baby and environment, the baby's developmental potential is realised. This is a route full of pain, which is full of meaning, and this is contained in the emotion. Our creative activities can be understood as the representation of these meanings.

To summarise what I have said so far: Fordham inferred there was an original self in infancy. He studied this at first through children's pictures, then reconstructively through analyses and finally through infant observations. The result of his study was that he found evidence for the self helping to create the environment in which the infant's emotional development took place. This is the most radical aspect of Fordham's model.

Fordham is implicitly rejecting Jung's idea that ego development consists of the coalescence of *islets of consciousness*, for this suggests that there is no centre to the infant. Jung thought that there was no centre to the infant until the ego developed. Fordham, however, thought of the infant as having a centre and of his or her experience as being on a continuum, with a sliding scale for the degree to which a perception was suffused with real qualities as distinct from having primarily a self object quality. Fordham described a self object as follows:

> When the object is mainly a record of reality, it may be called a reality object; when it is mainly constructed by the self and so records states of the self, made out of exteroceptive and introceptive sense data, then it may be called a self object. . . . It appears that self objects increase in affectively charged states, while in quiet contemplative exploring activities real objects predominate.
>
> (Fordham, 1985a: 56)

Here is an account of Baby G taken from Fordham's book *Explorations into the Self*.

> Baby G was an active aggressive baby who could make his wishes known in no uncertain manner especially over nappy changes during which he made loud and noisy protests. One day a health visitor arrived during a breast feed and demanded information immediately.

Mother interrupted the feed lying her baby down for a short period. He made protesting cries which escalated into screaming and drowned all conversation; in addition he soaked and dirtied himself. At first he was not to be calmed down and mother became worried though in an appropriate way; she initiated and persisted in efforts to relieve her baby's distress. Finally she was successful so that the feed could be continued and was followed by sleep. Thus a potential disaster was well and adequately dealt with – integration took place.

(Fordham, 1985a: 57)

The process of integration in this example is facilitated by the mother's actions and by her thinking about her baby's pain. But suppose the mother had not persisted and had not been able to retrieve this situation. Suppose too that this had been repeated over a number of occasions, then what would be likely to happen would be what is called splitting of the ego. (For a fuller description of this and a comparison of splitting and deintegration see Fordham, 1985b.)

The feeling of badness clearly had a reality for Baby G which was subjective and infused with violence and rage. He is not able to distinguish the thing in itself, the absent breast, from his feeling of its absence. In that sense the absent breast is a true archetypal image (and in Jung's sense primordial). When the breast is removed only its badness remains, good feelings and memories of it being lost to his mind. He is inside the badness.

I hope it is clear that the fantasy that the infant is part of the parent's unconscious (that is, that there is a state of fusion between mother and infant) is incompatible with the infant having an original self. This does not mean that *experiences* of fusion do not occur; they do. There is an early stage when subject and object are less distinct and when the experience of the baby is mainly pleasurable, which has come to be thought of as a blissful fused state. For Fordham, fusion is not the initial primary state of mother and infant, such as is meant by the phrase 'participation mystique' or primary relationship. Following on from this it ceases to be tenable that mother and infant are in a state of primary identity. If the infant's self is an integrate then it cannot be carried by the mother. Fordham is therefore rejecting Neumann's idea (Neumann, 1973) that the infant lives in a mythological world, and has cogently criticised this theory arguing that it is derived from applying a theory about the development of culture to the development of an imaginary child (Fordham, 1981).

Whole objects and part objects

Fordham conceptualises the infant's first relation to the mother's breast or feeding experience as a whole object relationship. This is because the first experiences are very close to the self and are therefore permeated with a quality of wholeness. Initially the breast is the main preoccupation of the infant, then this broadens out to include the many other aspects of the mother and of the baby's internal experience of her. All of this constitutes the experience of wholeness for the baby. Fordham says of this: 'The whole object might then be compared with a mandala that has a nipple at the centre and various objects placed within the magic circle' (1988: 65).

The move from whole objects to part objects and then to a combined object does not have to be via splitting of the ego. Rather, as we have seen with Baby G, the deintegrates become classed as good or bad. In Fordham's thinking, splitting occurs when there is an observable change in the personality of the child, that is, that something has changed structurally within the personality. This keeps development independent of pathology and focuses on adaptation, in the biological meaning of learning to live in a particular environment.

Why do we need a model like this, and what does it add to our existing conceptions of infancy? First it focuses attention on the infant and what it does. We start our enquiries from the same position as the ordinary mother, thinking of the baby as a separate person. This leaves room for the baby's capacity for discrimination. Next, by having a theory of deintegration we are able to think about the observed behaviour of the infant as being continuous with the self. What this means is that the development of the individual baby is in effect an early form of individuation, as experiences are being reintegrated within a continuum. So this model lets us proceed on the basis that the infant is a separate person but it also takes into account the fit between the infant and its mother and how actively the baby contributes to this. Why is it useful to think of experience as being on a continuum? Because it takes us away from linear thinking where one developmental stage replaces another and puts in its place a model which allows previous experience to coexist with contemporary experience such that each may modify the other.

Summary

Fordham's model begins with the primary self. This has no features. It cannot be experienced. But when parts of it are brought into relation to the environment it initiates a process which leads to the structuring of the mind. From the observation of this process its features can be inferred. It is a psychosomatic entity, having the potential to form a body and a psyche. The exteroceptive skin experiences are important in infancy as they help define the boundary of the infant and the feeling of its body being a container. Inside this container an inner world can develop. In response to environmental conditions the self responds in pre-formed ways. The dynamic of this self, its way of acting, Fordham called deintegration to preserve the idea that the self did not disintegrate in action.

Each deintegrate would have a physical and a psychic dimension. Thus far Fordham seems to have been widely understood and his ideas taken up by other analytical psychologists. What is radical about his model is that he suggested that the infant self contributed significantly to the environment in which it developed. Of course it doesn't quite work out like that and failures, disappointments and misunderstandings occur. This model respects the individuality of the infant and the interactive nature of the nursing couple. I like it too because it removes the study of behaviour from the realm of causal explanation and has made the study of the self into a unified field theory.

References

Astor, J. (1995) *Michael Fordham – Innovations in Analytical Psychology*, London and New York: Routledge.

Fordham, M. (1944) *The Life of Childhood*, Kegan Paul, Trench, Trubner and Co.

—— (1957) *New Developments in Analytical Psychology*, London: Routledge and Kegan Paul.

—— (1969) *Children as Individuals*, London: Hodder and Stoughton.

—— (1976) *The Self and Autism*, London: Heinemann Medical Books.

—— (1981) 'Neumann and childhood', *Journal of Analytical Psychology*, 26(2).

—— (1985a) *Explorations into the Self*, London: Academic Press.

—— (1985b) *Abandonment in Infancy*, Wilmette, IL: Chiron Publications.

—— (1988) 'The infant's reach', in *Psychological Perspectives*, Journal of San Francisco Institute for Analytical Psychology.

—— (1993) 'Notes for the formation for a model of infant development', *Journal of Analytical Psychology*, 38(1).

—— (1994) *Freud, Jung, Klein. The Fenceless Field: Essays on Psychoanalysis and Analytical Psychology*, London: Routledge.

James, W. (1902) *Varieties of Religious Experience*, London: Collins.

Jung, C.G. (1960) *Psychological Types, Collected Works* 6.

—— (1951) *Aion, Collected Works* 9.ii.

—— (1954) 'The Development of Personality', *Collected Works* 17.

—— (1963) *Memories, Dreams, Reflections*, London: Collins and Routledge and Kegan Paul.

Neumann, E. (1973) *The Child*, London: Hodder and Stoughton.

Infant Observation and Countertransference

Veronika Marlow

In this paper I would like to present what I have learnt from the two infant observations I have completed, one lasting two years and the other twelve months, and of the two infant observation seminars I have subsequently led.

It took quite some time to appreciate the meaning of what happened then, and how infant observation has shaped my analytical work. Observing an infant in his or her family setting from birth to two years of age, and attending weekly seminars to present this material, have become part of many analytical and psychotherapy trainings. It is not compulsory for members of the adult training course at the SAP.

While observing these infants I held the following goals in my mind: to trace the developmental steps of the baby from birth to the end of the observation; to observe the formation of the relationship between mother and baby, and, moving on from that, to his extended family; and to make the material meaningful to myself in my inner world through my analysis.

For a long time I was enchanted by the processes unfolding before me. I felt very privileged to be invited by a family to share its most intimate events, to be trusted and accepted by them. My analysis was enriched and deepened by the observation, and theoretical concepts of child development took on a new meaning.

It was only when I had completed my training and was 'on my own', working with patients, that I found myself returning time and again to my 'inner infant observation'. Here I found a space to think about me, about my reaction to what had been going on, to sift through the feelings of anger, frustration, rage, violence, love and desire which I had experienced years ago when observing a baby and his mother.

It was not the observation of theory in the making, nor the conjecture of what inner processes might at this point occur in the infant, nor the privilege of being part of a family's dynamic, enormously worthwhile as all these undoubtedly are. It was, rather, the creation of what I call analytic space that was so important then, and so necessary for my analytic work to follow. Here, in a room with a mother and an infant, there was time – time to observe without the need to interpret, time to look at the dynamic of their interaction but not to intervene, time to acknowledge the feelings they had for me, and time to learn of my countertransference without having to work with it. And so the hour of observation offered this space that is so like the analytic space of a session, and it taught me the waiting for and the being with another's dynamic and how it interacts with mine.

Every hour of an infant observation is different, as is every analytic hour, but whereas sessions with a patient take place several times a week and so offer more consistency, an infant is observed once a week. For a small baby, seven days is an enormous amount of time in which significant developmental changes can take place, let alone if the observation is interrupted for a longer period because of holidays. This gives a true sensation of the unexpected, and of never knowing what might happen. Another aspect of this is that, apart from mother and baby, any number of other people might be present during an observation – grandparents, siblings, neighbours dropping in for a chat. Every observation is an experience standing on its own – without past or present.

It was a pleasurable shock to come upon Michael Fordham's paper 'On not knowing beforehand' (1993). In this paper Fordham reported studying 'not knowing beforehand' as a way of investigating mutual projective identifications. He derived this notion from a phrase in Jung's essay on the transference where he writes: 'Inseparable from the persona is the doctor's routine and his trick of knowing everything beforehand, which is one of the favourite props of the well versed practitioner and of all infallible authority' (Jung, 1946: 176). Jung went on to say that this was impossible in psychotherapy as both patient and doctor are involved in the same unconscious processes and are both affected by them, and that each individual patient needs an individual approach. Fordham takes this further by stating that not only does each patient need an individual approach but that in each analysis, each hour needs to be approached in an individual way. He writes: 'I focused on single interviews. I considered what might happen if each time I met a patient, I tried to perceive him as if I had never seen him before and had no knowledge of him; attempting to do this would mean that I would have to develop an attitude of, as Bion puts it, eschewing knowledge, memory and desire' (Fordham, 1993: 130). Fordham then cites a case where he was just about able to sustain this attitude, and he goes on to say:

> I succeeded in blocking off all that material but I had to be very alert to do so for I could soon have had enough material to make quite a number of interpretations and so could have relieved myself of the effect of not knowing. My point is that if I had started intervening I would have shaped the interview myself instead of leaving the patient to do so. It turned out that none of my memories, knowledge or

desires were relevant to the shape of the interview . . . all I have done is put into words a general procedure – a piece of what may be called microanalysis hardly worth mentioning. Yet, if you proceed thus, I consider that you must have learned to do so. That was so in my case at least, and I think it is so for others.

(ibid.)

It was certainly so for me, and I began my learning during infant observation which allowed me the space to do so. I am going to present three infant observations of the same child at various stages in his development and my inner reactions to these.

I would now like to quote from my first observation of Paul whom I observed from birth until the age of two, prior to commencing my training with the SAP.

Paul was Janet's third child, and during one of my visits in the late stages of her pregnancy, Janet confided that she had not really wanted this baby. The other two children were older and at school and she did not want to start baby care all over again. This resulted in feelings of extreme guilt which made her cling to Paul so that it was impossible for them to separate out for quite a long time. During the height of this symbiotic state she was unable to put Paul down at all, and even had to take him to the lavatory with her. Janet was a childminder and during my two-year observation I was rarely alone with her and Paul, except in the first nine months. The other children she minded were older than Paul, toddlers, and those waiting to be picked up after nursery school, which meant that Paul's position as the baby and the one needing most attention was undisputed.

I became interested therefore, when Janet mentioned Robert, nine months old, three months younger than Paul, such a 'good little boy, no trouble at all'. I arranged an observation when Robert was there.

Janet opened the door. I had been away on a fortnight's holiday. Behind her came Paul, walking alone. He had grown and his face was more rounded. Mother picked him up and I greeted him. He looked at me for quite some time, then gave me half a smile and turned away, putting his arms around Janet's neck. The dog nearly knocked me over with excitement, and we all went into the living room. On the floor by the gas fire was Paul's changing mat and on it lay Robert who regarded us solemnly with his huge dark eyes. He wore a jumper and a bib and was kicking with his bare legs and bottom – I assumed that Janet was about to put a nappy on him.

We sat down on the floor next to Robert, and I looked at Paul who was between mother and me. He sat, patting his mother's knees with both hands, smiling at her. She smiled back at him. I said how well he looked. Janet said yes, he was well, nothing much had happened during my absence.

I smiled and said nothing but was wondering about Robert's arrival and what it meant.

Paul moved over to me and pulled himself upright on my cardigan. He got hold of my right thumb and walked round me in a circle so that I had to turn with him until he landed by the settee, where he halted, let go of my thumb and stood patting the cushion. Janet laughed and said that he'd found someone to hold on to again – she'd stopped holding him as he could walk perfectly well by himself, and would have walked months ago if he weren't such a Mummy's boy. Her remark made me feel wary.

Paul now came from behind us and walked towards the window. I noticed that he walked mainly on tiptoe, and only now and then did his whole foot touch the floor. He took rapid, small steps, wobbled a bit but got safely to the radiator by the window. He stood there for a moment, then turned and came towards us, walking straight at Robert, looking at his mother and not where he was going. Janet said 'Careful', but Paul had caught his foot on the mat, fell halfway on to Robert, grabbed his penis and kept hold of it. Janet picked Paul up, saying, 'Don't pinch him.' Robert had remained quite calm and looked very seriously at all of us.

Paul was now sitting on his mother's lap and patted her face with both hands. She kissed his hands, and he slid down from her lap back to the settee. He now walked again over to the window and came back to us, again looking at mother. He stumbled when he got to Robert and sat down by his side, then lay flat on the floor and started kicking, in the same rhythm as Robert. Janet said to me: 'He's making out he's a baby now.' I said: 'Yes, maybe he's realised that someone else is lying on his mat.' She said: 'That's a long time ago.' I said: 'Yes, it does seem so.'

Paul was kicking and looking at us gravely. After a short while he stopped, and Janet pulled him over to her. He sat on her lap for a few minutes, then wriggled off and went over to the settee. Janet got a nappy ready to put on Robert. She turned to him and smiled. Paul came over to her and wanted to sit on her lap. Janet took him on her lap, turning away from Robert who had looked at her expectantly. By now I felt extremely anxious about what was happening, and what I should or should not do. Until now I hadn't taken much notice of Robert, but kept my eye on Paul, and was talking to him, aware that he hadn't seen me for a fortnight and wanting to re-establish my relationship with him, and to let him know that I had come to see *him*. At the same time I felt very moved by this delicate, very appealing infant who had lain there so patiently without making any demands while two adults were occupied with another, stronger child who could move about at will and who seemed so important to these two people. I was also conscious of Janet's predicament, as I could see that she felt torn between completing the nappy change for Robert who must be getting cold, and attending to the demands of her own son.

It would have been so easy for me to put the nappy on Robert and let her sit with Paul, and I felt that Janet expected me to do this. I managed to keep on sitting but it was very hard. Paul had moved away from mother again and was behind her. She put a nappy under Robert. I shifted my position slightly and Robert noticed my movement, gave me a huge smile and waved his arms in my direction. My hand brushed his and he grasped my index finger tightly with his left, very cold little fist. This took about thirty seconds, and then, still holding Robert's fist, or rather being held since he wouldn't let go of me, I turned round to Paul as I could feel that he was looking at me. He had sat down by the settee, with so much hurt and anger in his look that I was taken aback. I felt so guilty.

For a moment he was silent, then he started to cry, putting his arms out to mother. She turned round to him, saying: 'It's all right, don't worry, just a minute', and continued with the nappy change. I don't recall what I did next, but Robert must have let go of my finger and I must have moved over to Paul, and I think only a mintue had passed. I sat next to Paul who was now screaming, getting red and then blue in the face, holding his breath and letting it out in huge screams with big tears rolling down his cheeks. I spoke to him, saying: 'I know it's hard, it's all right, just a second', but he didn't hear me. I stroked his hair and put my arms around him, while he sobbed bitterly. Janet also spoke to him, saying: 'Paul, for goodness sake, come on now', and to me: 'I haven't heard him cry like that for a long time.'

She had got a nappy on Robert and was putting on his babygro suit which took a little longer as Robert had pulled up his legs and was clinging to Janet, like a little monkey, she said, wanting presumably to make the most of what holding he could get. Paul's screams continued, and now he turned to me with a helpless gesture. He stretched his arms out to me and buried his face in my cardigan. I picked him up and held him tightly to me. He kept on crying but his colour improved and for a moment he lay quite still and heavy in my arms, then he struggled and I let go of him. He sat on the floor and I wiped the tears off his face.

Janet had finished with Robert and had put him down on the mat again. She picked up Paul who clawed at her jumper and her breasts, still crying and sobbing. Janet cuddled him and made soothing noises, asking if I wanted some coffee. I said yes, and offered to put on the kettle but she said she would do it. She went into the kitchen with Paul, now no longer crying, in her arms. I felt they needed to be alone for a bit. I heard Janet speak to Paul, asking if he wanted a biscuit. I heard the kettle boil, the rattle of mugs – all was calm again.

This observation moved me deeply and I struggled at home and in my analysis to gain clarity in my thoughts and feelings. There was Janet's irritation with Paul's regression and her seeming incomprehension of why this had occurred. I also wondered why she had taken care of a child younger than Paul just when she seemed to have welcomed separating out from him which had taken so long to achieve. Was the younger child to be the proof of Paul's hard-won independence – proof that she had an older, stronger son? What a cruel burden she was placing on him, when his moves away from her were still so very tentative and fragile – liable to break down the moment they were challenged.

I felt criticised by Janet for allowing him to hold on to me. Walking round me, holding on to my thumb, was a game we usually played, and he seemed to have remembered it when he saw me. But it was Paul's struggle to usurp his rival, his frantic attempts to have Janet for himself that I felt so powerfully projected into me, and with which I was alone. I could not make sense of them for him, as I would have done in an analytic session. A baby has to struggle to maintain his bond to his mother and he does not always succeed. It is only over time that the capacity to struggle can be developed as a part of emotional maturing. The need to keep going in the face of disappointment and loss, to continue to hope, to love and be creative in difficult times is a continuing problem in adult life.

The second observation had a very different flavour, and left me feeling calm, serene and peaceful. Paul, now about nineteen months, went over to the toy box and picked up the small blue rubber ball. Janet said: 'Oh, here it is again. I found it this morning behind the chair.' Paul seemed delighted to have the ball again, and tried to bite into it without much effect, for it was too hard and round for him to get his teeth into. He threw it down, crawled after it and retrieved it. He picked it up, tried to bite into it, couldn't do so, threw it away and crawled after it again . . . When he'd had enough of playing on his own, after about five minutes, he came back to Janet, holding the ball. She picked him up and sat him on her lap facing me. Janet groaned when he started to throw the ball down in front of him, expecting her or me to pick it up and give it to him, so that he could repeat the process. Janet said that once Paul got into this game he would be at it for hours, and he was certainly at it until I left half an hour later. Janet and I took it in turns to pick up the ball for him, the only difference being that I would hand the ball to Janet after picking it up and that she would give it to Paul.

This was one of the happiest observations in these two years. I really felt the space that opened up between Janet and Paul, and a sense of gathering together all the good feelings that existed between the three of us, and how the little blue ball mediated these. I also felt into my own psychic space and could rest there, without having to use it, as I would in an analytic session. I was wondering if, in this observation, Paul was showing that he had internalised the earlier experiences of being held, fed, looked at and talked to by his mother, and that he could contain these moments within himself, so that the space which was created between him and his mother, by playing with the little blue ball, re-created these aspects of the relationship for him. We all need to create such moments throughout adult life and return now and again to the vibrancy of these early experiences.

James Astor, in his book on Michael Fordham (1995), mentions Fordham's 'pioneering work on the micro-analysis of countertransference [which] opened up the discussion of what analysts did with their patients and made possible the teaching of technique for future generations of trainees. Technique became not so much what was imposed on patients, as Jung had originally feared, but rather 'the distillate of habitual behaviours by an analyst with different kinds of patients' (Fordham, 1974: 270). Astor goes on to quote Fordham further, saying that the purpose of technique had been shown 'to increase the capacity of the patient for reflection about himself, first in his relation to his analyst, and, as a consequence, to his wider environment and his inner world' (ibid.: 271). I feel the sentence also makes sense the other way round, namely 'to increase the capacity of the analyst for reflection about himself, first in his relation to his patient, and, as a consequence, to his wider environment and his inner world'. I think this is a valid definition of countertransference, which I experienced very powerfully for the first time in infant observation.

The last observation I wish to quote from shows my struggle to reflect on and contain my feelings of anger and anxiety, and of guilt at deserting my task of observer in order to tend to another's needs.

This observation took place in the summer holidays, on a very hot day in August. Paul's siblings, Tracy, aged 12, and Tommy, aged 6, were at home.

I heard Paul crying as I walked up the path. Tracy opened the door, followed by a tearful Paul. Janet was on the phone. I said hello to Paul and picked him up. He looked very sullen and didn't return my greeting but let me hold him and put his cheek against mine. We walked into the living room where Janet was finishing her call. Tommy called to me to come upstairs to see his car track, Tracy had returned to the corner of the room where she was sorting out toys from the toy box.

Janet walked into the kitchen to make coffee, and Paul wanted to get down on the floor next to Tracy. I put him down and he started to pick up some of the things she had spread out. He got hold of the little wooden men who belonged to the fire engine and looked at them, one by one. I said hello to Janet in the kitchen who said that life had been dreadful. Paul had been crying for two days without any obvious reason. He was in a bad mood, nothing could please him, and she was at her wits' end. We went back into the living room where Tommy had waited very patiently to show me his car track. I went upstairs with him to his room, where he had laid out the track with an underpass and a bridge, and demonstrated a car moving over and under. I admired all this, rather hastily, as I was not in role as Paul's observer and was being side-tracked by this child's need for a bit of attention. I felt guilty for not giving Tommy his due and also felt guilty for not being with Paul.

When I came back Paul was on the floor playing with the peg men. He tried to fit these into the slots of the fire engine, then took them out again, then tried to put a man in the front seat. This was difficult, as there was a man fitted into the driver's seat which was inaccessible from the side, but Paul tried to push another one in all the same. He seemed quite patient at first, but suddenly lost interest and climbed on to Janet's lap, wailing and moaning. Janet said: 'What is the matter with you, what do you want?' Paul was looking around restlessly. I moved the fire engine, which he had left by my side, back and forth, and it made a tinkling sound which he used to like. Paul glared at me, got off Janet's lap and kicked the fire engine under the chair, glaring at me all the time. Janet remarked how sullen he looked.

There was then some interaction with Tommy about eating a biscuit, and the observation continues:

Paul went to the French doors and banged them to get out. Janet got up and opened one half. Paul started to open and shut the door quite force-fully and put his head against the window pane from outside to look in. He rattled on the closed half and banged against it. Janet got up and opened it. I felt irritated and surprised that she should do this as Paul had caught his thumb in the French doors just a couple of weeks earlier, and I would have thought she would want to avoid this happening again. Just then she said: 'One of these days I'll go up to the hospital with his fingers in a bag, the ways he plays with these doors. . . .' My anger and anxiety about allowing him to play like this increased still further, but I said nothing. Paul kept on banging the doors, not looking what he was doing. Janet said: 'Any moment now he's going to hurt himself', but made no attempt to stop him. I could not believe what was happening. From somewhere I heard myself suggesting that we go out to watch Tommy ride his bicycle, some-thing he had only just accomplished. Paul hestitated before coming away from the door but followed us quite soon. Tommy rode his bike very confidently around the front lawn and we all clapped and cheered. Paul had found his baby walker and was careering around the garden with it, not to be outdone by Tommy.

The rest of the observation did not materially add to the dynamic and I left with a sense of relief. When I got home and had settled down a bit, I remembered feeling enraged about Janet's inability to stop Paul from playing with the dangerous doors, especially as he had hurt himself in this way not so long ago. It seemed almost as if Janet wanted him to get hurt, as if she wanted to pay him back for hurting her.

At that time I had not commenced my training and had not heard of Bion and his theory of a container–contained relationship. What I now understand it to mean, at least in part, is being receptive to being stirred up emotionally, and that this is at the basis of our capacity to be responsive when we are brought into close contact with someone else's state of mind. This contact is not a comfortable feeling, there is something disturbing about it, so we want to avoid the emotional impact and with it the capacity for containment of the discomfort. I assume that something of this sort happened with Janet when she saw Paul playing with the French doors. She could not contain her feelings of caring for him any more, after a week of depression and misery all round. She, as the 'container', needed some containment. I think the observer often becomes the 'container' for some of the mother's experiences and finds this disturbing, as I did. I was so emotionally stirred up by what was going on that all I could do to contain it was to bring about a relocation of the action to a more benign area of activity, yet it did not feel right.

Next day, I suddenly recalled my mother telling me, quite some years ago, that I had shut my fingers in the kitchen door one morning when I must have been Paul's age, around twenty months. My father had just left on a business trip and she felt sad, isolated and was not paying attention to me. I had bruised one of my fingers rather badly and was screaming with shock and pain. For a moment or so she just stood there, then she took me into bed with her where eventually I could be comforted. I have never been able to call this event into consciousness but it was a relief to locate my countertransference to what was happening that afternoon in Paul's play and so to understand why I reacted the way that I did.

If the seminar leader presents as the main purpose of the observation a becoming aware of countertransference, of observers discovering the many painful hooks of a childhood long past on which the mother/infant dyad now hangs their projective identification so effectively, then it is essential to discuss these issues in the seminar because this is where they belong. It is not sufficient for the seminar participants to be in personal analysis, although this is essential for working through what can be very traumatic material. The sharing of deeply painful as well as extremely joyous experiences welds the group together and strengthens the ongoing task.

Astor writes about Fordham that 'The further refinement of Jung's statement about the significance of the personality of the analyst – since he was as much in the analysis as the patient – came from his work. This showed him that it was not so much the qualities of the analyst per se which were therapeutic as his abilities to manage them' (1995: 126).

An infant observation offers an observer the chance to learn to 'manage his abilities'. It creates an analytic space where sensitivity to emotion can be developed and feelings are perceived by a reflective state of mind. This in turn develops a capacity to hold anxiety, discomfort, helplessness and above all to tolerate 'not knowing beforehand'.

References

Astor, J. (1995) *Michael Fordham – Innovations in Analytical Psychology*, London and New York: Routledge.

Fordham, M. (1974) 'Technique and countertransference' in *Technique in Jungian Analysis*, Library of Analytical Psychology, vol. 2.

—— (1993) 'On not knowing beforehand', *Journal of Analytical Psychology*, 38(2).

Jung, C.G. (1946) 'The Psychology of the Transference', *Collected Works* 16.

Chapter 2

The Body–Self Relationship

Jung was inspired by the principle of opposing forces in dynamic relationship. Fordham explored this idea in developing a psychological understanding of the body in infancy. Mind and body were seen as a pair of opposites and the dialectical processes operating between them were key to the quality of emerging consciousness and to pathological states resulting from faulty early interactions. Catherine Kaplinsky weaves the dialectical processes into an exploration of the body in the consulting room with illustrations from clinical material. She shows how changes occur when the opposites collapse into one another constituting a *coniunctio*. Out of this process a symbol is born, facilitating the transition from one psychological state or attitude to another.

For Jung, body experience was sometimes I-experience, sometimes not-I or even shadow. Maturation involved differentiation between 'I' and body. Joseph Redfearn describes how the early 'I' has different core and boundary body-experiences, giving rise to different, but partially united, 'subpersonalities' or 'I's. As the subjective need for oneness, or normal autism, remains throughout life, we surround ourselves with numerous 'self-objects' – things, persons, interests etc. Oneness with these is experienced as healing, severance as bodily damaging. An 'I' is conscious in Jung's sense of the word if able to move in the symbolic boundary area between 'I' and 'not-I' without confusion of image and object.

The Body–Self Relationship

Joseph Redfearn

Introduction: mind and matter

In order to begin the discussion of the relationship between the actual body, which is or has to do with matter, and the self, which has to do with the mind, we shall refer briefly to the relationship between mind and matter.

The widespread experience of ghosts of the dead, who can be influenced by the living, is evidence of extracorporeality, but does not of course exclude the powerful influence of projection.

Material effects of mind, such as poltergeist and psychokinetic phenomena, were regarded by Jung in his *Memories, Dreams, Reflections* (chapter 11) as the action of exteriorised libido. In a conversation with Esther Harding in 1948 (McGuire and Hull, 1977: 184) he mentioned that whenever there was an important idea that was not yet quite conscious, the furniture all over the house creaked and snapped.

The well known psychokinetic expression of the tension between Freud and Jung at their Vienna meeting in 1909 (Jung, 1963: 152) takes us another step forward in our argument. It will be recalled that Freud's 'materialistic prejudice' against parapsychology at that time brought a sharp retort to the tip of Jung's tongue, which he checked with difficulty. He then had a sensation of increasing heat in the region of his diaphragm culminating in a loud report from the nearby bookcase. Jung called this a catalytic exteriorisation phenomenon, and when Freud said that was sheer bosh Jung predicted another loud report which duly occurred. From a clinical viewpoint we suppose that these reports were of a poltergeist type and were due not to the mere projection outwards of Jung's anger but to an actual exteriorisation of it after its initial bodily expression as the sensation in the chest.

The hypothesis suggested, if these and other paranormal phenomena are validated, is that meaning is prior to matter/energy in the physicist's sense. Meaningfulness could, according to this hypothesis, take discarnate form, and when incarnated it could be 'acted out', somatised in suffering or healing depending on its negative or positive form, or integrated and contained in other ways. To view matter/energy as discarnate meaningfulness gives rise to the question, 'Meaningful to whom?' We are left either with a solipsistic universe or some sort of primal cosmic experiencer for which God might be a suitable name. (See Peat, 1987, for a more adequate discussion.)

The brain and the 'I'

Coming now to the narrower question of the relationship between the experience of self and the brain, the neurosurgeon Wilder Penfield (1975) produced many movements, sensations, memories, and inhibitory phenomena in the course of his experiments on the electrical stimulation of different areas of the brain in conscious human patients. He claimed never by such means to have produced an experience of an I in the sense of personal causative agent. His patients found their muscles, etc., doing things, but never experienced an I doing them. He thus found himself taking a dualistic mind/brain position.

The work at the Neurosciences Institute, and the publications of the Nobel prizewinner Gerald Edelman (1993) typify the mind-as-matter viewpoint. He sees the nervous system as an organ of selection, choosing between the myriads of available stimuli for its response. He distinguished between two kinds of selection, innate and developmental (corresponding to our 'archetypal') and experiential, or learned. The selection biases he calls 'values', and like archetypes they are instinctual in their roots. By the selectivity and reinforcement of the neuronal connections the animal builds up ways of perceiving grouped into 'maps'. There is a continuous process of modification by other maps which he calls 're-entrant signalling', and it is by virtue of higher and higher orders of this that self-categorisations and aspects of what we might call self-awareness could come into being.

Edelman's model brain can, he claims, not only be conscious at lower levels but, because of its re-entrant inputs, can be aware of being aware.

No doubt the model can help us understand something of the hierarchical structure of the experience of I-ness. For example, anaesthesia or paralysis of a part may cause a disturbance in lower-order I-ness of a localised nature, whereas some cases of migraine exhibit a scotoma in the field of I-feeling of a much higher order (Sacks, 1995: 98). Massive damage to the sensory areas of the right cerebral hemisphere also produces higher-order abnormalities of I-feeling in which, for example, the patient is unaware that one side of his body is without sensation. His/her I simply does not include that side of the body or sensorial world.

I, sense of self, and body-image

In this section I hope to demonstrate that the I is not a static entity, any more than the bodily state or the body of subjective experience is fixed or steady in its behaviour. Nevertheless a sense of intactness and of continuity of the I is normally taken for granted. Most of us are familiar with Freud's (1923: 26) statement that 'the ego is first and foremost a bodily ego'. Writing in 1906, Jung, aged 31, also bases the healthy ego in the sensations arising in the body.

> The ego is the psychological expression of the firmly associated combination of all body sensations. One's own personality is therefore the firmest and strongest complex, and (good health permitting) it weathers all psychological storms.
>
> (1906: 40)

Jung's own out-of-body experience at the time of his heart attack (aged 69) may be used to illustrate his views on the relationships between a higher, objective I, a lower, personal, body-based, conscious-I, and the 'real' external world of time and space. While he was just being kept alive by means of oxygen and injections of stimulant drugs, he entered a visionary state in which he experienced himself as being high above the earth.

> The whole phantasmagoria of earthly existence fell away or was stripped from me. . . . Nevertheless, something remained; it was as if I now carried along with me everything I had ever experienced or done, everything that had happened around me. . . . I consisted of my own history, and I felt with great certainty: this is what I am. . . . There was no longer anything I wanted or desired. I existed in an objective form.
>
> (1963: 271)

In this state Jung felt free of his body-based 'ego-complex', and free of his body-based 'character defences' and 'ego-defences'.

Concerning the relationship between the body and ego-consciousness, Jung makes superficially contradictory statements in different contexts. On the one hand, he is saying that a securely embodied ego-consciousness is necessary if the unconscious is not to have destructive effects on ego-consciousness through inflationary and other malign effects.

> The body is necessary if the unconscious is not to have destructive effects on the ego-consciousness, for it is the body that gives bounds to the personality. The unconscious can only be integrated if the ego holds its ground.
>
> (1946: 292)

And only after the body-grounded individual ego-consciousness has been safely differentiated from the shadow-unconscious and from general truths in dangerous form can a reuniting of mind and body occur.

On the other hand we have such pronouncements as:

> [Unintegrated] unconscious contents lurk somewhere in the body like so many demons of sickness, impossible to get hold of, especially when they give rise to physical symptoms the organic causes of which cannot be demonstrated.
>
> (1955–6: 238)

> [People who have lost their shadow] are only two-dimensional; they have lost the third dimension, and with it they have usually lost the body, [which] . . . produces things we do not like. The body is very often the personification of this shadow of the ego.
>
> (1935: 23)

Dreams may of course help us span the gap between consciousness and the 'ultimately physiological foundations of the psyche'. Here he is referring to bodily instincts (ibid.: 209).

The clinical facts which reconcile the above two typical, apparently contradictory statements could be formulated as follows: an I with a creative working relationship with the body (image) can contain and then integrate unconscious conflict better than one for which bodily and affective aspects of the total personality are repressed or split off and which are shadow contents. By 'creative working relationship' I mean an I which is securely embodied but differentiated from the body image. The I–body relationship is then a consciously symbolic one in other words. The body imago is not confused with the body or identified with the I.

Time after time in his quotations from alchemical texts Jung refers to the need to separate mind and body before they can be reunited on a higher level. (See, for example, 1942: para. 157, pp. 122–4; 1944: 120; 1946: 299; 1946: para. 499, p. 288.) The need to separate I from 'body' before reuniting them in the transitional, aware, symbolic area, where I and 'body' both have space, is only one example of the I/not-I (or ego–Self) differentiating and reuniting required by Jung's individuation process.

A strong I, who can be a powerful agent and who also has adequate defensive stability without needing to split off and project pain or 'badness' into others, is an I who is in contact with his/her feelings and emotions, both of which have all-important bodily components. The increase in bodily well-being which a patient can have when angry feelings, with their corresponding bodily impulses, can be experienced and 'owned' without too much fear of rejection or retaliation, is a commonplace, though none the less gratifying experience in therapy. Of course this does not only apply to angry feelings, but to other feelings as well.

I well remember that the need to establish a real, three-way, preferably living, talking or at least vocal, relationship between the patient, his feelings and his psychosomatic symptoms, akin to Jung's active imagination, was stressed in the training seminars at the SAP which I attended in 1951. While a not-too-disembodied therapist is the first requirement (Redfearn, 1994b: 314), it often helps if the therapist has an accurate 'feel' for the level at which the interaction, or the block, is happening.

In therapy, the recovery of lost parts of the self always means the re-establishment of a lost link between I and body part or function. This applies whether we are talking about integrating shadow, anima/animus, baby or parent parts, or good or destructive omnipotent subpersonalities. To take a few examples, a slug, a teenage hooligan, a regicide in the basement, an incendiary, a lion, a plant, trickster-figures and babies in various states and circumstances, have all occurred lately in the dreams of my patients or those of my supervisees, and each of these 'subpersonalities' (Redfearn, 1994a and b) means a different and easily recognisable bodily posture, attitude or behaviour. There is a close relationship in practice between the Jungian aim towards an ego which relates well and as fully as possible to the Self, and the aim of analysing or otherwise undoing character defences and liberating energy flow (Reich, 1933), so attention will now be paid to the early I and the development of I/not-I interactions and their relation to the body and body-image.

I, not/I, transitional area, body-image, real body

In the dyadic relationship of analysis both parties are, hopefully, making steady progress in intersubjectivity, a transitional area between, on the one hand, the somewhat autistic assumption that the other is having the same experience as we are having, and, on the other hand, the annihilation of the other as a person with any sort of inner life. In other words, we are strengthening the transitional structures between absolute 'sameness' and absolute 'otherness'. I argue elsewhere (Redfearn, 1982; 1992, chap. 9) that the ascription of personhood to the Other precedes the division into I and not-I, but that later it is a subjective judgement depending partly on being in touch with one's body-image and one's feelings. The infant makes this leap forward in the first year, when I first discover that mother and I are not always the same, and then that mother has somewhat similar affective states as I, and that I can make mummy smile by smiling or pulling a face (or upset her by screaming). Furthermore, when she smiles lovingly at me I feel really good and smiley – but then I have experienced that as far back as I remember (or rather, as my body and behaviour 'remember').

Nowadays, ultrasound scanning of foetal behaviour shows how differently one foetus behaves from another (Piontelli, 1992). In Piontelli's study, feelings and motivations tended to be spontaneously ascribed to the foetus even by the participating doctors, let alone the parents. That these subjective reactions were not merely based on projection was shown, or at least powerfully suggested, by the fact that these foetal temperamental differences were continued into extra-uterine life. Ways of interacting with cord, placenta, and parts of one's own body were continued into post-uterine 'object relations', and this was very marked between twins. For example one pair of twins stroked and 'loved' each other, and another pair pushed each other about and were antagonistic from the start.

Viewing the foetus as a unique person does not of course mean ignoring the fact that maternal attitudes and emotions, and traumatic events during pregnancy, are clearly crucial, as Kay (1984) pointed out.

Watching the parent and child interacting from the moment of birth, one can understand statements such as 'There is no such thing as an individual baby, but only a nursing couple.' Of course, exactly the same statement could be made about each one of us adults – we are all interacting socially all the time, and sociologists can easily point out that there is no such thing as individual psychology. I believe Jungians more than Freudians might seriously allow for an appreciable paranormal element in the interaction between parent and child, and acknowledge, with Neumann (1973: 23), that sometimes, when we are in a psychotically regressed state, we are more in touch with the unconscious of others than we are when not regressed. Be that as it may, when we reflect that the carer for the neonate and young baby hardly knows from one hour to the next what will need to be done, it seems amusing to read that the period from birth to three months is referred to as the stage of homeostasis by Greenspan (1981) although, to be fair, he is only using the term to contrast this phase with the next phase, that of emotional attachment. Nowadays, stress is more likely to be laid on the behavioural, emotional and autonomic state of the baby being 'regulated', kept in equilibrium, by the behaviour, etc., of the carer and the way this is determined by the signals coming from the baby as well as by the needs of the carer herself (Taylor, 1987). In this sense we could include the mother in the baby's self-regulating system.

Let us take the simple case of a baby who is sleeping, stirs, wakes and is restless and whimpers perhaps. The mother thinks she is hungry and it is about time for a feed, gets her into a comfortable position, offers the nipple which the baby latches on to hungrily and sucks. The mother is talking and smiling, and later when not so hungry the baby plays and exchanges sounds and smiles, etc.

This commonplace, idyllic vision of the dyad may serve as a symbol of goodness, harmony, wholeness, and bodily well-being, and it may evoke or help to create good memories and good behaviour in us. But when we try to imagine or reconstruct the baby's I-feelings and I-experience in this scene we have to fall back mainly on our own experience, memories and empathic imagination. Fully aware of these limitations, let us nevertheless hypothesise about some early I-feelings.

When speculating and theorising about the I and its vicissitudes I find it helpful to reflect upon how far what I am saying would apply to, say, a puppy or a kitten. Much of the foetal and infantile behaviour and relating which we observe in the human would be true of other mammals, until we reach transitional phenomena and verbal symbols. This leads us to conclude that the early I of the human and that of other mammals is basically similar, as all who can relate to animals know.

Waking, sleeping, generalised states

Ultrasonographic studies since those of Reinold in 1971 (see Piontelli, op. cit.) inform us of the increasingly rich life of the foetus especially as term approaches. Well before this, a full range of movements, some purposive (for example thumb and cord sucking, pushing and stroking other objects), and some preparatory, such as 'breathing' amniotic fluid, are being practised and perfected. Each of these movements will be causing sensations from body surfaces making contact with things outside, and also sensations of what we might later call effort, from muscles, joints, etc. Finally, there are sensations from internal organs mediating autonomic, perhaps early 'affective', functioning. An early experience of boundaryless watery nothingness might be inferred from some creation myths (for example that in the Book of Genesis), to be followed by alternating wakefulness and sleep (the biblical light and darkness). We know that regular daily cycles of reactivity and quiescence occur in the foetus from quite early in pregnancy, but the emergence of the different kinds of sleep only occurs near term. From all this one wonders whether, although many detailed and differentiated conative, cognitive, and affective patterns are being learned and laid down, what is being experienced is more of the nature of different 'worlds' at different times, corresponding to the varying behavioural/ affective states. The sensory and motor pathways are organised in the nervous system topographically, even up to and including the approximately point-for-point representation of the surface of the body on the surface of the cerebral cortex. The limited ability in the foetus and neonate to form sharp gradients of excitation/inhibition would result in events and, eventually, objects, being experienced coenaesthetically, transmodally, and also affectively shaped and coloured. This 'world' I have called the coenaesthetic body–world scheme of affective experience (Redfearn, 1970). The transmodal transference of information (for example, lumpy object felt, then recognised visually) suggests that there may be even more primitive, perhaps paranormal, transference of information. With increasing maturity, increasing inhibitory capability reduces generalisation and sharpens boundaries, but the containing, holding, inhibitory function is at first carried out by the sensations from actual holding, skin contact of a warm, soothing quality, and instinctual satisfactions, etc. *In other words a combination of (1), keeping arousal and excitation within limits and (2), reinforcing boundaries by (a) loving holding and skin contact, (b) a positive emotional environment, and (c) the sights, smells, and mirroring affects of the carer, all help to bring about a good yet bounded body–I experience (affect–I).*

From the point of view of the well-embodied, secure feeling of I it is important to recognise the over-alert child of the first year whose narcissistically needy carer has in trying to satisfy her own needs failed to maintain the graded balance between greedy love and catastrophic abandonment which has been so well described in Winnicott's books. Daniel Stern, whose study was mostly of children in an optimal state of arousal for mental functioning (1985: 195), describes such a child's difficulties with an over-stimulating, over-intrusive mother. Joyce McDougall (1989: chap. 5) makes the point that the act of falling asleep must be libidinally invested (oneness with good world-mother, with consequent bodily well-being), and that life-threatening insomnia can manifest itself in the first weeks of life.

The early feeling of I, normal autism and the body

If by narcissism we are referring to how one feels about oneself, we observe that most of our everyday life is narcissistically neutral. This would apply even more to the puppy whose body and instinctual and conditioned reflex functioning are well integrated. How one feels about oneself is not at issue. This does not mean that the baby and the puppy do not have different states of happiness and unhappiness, but let us say that these depend largely on how much the young one is being loved by its 'self-objects', those on whose love it depends.

Our observations of foetuses', puppies' and babies' movements do not suggest any confusion between self and not-self. The thumb, or nipple as the case may be, may be sucked without any problems of whether it is I or not-I; the foetus has not yet learned the more sophisticated definition of self and not-self which it will adopt later. Stern (1985: 10) writes;

> They [infants] never experience a period of total self/other undifferentiation. There is no confusion between self and other in the beginning or at any point during infancy. They are also predesigned to be selectively responsive to external social events and never experience an autistic-like phase.

(In other words they are like our puppies.)

But there are times when, babies and adults alike, we are, subjectively speaking, not differentiated from the Other. We assume or demand oneness in some sense. This part of ourselves I call the normal autistic part-self or subpersonality. In this state the Other is a self-object, and we have a no-boundary, no-space situation. Fordham (1976: 81) describes this autistic subpersonality, but does not mention that it is present in us all.

> The autistic child's relation to objects has been extensively studied. It has been observed that any object that engages the child's interest must comply with what he wants to do with it: the object can be anything from a toy to a part of a person – his hand or arm, for instance – which the child will manipulate to his own ends. If the object does not comply with the child's needs, he will either cease to be interested and treat it as if it does not exist or he will fly into a rage or panic. The objects that are used and that comply with the child's needs are called autistic or, as I would prefer, self-objects.

Frustration of the need for oneness may pathologically augment the demand that you should 'be like me', comply exactly with my needs, and furthermore want to do so, that you should think as I think, know what I am wanting, etc., etc., or else I will destroy the world, myself included. (In the infant this means getting into a screaming temper.) The clinical fact that this omnipotent subpersonality in ourselves is usually part of the collective shadow, and is therefore acted out, or projected, either on to God or the State or whatever, with panic fears of nothingness and annihilation, is the subject matter of my book, *The Exploding Self* (1992).

All our 'objects', things or persons, are self-objects (in the above sense) to a certain extent. From the body's point of view, they are part of us. They heal us or damage us according to whether they are behaving positively or negatively.

This need for oneness is obviously closely related to the 'instinct of imitation', for example of the mother's smile and affects, and to the subjective state of I–world–body–mother undifferentiated 'harmonious mix-up', or 'participation mystique' perhaps. The 'security blanket' provided by the environment, and the mother's own stage-appropriate felt need for oneness (identification) with the baby, produce an I which expects and needs to be satisfied. But when this does not quite happen the potential explosion is bounded and contained by sufficient holding, skin contact, loving sounds and behaviour, etc. (Following Anzieu (1989) we are permitting ourselves to use the word 'skin' in a literal as well as a metaphorical sense to refer to the boundary between I and not-I. The more violent the autistic demand, the more physically literal the holding may have to be.)

The obverse of what I have called the autistic demand for the other to be at one with oneself, etc., is the need to be just like the other person, do exactly what she wants, be part of her or more exactly completely identified, and so on, otherwise one might be annihilated. One might call this 'reversed autism' or autism with the I/not-I positions reversed, and it may as I said be based on primal imitation and a basic need for oneness. It is not usually appreciated clinically that the fear of annihilation is the other side of the wish to annihilate if the demand for oneness is frustrated. Thus both the need to explode and the fear of annihilation derive from the primary need for oneness with the Other.

Although the early I is body-based, motored by appetite, and bounded by skin and environmental containing and satisfying, the almost as early I can move across the particular I/not-I boundary which is present at any one time. In other words self and other can be interchanged to some extent, almost reversed one might say. But whichever side of the early boundary the I is, it is usually strongly bodily based and bodily identified. But the actual bodily feelings, which are the basis of affect and emotion, are different according to which side of the boundary the I of the time is situated. The demanding hungry I has different bodily functioning and experiencing from the loving, identifying I, and one might say the two are designed to fit together, when 'enacted' by different people (and the bodies of the different people are equipped to so enact, as with mother and child). The different part-selves or subpersonalities have different body I's in this sense and they may be on opposite sides of the same boundary, for example that between good child and naughty child, or that between naughty child and censorious adult.

This need for oneness and the imitative 'reflexes' soon gives rise to what one might refer to as 'normal tricksterism', and later to intersubjectivity as well as to the building up of mental structure and metaphor at the I/not-I boundary which progressively becomes a transitional one.

It goes without saying that each subpersonality has a different physiology, a different quality of I/not-I boundary. For example, for a fighting situation we need to 'stiffen the sinews', become hard, oblivious to pain. For another situation we may need to get into a much softer, merging, loving subpersonality. 'Tough-mindedness' and 'tender-mindedness' are physiologically opposing subpersonalities which, as we know, may become set habits of mind.

Libidinal cathexis and the well-being of the body-I

At the hypothetical (or perhaps merely didactic) stage of I/not-I undifferentiation, or of I–mother–body–world unity, physiological state, emotional state, and the well-being of the fused self and other would be experienced coenaesthetically as a sort of world body self–other, with pleasant, rolling, curved hillsides and beautiful bright points during a Kleinian 'good-breast' experience, and as jagged peaks, or shattered buildings, or desolate places, etc., during various kinds of 'bad-breast' experiences. The image of the good breast or good round whole and the experience of wholeness and well-being in the 'good-feed' go together coenaesthetically so well that the Jungian mandala is often interpreted by psychoanalysts as a 'good breast' image. When there is something resembling a nipple at the top or in the middle the connection is even more obvious. The reader will appreciate that I am writing in a clownish way of something very real, the coenaesthetic body–world scheme of affective experience towards which the adult I may reach and expand in art and poetry. As I write I am listening to someone on the radio reading a passage by Christopher Isherwood about the bleak Prussian mid-winter landscape creeping into the body of Berlin, where he is and with which his own body and bones are achingly and creakingly identified. Not only do the landscape and the emotional environment enter our bones, but they *are* our experiential bones and, furthermore, now, not only at the time before we were 'separated from the mother'. We are describing adult experience, not simply pathological regression. This, to my mind, is an important empirical truth concerning psychosomatic phenomena.

But at the same time, at the surfaces and at the places where sights, sounds, and smells meet us, the I and the actual mother are separating and interacting. In her caresses the mother excites the boundary experience, communicates her feelings through it, and makes the I whole and at peace. (Or not, as the case may be.) The most exciting and whole-making boundary, I/not-I experiences, are of course the paradoxical experiences of merging plus meaningful communication, rather than of separation and impermeability, although feelings of integrity, strength and independence, for which anger and frustration are essential components, are necessary in building up the healthy body–I with a strong and yet flexible and communicating 'ego-boundary' or 'skin' at a later stage.

The 'self-object' or 'autistic' stage of somatic dependence is well discussed by Ogden (1992: chap. 3, 'The autistic-contiguous position') and by McDougall (1989: chap. 3, 'The body–mind matrix', and the sections on the one-body-for-two fantasy). The same stage is also covered well by Neumann in his books *The Child* (1973: chaps 1 & 2) and *The Great Mother* (1955, first four chapters). See also Newton and Redfearn (1977), Newton (1965), and Redfearn (1985: chap. 5, 'The body, the body image and the self').

Space between I and not-I. The symbolic attitude

Some of the later stages of I/not-I differentiation are described or creatively reconstructed by Stern (1985), and by Anzieu (1989), in his description of the boundary as the skin ego. One important aspect of Anzieu's clinical work lies in his demonstration of the somatic link between skin ego and actual skin. But both for psychosomatic well-being and for the development of consciousness it is the space between I and not-I which is vital.

Our self-objects are zones of no-boundary, so that separation can be experienced as a tearing or severing if the I is strong enough to bear the pain, but if not, produces destructive or violent, disintegrated behaviour together with absence of actual mental experience of pain or disintegration (Redfearn, 1992). But another result of the inability to handle the affect creatively is somatic illness, so that destructiveness or somatic illness are the alternative eventualities of the no-boundary, non-symbolic I/not-I situation for any particular subpersonality of the total self. Loss of self-object means somatic damage (Taylor, 1987), or externally directed destruction. The *experience* of pain means that a containing, transitional boundary zone is in operation and we are not dealing with a 'pure' self-object. Of course, the need to suffer and process pain for the sake of one's best interests or those of others is a large and sociologically vital subject.

The pragmatic, operatory I who is not in contact with the body-I, the affect-I, is the I who oscillates between fusion and cutting off or destroying, or as it were unconsciously self-destructing in somatic illness. But this I/self-object situation may only pertain to some subpersonalities, and not to others. *The fact that the no-space, no boundary, self-object situation usually applies to some subpersonalities and not others is vital to an understanding of the role of the self-object in healing and damaging the body.*

Depersonalisation: the location of the I in relation to the body

The feeling of aliveness in the body is a background to self-feeling we can usually take for granted, but in some disorders of self-feeling, bodily I-feeling is noticeably obliterated, the body feeling like a robot and the I being located in an abnormal situation in relation to the body, commonly out of the body even. One may feel like a disembodied eye. I investigated many such patients about thirty years ago in work which I only partially published (Redfearn, 1965, 1994a and b; see also Ledermann, 1981). Here again we are dealing with deadening of the normal affective relation with the bodily self, often spreading from a localised deadening of body feeling. For example, instead of fear of loss of or damage to a particular body part or function, for example castration anxiety, there developed dead or robotic feelings in that part of the body, which usually spread to the entire body–self. In other words, anxiety is to depersonalisation as fear is to 'coming to pass'.

Understanding the relationship between feelings towards oneself and bodily aliveness takes for granted that affect is to do with conscious or subliminal messages from the actual body, and that different affects have to do with different 'chakras' of the body (rather, different bodily zones of potential I-ness). I described movements of the feeling of I in relation to the body in the 1965 and the 1994b articles.

Often in the course of therapy, affective contact with the Other is restored, with interesting somatic concomitants. For example, for a patient in whom dependent feelings have been denied because of old hurts, holiday breaks may, when the stage in therapy is being reached when denial of dependence is being forgone, be accompanied by somatic illness, which at the next break will be replaced by actual feelings of missing the therapist (Sidoli, 1993). As affect is restored, the body returns to life, usually at first in a negative way. In other words, patients seem to be 'healthy' in body so long as they can maintain their schizoid, paranoid, or manic defences, but may suffer bodily illness when they begin to care for the Other, and to suffer and put themselves out for other people. The numerous books of Alexander Lowen (for example 1967: chap. 12) are very illuminating in respect of the restoration of bodily I-feelings and of affective awareness.

Conclusion

The emergence of the conscious I out of the state of primitive identity, and the separation thereby of the outer object from its imago, for example mother imago from mother, is just as necessary for the body-image and the body. Just as with the mother imago and the real mother, where a continual dialectic must be maintained, the communication between actual body and body-as-experienced is vital, in what we call the symbolic attitude. Jung saw clearly the need to separate I from body-self as a prerequisite to a higher union in which the body is no longer a self-object. However, he tended to equate (mistakenly) feelings of wholeness (expressed coenaesthetically as the mandala, for example) with total self. He perhaps did not take sufficiently into account the infantile autistic core in us all which 'needs' to explode and destroy everything at moments when powerful needs for feelings of oneness, wholeness and well-being are not being met. This destructiveness can take the form of somatic illness and other forms of self-damage when they are neither acted out nor integrated in the symbolic space between the I and the not-I.

References

Anzieu, D. (1989) *The Skin Ego: A Psychoanalytic Approach to the Self*, trans. C. Turner, Newhaven: Yale University Press.

Edelman, G. (1993) *Bright Air, Brilliant Fire: On the Matter of the Mind*, New York: Basic Books.

Fordham, M. (1976) *The Self and Autism*, London: William Heinemann Medical Books.

Freud, S. (1923) 'The Ego and the Id', in *Standard Edition* vol. XIX, London: Hogarth Press.

Greenspan, S.I. (1981) *Psychopathology and Adaptation in Infancy and Early Childhood*, New York: International University Press.

Jung, C.G. (1906) 'The Psychology of Dementia Praecox', *Collected Works* 3, English edition, London: Routledge and Kegan Paul.

—— (1935) 'The Tavistock Lectures', *Collected Works* 18.

—— (1942) 'Paracelsus as a Spiritual Phenomenon', *Collected Works* 13.

—— (1944) 'Individual Dream Symbolism in Relation to Alchemy', in *Psychology and Alchemy* (2nd edn, 1952), *Collected Works* 12.

—— (1944b) 'Religious Ideas in Alchemy', in Psychology and Alchemy (2nd edn, 1952), *Collected Works* 12.

—— (1946) 'The Psychology of the Transference', *Collected Works* 16.

—— (1955–6) 'Mysterium Coniunctionis', *Collected Works* 14.

—— (1963) *Memories, Dreams, Reflections*, London: Collins and Routledge and Kegan Paul.

Kay, D.L. (1984) 'Foetal psychology and the analytic process', *Journal of Analytical Psychology*, 29(4): 317–36.

Ledermann, R. (1981) 'The robot personality in narcissistic disorder', *Journal of Analytical Psychology*, 26(4): 329–44.

Lowen, A. (1967) *The Betrayal of the Body*, London: Collier Macmillan.

McDougall, J. (1989) *Theatres of the Body*, London: Free Association Books.

McGuire, W. and Hull, R.F.C. (eds) (1977) *C.G. Jung Speaking*, Princeton: Princeton University Press.

Neumann, E. (1955) *The Great Mother*, London: Routledge and Kegan Paul.

—— (1973) *The Child*, New York: Harper Colophon Books.

Newton, K. (1965) 'Mediation of the image of infant–mother togetherness', *Journal of Analytical Psychology*, 10(2): 151–62.

—— and Redfearn, J.W.T. (1977) 'The real mother, ego–self relations and personal identity', *Journal of Analytical Psychology*, 22(4): 295–315.

Ogden, T.H. (1992) *The Primitive Edge of Experience*, London: Maresfield Library, Karnac Books.

Peat, F.D. (1987) *Synchronicity: The Bridge between Matter and Mind*, New York: Bantam Books.

Penfield, W. (1975) *The Mystery of the Mind*, Princeton: Princeton University Press.

Piontelli, A. (1992) *From Foetus to Child: An Observational and Psychoanalytic Study*, London/New York: Tavistock/Routledge.

Redfearn, J.W.T. (1965) 'The patient's experience of his "mind"', *Journal of Analytical Psychology*, 11(1): 1–20.

—— (1970) 'Bodily experience in psychotherapy', *British Journal of Medical Psychology*, 43: 301–12.

—— (1982) 'When are things persons and persons things?', *Journal of Analytical Psychology*, 27(3): 215–38.

—— (1985) *My Self, My Many Selves*, Library of Analytical Psychology, London: Karnac Books.

—— (1992) *The Exploding Self*, Wilmette, IL: Chiron Publications.

—— (1994a) 'Introducing subpersonality Theory', *Journal of Analytical Psychology*, 39(3): 283–309.

—— (1994b) 'Movements of the I in relation to the body image', *Journal of Analytical Psychology*, 39(3): 311–30.

Reich, W. (1933) *Characteranalyse*, New York: Sexpol Verlag. (Many English editions, e.g. New York; Farrar, Straus and Giroux, 1949.)

Sacks, O. (1995 edition) *Migraine*, London: Picador.

Sidoli, M. (1993) 'When the meaning gets lost in the body: Psychosomatic disturbances as a failure of the transcendent function', *Journal of Analytical Psychology*, 38(2): 175–90.

Stern, D.N. (1985) *The Interpersonal World of the Infant*, New York: Basic Books.

Taylor, G.J. (1987) *Psychosomatic Medicine and Contemporary Psychoanalysis*, Madison: International University Press.

Emerging Mind from Matter
Dialectical processes

Catherine Kaplinsky

> The connection between spirit and life is one of those problems invol-
> ving factors of such complexity that we have to be on our guard lest we
> ourselves get caught up in a net of words in which we seek to ensnare
> these great enigmas. . . .The mistrust of verbal concepts, inconvenient
> as it is, nevertheless seems to me to be very much in place in speaking
> of fundamentals.
>
> (Jung, 1926: para. 601)

Introduction

Before starting this paper, I was overcome with an unusual desire to sleep.
An archaic struggle began between the desire to fall back into oblivion and
a push out and forward to separateness and 'me' who could think and have
ideas. I realised this was the essence of the very process about which I am to
write – this on-going dialectical rhythm which is life's pulse and out of
which, I believe, we develop our sense of self in our body.

The Jung/Freud split itself can be seen in terms of a dialectical movement, with Jung reacting to Freud's drive model and its relation to eroto-
genic zones. Jung emphasised instead the transformation of libidinal
energy to symbols in the service of forward and upward development.
The fact that Jung did not work very much with children and tended to
neglect infancy, further propelled him away from the body. Now, in analytical psychology, with the evolution of the Developmental School, there
has been a swing back to the soma, compensating for this lack (Fordham,
1957; Astor, 1990). As a consequence of this dialectical interplay a new
integration is possible. This expands our understanding of the mind/body
relationship in analytical psychology (Gordon, 1993: 159).

Jung did provide us with a basic dynamic frame in which to explore the
'fundamentals'. Underlying the body of theory in analytical psychology is
the principle of opposing forces and the dynamism which exists between
them. This dialectical process is key to understanding an emerging consciousness and an embodied self. It was from within this frame that Fordham

developed his ideas about the deintegrating/reintegrating processes. My sleepiness which was followed by a push to separate out, seemed to be part of this process. Jung wrote that 'Mind and body are presumably a pair of opposites and, as such, the expression of a single entity' (Jung, 1926: para. 619). The concepts he used to address this original fusion are difficult to grasp, sometimes overlapping, and the confines of this chapter prevent their proper exploration. They include such ideas as the psychoid, the collective unconscious and the archetypes (Samuels, 1986) out of which dialectical processes emerge. The Kleinian term 'preconceptions' or Bion's 'unthought known' seem to correspond to the archetypes which are themselves bipolar, having a somatic–biological–instinctive pole and a psychic–spiritual–image pole.

Psychological and somatic unfolding require interaction with the external world – a meeting of opposites, of internal with external. The nurturing and mirroring processes in the mother–infant dyad, for instance, involve a myriad of dialectical interchanges as each reaches towards, reacts against and has ambivalent reactions to the other. In turn this sets up *internal* complicated, dialectical interchanges between psyche and soma bringing about transformation. In analysis, the secure, holding setting fosters the expression of unlived archetypal strivings. The dialectical interplay between analyst and patient, if intelligently reworked, can then make space for internal unfolding and a freeing up of libido which had previously been blocked. I hope to illustrate this in the clinical section to follow.

The inspiration for Jung's use of the dialectic came originally from his interest in alchemy though he must also have been influenced by Hegel – as was Freud (Soloman, 1994). It was via alchemy that he came to understand change in the transference/countertransference interaction (Schwartz-Salant, 1988; Jung, 1946b). Crucially, change occurs when the opposites meet and the dialectic collapses. This constitutes a *coniunctio* – again derived from the alchemists. Out of this process the symbol is born whose meaning adheres to neither one side nor the other. The symbol often facilitates the transition from one psychological state or attitude to another (Jung, 1943: para. 121).

Dialectical processes and the body

In 'Principles of Practical Psychotherapy' Jung wrote that 'psychotherapy is a kind of dialectical process, a dialogue or discussion between two persons. . . . A person is a psychic system which, when it affects another person, enters into reciprocal reaction with another system' (Jung, 1946a: para. 1.) In the consulting room there are two bodies, two dialectical systems in which 'the psyche depends on body, body on psyche' (ibid.: para. 1). Our togetherness in the analytic hour creates numerous other dialectical processes as we experience and try to make sense of our 'fit'.

And just as there are dialectical processes, so there are possibilities for *coniunctio*.

Our original sense of togetherness drew on all our bodily senses – smell, taste, touch, sound and sight – messengers about the outside world. In infancy, they are not yet differentiated and 'mind', as such, is still sub-jugated to the body – at least until about the end of the second month (Gaddini, 1992: 124). At this stage fantasies and physical experience, such as suckling, are not differentiated. Frustrated infantile, pre-verbal states capable of development become manifest in the transference and counter-transference. These are the complex archetypal strivings which essentially are about becoming who we really are.

During the togetherness of the analytic hour, the dialectical processes hint at the history of our patient's early deintegrating/reintegrating pro-cesses (Fordham, 1957). Our eyes meet, or do not. If not, is there a sense of hurt or shame? Or is it hostility? We hear each other, or do not. If not, is there a sense of having been overridden, robbed of ability to express, of not wanting to hear? We smell each other or do not and occasionally touch; we do not taste. Together, we are in the same atmosphere, breathe the same air and sometimes use the same toilet. But our different senses have differing significance. In infancy the taste and olfactory senses are more developed than in adulthood so that when issues of smell or taste emerge, one is alerted to their early origin. Additionally, our senses interpenetrate in different ways – the dialectical processes vary. We can smell, touch and look at each other at the same time – each taking in the other simulta-neously. But we cannot know very directly if we are being smelled. Two different patients in a state of paranoia have asked if they smell bad. With the other senses we can be aware, to some extent, if we affect the other. Looking into the eyes of another as they look into ours is the most directly interactional and simultaneous communication. But to be heard, the other is required to be passive and listen. We cannot both be heard at the same time. Key to the analytic venture is the idea that one is heard.

Faulty togetherness – whether it be unresponsive, abandoning or inva-sive – hampers the deintegrating/reintegrating processes and archetypal unfolding (Fordham, 1957). Other solutions are found which I have come to think of as 'perverted' solutions. The aim of such solutions is to avoid traumatic togetherness. These defences of the self involve the dam-ming or blocking of libidinal energy. At the early pre-verbal stage, faulty togetherness inevitably involves the way bodily sensations are mediated which affects the infant's own ability to internalise a mediating process. The capacity to imagine is likewise impeded. The infant left for too long, for instance, gives up its rage after a while and becomes apathetic. Later he/she may refuse to eat. This is the stage when defensive psychosomatic illnesses can develop. (The literature is extensive on psychosomatic illness. See McDougall, 1989 and 1995.) In therapy, the faulty constellation is replayed in the transference/countertransference relationship and the *feel* of this constellation, always in flux, points to complex strivings which journey along with us in our psyches. In states of projective identification, we must, in part, be dealing with undifferentiated sensations and the repeated searching for appropriate, compensating responses. In the analytic journey we will be required to repeat these early struggles.

In the clinical section to follow I hope to illustrate how the infantile, faulty, taking-in, swallowing sensation affected the psychological, emotional capacity to take in and integrate. These processes of taking in and integrating thus have both somatic and psychological poles. Jung wrote about sensation when exploring what he believed to be our four basic psychological functions. These are thinking, feeling, sensation and intuition. 'Sensation is the psychological function that mediates the perception of a physical stimulus' (1921: para. 792–6). It therefore represents bodily changes and impulses to consciousness. He believed that, together with intuition, sensation is strongly developed in children and that it predominates over thinking and feeling. Thinking and feeling, he regarded as rational; sensation and intuition irrational. But, to my knowledge, he did not suggest that the latter are the two irrational functions because they 'belong' to an earlier stage of development as such – though it is implied. He also says that the functions of thinking and feeling are developed 'both ontologically and phylogenetically, *from* [my italics] sensation (and equally of course from intuition as the counter part of sensation)' (ibid.: para. 795). The rationality of feeling and thinking comes about with consciousness and therefore emerges later, so to speak, *out of* sensation and intuition.

Clinical example

I should like to describe some clinical material which I believe illustrates the momentary movement from a defensive position in which libidinal energy is 'perverted' into the body so as to avoid interaction, to a more appropriate solution which allowed integration. The example illustrates some aspects of the journey from sensation to perception, the development of a symbol and the struggle to emerge. This comes about via dialectical processes mediated by the Self and replaying unmet archetypal needs.

Relevant background factors: Susie came from Ireland. She had suffered from projectile vomiting (congenital pyloric stenosis) as an infant. The cause of this condition is unknown but it begins when the infant is two to eight weeks old and involves fierce stomach contractions and an inability to force milk down a thickened pyloric tube. Just prior to the decision to have the condition operated on, she improved, which seemed to imply that the problem was not primarily somatic. It meant therefore, she had been deprived of an easy swallowing, taking-in sensation and that she could not process what she took in. Youngest of four, she complained that she had been terrified of her mother who often hit her and threatened to cut off her tongue because she talked too much. She felt her mother controlled her body, put words into her mouth and 'pulled her body to bits'. When she was 9, her father left the family and she was instructed not to let anyone know. As a child she suffered from tummy aches and diarrhoea which have continued through adulthood. She remembers often lying tummy down on the floor, her hip bones pressing the floor so she would have a sense of boundary and being 'there'. She found this sexually exciting. She also liked to sleep with a small ceramic rhinoceros whose horn would poke her. 'Teddy bears', she said, 'didn't work for me.' This indicated to me that her sensory, infantile world had been inadequately mediated and was filled with anxiety. It had therefore been difficult to find a satisfactory way of linking separateness and togetherness – which was why the teddy 'didn't work' (Winnicott, 1971). The hardness of the floor and the rhinoceros on the other hand had an immediate confirming effect on her being and boundary. I related this to the autistic objects Tustin talks about – the 'not-me' possessions which serve to protect from danger (Tustin, 1986). As an adolescent she felt there was something 'wrong' with her body and she was often preoccupied with how it worked. She frequently examined herself and sometimes arranged to be examined internally by doctors for her tummy aches. She was never able to confront her mother, father or partners with her anger – she was terrified of retaliation or abandonment.

Now an attractive, sensitive and intelligent woman, she is well qualified and holds down a responsible job. In our sessions, she locks me in a fixed stare as she lies on the couch turned sideways, seductively, sensitively taking in my every move and demeanour, often clutching her tummy with the one hand and touching her mouth with the other. In the early stages, while being conscious of feeling tied down – particularly at the beginning and end of sessions – my countertransference feelings were governed mainly by what felt like the engrossed reverie of a nursing couple.

An on-going theme has concerned her difficulty in holding things in and processing things, in remembering what happened and in feeling she can keep a link with me. She struggles to hold on to our togetherness, going through the sessions afterwards in her head, writing down the connections we made. She is plugged into me. Unplugging feels unsafe and ending sessions is always difficult.

Two sets of dreams, a year apart, illustrate what seems to have been an internal shift when early defences of the self softened, allowing a more appropriate interaction and a firming up of ego boundaries. This in turn meant she could be liberated, at least momentarily, from her bodily symptoms.

The first occurred in a session when she had been complaining that she felt the security in my rooms was not good enough and that she felt 'funny'. We understood this to be to do with having different feelings she could not make sense of, and I had thought of her different 'selves' (Redfearn, 1985). She remembered a dream.

> I was in the house of a flatmate who had recently left. His father was not there. Pipes and tubes were tangled everywhere – coming out of the walls and milk and water gushed chaotically.

This illustrated the sense of terror and confusion in relation to her body, being left on the outside, and to me. There was no ordering function, no authority; a muddle and flooding of bodily fluids. I struggled with images of her vomiting, her horror and panic at her bodily rebellion. When I managed to link her infantile experiences to the transference situation and being repeatedly unplugged, she was visibly relieved, asking for reassurance that we could talk about this again.

Two sessions later, complaining again that the buzzer on my door was not working properly, she was fearful of being left anxiously waiting. She had a dream she would not tell me till the following session.

> I was in the woods. Someone was chasing me – a policeman, dark, in uniform. I was in a house and a man was tied up with his bottom in the air. I poured water over him so shit went into his eyes and mouth. Another blond policeman was at the door and going to punish me.

She was very disturbed about the implications of this dream. We related it to her persecutory feelings and the part of her that felt tied up, unable to express rage and having to recycle her own shit, orally and visually. When I was able to link her fears and rage at me for not being there when she needed me and for pushing her away repeatedly at the end of sessions, she again relaxed visibly and expressed gratitude.

A year later she was much more able to admit her attacking feelings. She was feeling more 'secure' with regard to being let in and out. My own sense of being tied up and trapped, led me to feel that at some level she had sufficient ego strength to be able to deal with the battles required in order to separate. She was managing to get under my skin by repeatedly attempting to break the boundaries by prolonging sessions, asking to borrow books, trying to find out about me, etc. I had been making interpretations around her need for me to keep the boundaries since she found it so difficult to do so. I also found myself leaving her in longer periods of silence and wondered whether I was being persecutory. She was enraged with me and, momentarily, I with her.

Around this time there were two significant developments. One was what she experienced when I linked things up and seemed to understand her rage – 'it feels like warm milk going down inside me and is sort of arousing sexually', she said. Inevitably this made me think of the sensations of 'taking-in' she had *not* experienced as an infant. The second development was her confessing that when she was really mad with me, she had fantasies of vomiting all over me, pissing on my carpet and killing my dog. She was later relieved to hear the dog bark, reassured it was still alive. Again this made me wonder about her infantile rage and projectile vomiting. She then had what felt like her first archetypal dream which she only told me four minutes before the end of our session.

> I was in your house. It was very big. You were showing me around all the rooms. There were lots of corridors. In the kitchen there were little girls. I was not sure whether they were yours or not. Then there was a chapel with a crucifix and two round things on either side of it. There were also statues in glass cages and a monkey type creature you were restraining.

Since it was the end of the session – a ploy to prolong it – we did not have time to explore this dream. But I had a sense of increased internal order (the corridors), an ability to contain and process (in the kitchen) and an ability to transform suffering, pain and chaos to a higher realm creatively (the crucifix in the chapel). The girls made me think of the *sorores* (helpers) of the alchemical process. Susie said she had not left it till the end on purpose. I said 'No, it was the monkey who did that', and as I said this I was thinking of Mercurius in the alchemical process. She laughed and then looked very angry which I knew was to do with her feeling pushed out by me. I said 'The monkey wants to bite now.' 'Oh all right then', she said, getting up, 'but what about arranging times for Wednesday?' 'We will have to leave that till next time', I said. She was furious.

A couple of days later she brought another dream:

> I was in a common room in a university. People were around. You were there having a session with me. I thought you were ill and asked you if you were and you said 'yes' but we carried on with the session. I then saw you had done something to yourself – shaved some of your hair perhaps. And I could not work out where your eyes were. Below them were painted two fishes. Disturbing. Also you were wearing a fifties old fashioned purple suit. I wanted a cuddle and got on top of you, lying on you, asking if I was too heavy. You said I was not.

There was a sense in this dream of me as wounded healer, of initiation and rites of passage (the shaved heads). She associated the fishes to being under the sea and to Christianity and purple to priestly robes. Instead of eyes there were fishes seeing into her depths. But it seemed that the most important aspect here was the fact that she could lie on me, and that she was not too heavy to be borne. This image constituted a *coniunctio* out of which she could be born in the other sense of the word.

Soon after this, she did give birth, symbolically, to what I felt was an ability to remember and symbolise, if only momentarily. Again it followed a session in which I had felt wound up by her and had been particularly firm when she had been attacking me by trying to find out more about me. She protested she could not help it; she was so muddled, etc. I said I did not think she was, that it was to do with her destructive envy and her need to unseat me. I was surprised at my harshness. But while on one level she was upset, on another she quite liked this battle. The next session she said it was funny but she had not had to write everything down afterwards. She had not wanted to and she had remembered it anyway. She also brought a dream.

> I was in bed. On the right side of my tummy there was a dome shaped lump as if pregnant. I badly needed to shit. I went to the toilet and did so, looking at it afterwards, trying to flush it but it would not go down. The brown mass then turned into something old looking, with crinkled skin. Then I realised it was a baby elephant. I saw it moving and saw its big brown eyes and big eyelashes fluttering. It was sweet. I took it out and was worried it would be all right. There was then a powerful sensation of space in my tummy where the elephant had been.

Her first association to an elephant was that it never forgets and then that she had been given a soft toy elephant, named Mandelay, when she was 8 years old. She associated Mandelay to mandala and wholeness. Once also her friend had told her about a baby elephant she had gone to greet in a foreign country. It had then charged her, becoming out of control, picking and tearing up plants and objects out of other people's gardens. As we explored further we realised that this elephant represented a number of opposites. It was female but masculine-looking with its long nose; it had old skin but was young; it was sweet but it rampaged out of control. And most importantly, it was bad bodily shit transformed to a symbol which stood for remembering. It represented something to be held on to in the mind, leaving a space in her tummy.

In later sessions the elephant was explored extensively. She also related it to Dumbo the elephant whose story she thought of as sad as it was about attachment and loss. Significantly too, Susie found it interesting that she had not been getting tummy aches or diarrhoea lately.

Discussion

This clinical example I believe serves to illustrate how Jung's framework and constructs, enhanced by the research of the Developmental School, throws light on mind–body interaction and the emerging consciousness.

First the material illustrates how in the pre-symbolic, pre-verbal stage of Susie's infancy, the deintegrating/reintegrating processes were impeded in such a way that she was apparently deprived of comfortable processing sensations which could enable the development of a healthy body ego. Inadequate bridging between togetherness and separateness also meant there had been insufficient opportunity for illusion, resulting in extreme anxiety about the 'spaces' which she desperately tried to control. Taking in and processing were frightening, so to protect herself it was necessary to set up barriers to intercourse with the outside world. Libidinous energy was therefore redirected or 'perverted' inwards to the body and symptoms developed. To create compensatory sensations aimed at confirming her being, she used the hardness of the floor to press up against, the rhino horn to poke her. She was able to control these things herself. Her diarrhoea and tummy aches were symptoms of this inability to process and resulted in an attack on herself.

The task in the analytic situation was to create a safe enough space to allow the redirection of libidinous energy outwards so she could feel received, could protest and attack and come to know that this attack could be digested, made sense of and that it did not annihilate. But to reach this stage I was first required to be the idealised good mother, there only for her. The gaze in which I was locked seemed to be a way of procuring a sense of interpenetration and fusion – as though I was being continually drunk in. It also prevented my having any other kind of intercourse which might cause envy. I came to think of our meeting eyes as an *ongoing coniunctio* in the sessions – as if in this fixed togetherness, early experiences of deintegration and reintegration could take place. Most pertinent to our dialectical processes was the fact that she came to experience my interpretations sometimes like a bodily sensation, 'like warm milk going down inside me and is sort of arousing sexually'. This seemed to be a compensating sensation which she searched out as a result of her traumatic projectile vomiting. This was satisfying for me too since I felt I had got it right. But only once we had had sufficient experiences of *coniunctio* in our togetherness, would she be able to experience an internal *coniunctio* and shift so that she could begin to separate out.

My ability to digest for her and feed back what I believed was going on was vital to her own growing ability to digest emotional experiences. This enabled her eventually to feel safe enough to express her frustrations with me. These grew to fantasies of pinching and smashing my things, pissing and vomiting on me and killing my dog – of whom she felt envious. These feelings were most powerful as she left sessions which she experienced as wrenching and cruel unplugging. The kitchen in dreams often represents the *vas* of the alchemical process or consulting room – the containing space where things are mixed up, heated and transformed. It is also the body. Containing the ferment in the 'kitchen' allowed for transformation. In

Susie's dream of my kitchen, the chaotic pipes and tubes from her first dream were now corridors, leading somewhere. And there was also a sacred place, the chapel, where suffering could be transformed to a spiritual level. But it was the mercurial monkey, trying to provoke and break boundaries, who got us embroiled in battle which hardened up the boundaries. Also my countertransference feelings of being frustrated at being tied down and invaded, had indicated a need for a battle to separate at some level. This clash enabled the shit (*massa confusa*) that previously clogged, poisoned and could not be processed, to be firmly expelled. Susie experienced its effect on me, giving her a sense of boundary and potency.

The non-retaliatory containment and the survival of our togetherness allowed the reintegration of her rage. This resulted in the *coniunctio* expressed in the dream when she could lie on me, was not too heavy for me and could be borne. And out of this *coniunctio* the third was born, the symbol of the elephant which remembered. Now the rhino with its rigid horn was replaced by the elephant with a flexible trunk. In this way opposites were brought together and she came to know that her rampaging, envious self symbolised by the elephant, was also experienced as sweet and lovable. Her momentary trust had enabled her to feel outwardly received so her body too could be freed up.

This material illustrates, I think, how pre-symbolic archetypal potential can journey along with us 'in readiness' to be 'met' and transformed from bodily experiences to symbols which give meaning. The transforming process is a mutual one of analysand and analyst since it is required of both that they become muddled and in ferment. This occurs in numerous ways, involving all our senses and dialectic processes, many of which cannot be brought to consciousness. Experiences of *coniunctio* between analyst and analysand are necessary first before they can then be digested in the service of internal *coniunctio* and shift. Transformation is possible because the moment of *coniunctio* is the moment when dialectic processes collapse into each other so there is an interpenetration. This must also be the moment when we tap into the deeper layers of the unconscious and reach into the unknowable collective and psychoid areas. Out of the collapse a new order and transformation can take place.

References

Anzieu, D. (1989) *The Skin Ego*, New Haven and London: Yale University Press.
Astor, J. (1990) 'The emergence of Fordham's model of development', JAP 35 (3).
—— (1995) *Michael Fordham – Innovations in Analytical Psychology*, London: Routledge.
Fordham, M. (1957) *New Developments in Analytical Psychology*, London: Routledge and Kegan Paul.

Gaddini, E. (1992) *A Psychoanalytic Theory of Infantile Experience*. London: Routledge.

Gordon, R. (1993) *Bridges; Metaphor for Psychic Processes*, London: Karnac.

Jung, C.G. (1921) 'Definitions'. *Collected Works* 6.

—— (1926) 'Spirit and Life'. *Collected Works* 8.

—— (1943) 'The Synthetic or Constructive Method'. *Collected Works* 7.

—— (1946a) 'Principles of Practical Psychotherapy'. *Collected Works* 16.

—— (1946b) 'The Psychology of the Transference', *Collected Works* 16.

Kaplinsky, C. (1992) 'Soul on ice, soul on fire: Abandonment, impingement and the space between', JAP 37 (3).

McDougall, J. (1989) *Theatres of the Body*, London: Free Association.

—— (1995) *The Many Faces of Eros*, London: Free Association.

Neumann, E. (1954) *The Origins and History of Consciousness*, London: Routledge and Kegan Paul.

Redfearn, J.W.T. (1985) *My Self, My Many Selves*, London: Academic Press.

—— (1994) 'Movements of the I in relation to the body image', JAP 39 (3): 311–30.

Samuels, A. (1985) *Jung and the Post-Jungians*, London and Boston: Routledge and Kegan Paul.

—— Shorter, B. and Plaut, F. (1986) *A Critical Dictionary of Jungian Analysis*, London: Routledge and Kegan Paul.

Schwartz-Salant, N. (1988) 'Archetypal foundations of projective identification', JAP 33 (1).

Soloman, H. (1994) 'The transcendent function and Hegel's dialectical vision', JAP 39 (1).

Tustin, F. (1986) *Autistic Barriers in Neurotic Patients*, London: Karnac.

Wiener, J. (1994) 'Looking out and looking in', JAP 39 (3).

Winnicott, D.W. (1971) *Playing and Reality*, New York: Penguin.

Chapter 3

Patient and Analyst

Transference and Countertransference

Mel Marshak's paper concentrates on contemporary formulations in psychoanalysis and analytical psychology around the patient–analyst relationship. She describes the shift from a subject–object perspective to one of intersubjectivity, recognising that the experience of transference and countertransference is nowadays explored and clarified in terms of a single system. Furthermore she suggests that Jung's use of alchemical symbols to describe the analyst–patient relationship anticipated the current emphasis on intersubjectivity.

Jean Knox traces the development of ideas about the analyst–patient interaction as it has evolved in the Jungian School. She follows the thread from the initial Freud–Jung collaboration, through their later differences and on to the very important contribution made by Michael Fordham. Knox follows up the effects of Fordham's theses on such particularly Jungian concepts as the transcendent function, the self and its defences.

The Intersubjective Nature of Analysis

Mel D. Marshak

Introduction

> Intersubjectivity has recently become a new flashword for many analysts of different schools for attempting to transcend the limitations of the concept of countertransference which itself derives from the one-person model.
>
> (Grotstein, 1994)

Though, at times, the word has become associated with some forms of analytic theory and practice with which I am not identified, none the less, within the frame which I want to address, it conveys the subject/intersubjective nature of the relationship between analyst and analysand.

My object in this paper is to describe the task of analysis which is to depict, as well as one can, and clarify the nature of the experience of the interacton between analyst and analysand, that is, the intersubjective as the primary 'subject of analysis' (Ogden, 1994). The prototype of the analyst–analysand relationship is the intersubjective relatedness of mother and infant, and it is my intent here to review some recent literature that has affected my thoughts and practice.

Historically, one of the major connecting links between Independent Object Relations analysts and Jungian analysts was their interest in and emphasis on what happens between analyst and patient. Both schools emphasised the interrelations between the analysand's and the analyst's subjective experience.

My own introduction to the interrelationship between analyst and analysand came from my early experience as an analysand in a classical Jungian analysis in San Francisco. As was usual in classical analysis, I read a good deal of Jung and became acquainted with 'The Psychology of the Transference' (Jung, 1946). At that time the Jungian School, certainly in San Francisco, had not absorbed much of the psychoanalytic literature, in particular Klein.

Michael Fordham came to San Francisco in 1950 and delivered his paper, 'Primordial images of childhood', making the connection between our notion of the archetype and Klein's idea of archaic images. I was struck by this and immediately made arrangements to go to London, where, in the fullness of time, I completed my training at the London Society of Analytical Psychology. What was unique about my training was that it occurred prior to the split in the Society of Analytical Psychology into two independent groups, so that I ricocheted between the best that the London Classicists had to contribute and the growing significance of Kleinian and Object Relations theory as it affected members of the SAP and their developmental orientation.

I want, then, to start this paper where I started long ago, with Jung and 'The Psychology of the Transference'. Jung (quoted in Jaffé, 1979: 125), said: 'the living mystery of life is always hidden between Two, and it is the true mystery which cannot be betrayed by words and depleted by arguments.' Symington (a member of the British Psychoanalytic Institute) describes this 'living mystery' in a similar way: he describes what he calls the X phenomenon – which suggests how very little we know about it (Jung's mystery). He says:

> At one level the analyst and patient together make a single system. Together they form an entity which we might call the corporate personality. . . . Transference and countertransference are two parts of a single system; together they form a unity, they are shared illusions which the work of analysis slowly undoes.
>
> (Symington, 1983)

Jung used alchemical symbolism, as found in the *Rosarium Philosophorum* (1550), to amplify his idea of the relationship of analyst and analysand (1946). According to Jung, by using alchemical symbolism he was trying to interpret by use of metaphor, a 'grand projected image of unconscious thought processes' (quoted in Jaffé, 1979: 87).

Briefly, some of the terms that have symbolic relation to analytic processes and the intersubjectivity of analyst and analysand are as follows:

- *Vas* – the alchemical vessel in which *prima materia, massa confusa* are mixed. It corresponds to the containment of the patient and analyst in the structure of analysis. In addition, the analyst's understanding, interpretation and holding of the situation created a *vas* for the patient (this is similar to Bion's concept of the analyst as container).

- The *Lapis* – became for Jung a metaphor for the actualisation of the self, the outcome of the process of individuation.

- The *Coniunctio* – (in chemical terms, it refers to the combining of disparate elements) symbolises for Jung the union of opposites: the interaction between the analyst and his or her analytical 'opposite', the patient, and the differentiation and integration within the ego of conflicted elements in the psyche of the patient; and, lastly, the interpenetration and integration of conscious and unconscious parts of the patient's psyche.

- The *Hierosgamos* – literally translated as 'sacred marriage', in alchemical terms referred to the process whereby opposite elements unite to produce a third substance. (Jung's use of this term seems to have anticipated what has come to be known as the analytic 'third' in psychoanalytic literature.)

- *Adept-Soror* – in alchemical terms the *adept* carried out the work in the context of a relationship with a partner. It is the notion of complementarity; the analyst and his unconscious, the patient and his unconscious and, in the external setting, the analyst and the outerworld patient. Once again, in the use of this complex symbol, Jung seemed to have anticipated the notion of the intersubjective which consists of the intrapsychic and subjective elements of both analyst and patient.

- *Nigredo* – from the alchemist's position, refers to stages of the alchemical process. *Nigredo* implies a sign of some significant event in analysis, for example, the emergence of a physical symptom, or a particularly significant dream, or a patient's sudden cancellation, etc.

- *Fermentatio* – in alchemical terms refers to the comingling of elements to produce a new substance. When Jung speaks of the analytic process as involving the altering of both analyst and analysand (1946: 176) one must bear in mind Jung's use of alchemical concepts to refer to their psychological meanings. The alterations take place because the personalities of analyst and patient are 'combined' like chemical elements to produce a new third substance. For Jung the 'third' is the transformed factor for both participants. 'The analyst in his combining with the patient . . . quite literally "takes over" the sufferings of his patient and shares them with him' (ibid.: 358).

Since unconscious content is projected it leads to an 'atmosphere of illusion' and, I would add, a loss of the capacity to symbolise. My own view is that projections work both ways – it's not only the patient who projects into the analyst, but also the analyst into the patient. What constitutes the 'third' is not that the separate entities or subjectivities of analyst and patient are combined, but that the 'third' is a product of a dialectic, or what Fordham has called the *'interactional dialogue'* generated between separate subjects.

To believe that the analyst quite literally 'takes over the suffering of his patient' is to enter into a delusionary countertransference. The central idea of the intersubjective is that analyst and patient are continuously defining themselves and each other. It is not so much combining elements to create a new 'third', but the 'third' represents the interplay between two subjects.

One of the multiple aspects of intersubjectivity maintains that psychotherapy is mutual (Jung's altering of both analyst and patient). This idea has, in some writings, given a kind of licence to the analyst for self-revelation, which is not what is meant by 'mutual'.

Though Jung's insight into the relationship between analyst and analysand is profound, I believe the notion of disparate elements combining to form the 'third' is an error. Rather, each individual is deconstructed and constructed by the other during the process of interaction.

I would now like to review briefly some of the ideas which have percolated through the literature, with increasing emphasis on the intersubjective nature of analysis. For a review of the ideas of countertransference I will, for the most part, refer the reader to Edmond Slakter (1987) who does an excellent review of relevant papers. In the main, the ebbing and flowing of the ideas of countertransference, or 'that which is to be got rid of' to 'that which is to be made something of', makes up the bulk of the history. I will only hit the highlights that are relevant to the theme of intersubjectivity.

This emphasis on subjectivity – the analyst's as well as the patient's – gave rise to the creation, development and re-evaluation of theoretical notions such as: countertransference as something of clinical relevance; acting out as a means of communicating something significant; modifications in technique – in order to adapt the technique to the patient rather than the patient to the technique, etc.

Laplanche and Pontalis trace three

> historical positions on the subject of countertransference: 1) Rid yourself of it by means of your analysis (Freud's 1910 position wherein countertransference is an impediment, to be overcome by the analyst's self analysis), 2) Use the therapist's unconscious as an instrument of research for locating the patient's unconscious (Freud's 1912 statement of the analyst adjusting himself to patients as a telephone receiver so that the analyst's unconscious is able to pick up on the unconscious of the patient), or 3) Stay with it intersubjectively, i.e. the resonating between unconscious as the only authentic psychoanalytic form of communication.
>
> (1983: 92)

Before the mid-sixties very few psychoanalytic writers disagreed with the view that countertransference must be considered an interference in the analytic procedure. Freud really never recanted his position that counter-transference was an undesirable impediment, although it is well known that Freud's clinical failures were sometimes products of countertransference interferences (Binswanger, 1956; Boyer, 1967). Fenichel (1945) was the first to note that analysts' countertransferences are largely determined by the influences on their unconscious conflicts by introjections of patients' attributes. Analysts have been concerned with the means by which psychological attributes of one person are assumed by another.

Meltzer (1948: 14) called introjection 'the most important and mysterious concept in psychoanalysis', and said that the process by which the child's experience of the external object is taken in, has not yet been described, Menzies-Lyth (1988: 1) said that 'introjection and introject have in no way found in psychoanalytical literature a place comparable to projection and project'. She notes, along with many other writers: 'Projection turns out to be more exciting, more innovative, more illuminating to our understanding of normal and pathological development' (ibid.: 3). It suggests why so many analysts were reluctant to study countertransference, preferring instead to investigate 'intuition' and 'enactment'.

Until the 1950s, some forty years after Freud introduced the term, there were few direct studies of countertransference. Hann-Kende (1933) seemed to be the first to suggest that the analyst's reaction to the patient's production might be helpful. Sharpe (1930) also reported a clinical case referring to the analyst's reaction. It was curiosity about intuition that captured the imagination, as it remains so today. Reiks (1948) 'listening with the third ear' – having a receptive attitude – found that an understanding of the analysand's message from the unconscious suddenly emerged. Balter, Lothane and Spencer speak of the analysing instrument operating within a subsystem of the analyst – who, therefore, 'is more likely to perceive connections between words, ideas and images which are products of the patient's primary process . . . because the (analyst's) subsystem is in part freed from the constraints of secondary process thinking, readily listening and so on' (1980: 490, 491).

Whatever their dominant orientation (ideas about object relations deriving from structural theory or from theories of the British Independent School) most people today who write about transference–countertransference interaction use one or another version of Klein's (1946) concepts of splitting, and projective and introjective identification. Although Melanie Klein firmly held the traditional view that countertransference constituted an obstacle to treatment (Klein begged Heinmann not to deliver her first paper on countertransference) and told Tom Hayley in the late 1950s that she thought countertransference interfered with analysis and should be the subject of self-analysis (Grosskurth, 1985: 388) none the less her subtle interpretations of her patients' inner words – especially pre-verbal feelings and ideas – can only make sense in the light of her ability to resonate with her patients' most primitive feelings. And Bion's injunction to 'abandon memory and desire' has to have been made in the name of countertransference. Whatever term we give to the process, Klein's work has been the most powerful single influence for the 'shift of perspective' (O'Shaughnessy, 1983: 281) that has led to interpretations now being directed toward the interaction of patient and analyst at an intrapsychic level. This has heightened modern understanding of countertransference, with its emphasis on the positive therapeutic uses of the analyst's reaction to the patient's verbal and non-verbal productions.

Bion's (1962) extension of Klein's work in finding projective identification to be not only a defence mechanism but also an infant's first way of communicating with objects, and in describing the role of the mother and the analyst as metabolising containers, further deepened understanding of the intrapsychic dynamics in the countertransference.

An understanding of the interdependence of transference and counter-transference emerged from Winnicott's ideas about the interdependence of subjectivities of mother and infant (1965) and the creation of a 'third area of experiencing in the potential space that exists (but cannot exist) between baby and the object' (1971: 107).

Psychoanalysis might now be seen as a combination of two perspectives, intrapsychic and intersubjective. The term 'intrapsychic' needs very little comment in that it is all we mean by internal objects and part objects. Intersubjective does not mean interpersonal, nor is it interactive or inter-action. Intersubjective means that two subjects relate, keeping in mind that there is a subject only for another subject. In this formulation the significance of intersubjectivity lies in intentionality. What is this for? Green quotes Sartre; 'en soi, pour soi, pour autre', that is, 'in itself, for oneself, for someone else'.

> The intrapsychic is for oneself, the intersubjective is for someone else; it means, 'what do you want from me?' Hence I'm not addressing the whole person, nor the personality, nor some global entities. I am addressing some very specific thing which is: 'What are you interested in me; what do you expect from me?' This is close to what Lacan described in terms of desire – desire for the other, desire of the other, desire of desire of the other. This dimension is important because it makes two subjects commensurate – not only two people, not only two bodies, but two subjects. The fact that it is two subjects changes the thing because it gives it its specific human condition, since only a human can be a subject.
>
> Nor does it mean that we do not depend on the more primitive, 'animal' drive part of us. This is the intrapsychic problem – the relationship of the id to the ego to the superego. What becomes interesting in

the intersubjective relationship is that as a consequent the two subjects will have to relate also through their intrapsychic dimension.

(Green, 1990)

'What do you want from me?' The question cannot be posed unless each of us considers our own intrapsychic world, our previous history, the organisation of our individual thoughts, desires, deeds, volitions, etc. And while each addresses the individual intrapsychic world in order to relate intersubjectively, each individual response will have an indirect and unknown effect, not only on the other's subjectivity, but also – though in a manner totally unknown – on their own intrapsychic world, inducing other intersubjective effects, and so on . . .

Green says: 'so you see, seen this way psychoanalysis really is an interesting thing.'

> Object Relations theories, even those interested in intersubjectivity, have not followed up on Winnicott's (1971) crucial distinction between the subjectively conceived object and the objectively perceived, outside other.
>
> (Benjamin, 1990: 37)

Benjamin calls attention to the troublesome legacy of intrapsychic theory, the term object. The term refers to the psychic interrelation and representation of interactions between self and objects. Though the 'real' environment and 'real' parents now play more of a role than in Klein's original theory, 'they have only taken us to the point of recognising that "where ego is; objects must be"' (ibid.: 46).

The tendency to collapse subjects into objects denies the difference between experience as perceived outside the self and the subjectively conceived object. Winnicott (1971) formulated the basic outlines of this distinction and the juxtaposition of two possible relationships to the object in 'The use of an object and relating through identification'. The distinction between the two types of relationships to the 'other' is significant. Both are natural psychic experiences and therefore both valid areas of psychoanalytic knowledge. Benjamin refers to these two categories of experience as the intrapsychic and the intersubjective (1990).

Intersubjectivity (brought into psychoanalysis from philosophy (Habermas, 1971a)) postulates that the other must be recognised as another subject in order for the self to experience fully his or her own subjectivity in the other's presence. The intersubjective theory contrasts with the logic of subject and object which has been predominant in philosophy and science in the western world. The intersubjective dimension of the analytic relationship aims to change the subject–object to: 'where objects were, subjects must be' (Benjamin, 1990: 34).

From the ego-object perspective, the child is the individual, seen as progressing towards autonomy and separateness, and psychic structure is seen as created through the internalisation of interrelations with the object, leading to greater independence. Thus separation-individuation theory focuses on the structured residue of the child's interaction with the mother as object – learning through experience of engagements, connection and active assertion that occurs with the mother as other.

The infantocentric viewpoint of intrapsychic theory leaves out the source of mother's responses (reflecting health or pathology) in her necessarily independent subjectivity. The intersubjective perspective, while not omitting the intrapsychic, transcends it since it focuses on the question of how persons become capable of enjoying recognition with an other. Recognising the parent as subject cannot simply be the result of internalising her as mental object.

This is a developmental process that has barely begun to be explicated. Benjamin asks where the theory is that tracks the development of the child's responsiveness, empathy and concern, and not just the parents' sufficiency or failure!

The self in psychoanalytical theory seems always to be the recipient, rather than the giver of empathy. The responsiveness of the self-object, by definition, serves the function of 'shoring up our self throughout life', but at what point does it become the responsiveness of the outside other whom we love? The pleasure in mutuality between two subjects gets reduced to its function of stabilising the self (hence love-object) rather than enlarging our awareness of the outside, or of recognising others as animated by independent, though similar feeling.

Stern (1974, 1977, 1985) and more recently Beebe (1985), Beebe and Lachmann (1988), Beebe and Stern (1977) have shown how crucial is the relationship of mutual influence for early self-development. The research on mother–infant interaction has revealed the significance of early reciprocity and mutual influence best conceptualised as the development of the capacity for mutual recognition. The studies have also shown that self-regulation is achieved at this point through regulating the other: 'I can change my own mental state by causing the other to be more or less stimulating.' Mother's recognition is the basis for the baby's sense of agency.

In Stern's view, early play does not yet constitute intersubjective relatedness (1985). He designates the next phase, affective attunement (which develops at eight or nine months) as intersubjectivity proper, that is, the moment when we discover 'there are other minds out there', and that separate minds can share a similar state. Yet the earlier interaction can be seen as antecedent, in the form of affective sharing. Certainly, when the infant returns the mother's smile, or vice versa, there is the beginning of reciprocal recognition.

The necessity of assuming a developmental point when infants acquire a theory or working sense of separate minds is not alien to philosophical inquiry. Psychology, on the other hand, has been slower to deal with this issue in these terms largely because the study of the development of subjective experience with persons, in comparison with the study of the development of knowledge of things, has been relatively neglected in academic psychology, although Baldwin (1902) designated subjective experience of the self and other as the starting units for a developmental psychology.

Psychoanalysis has always been intensely concerned with the subjective experience of individuals. Except in the very special case of therapeutic empathy, however, it has not conceptualised intersubjective experience as a dyadic event. This conceptualisation is necessary to a generic view of intersubjectivity.

Stern cites the dominance of separation/individuation theory to explain the emergence of this phenomenon as acting as an obstacle to a fuller appreciation of the role of intersubjectivity. Ego psychoanalytic theory viewed the period after seven to nine months as the time of emerging more fully from an undifferentiated and fused state that could interact with a more separated other. Stern, Fordham, etc., have shown that this undifferentiated or fused state is a fiction, and that the infant is an individual from birth. It is therefore not surprising that the former theory failed to notice that the appearance of intersubjective relatedness occurred very early in infancy, permitting the creation of mutually held mental states. 'Mutually held' does not mean mother's and infant's feelings are about the same thing: for example, baby experiences delight in a toy and mother experiences delight in baby's delight – a simultaneous affective experience about different aspects of the event. Cuddling and being cuddled, feeding and being fed are simultaneous affective events among many others. Both separation/individuation and new forms of experiencing union (or being with) emerge equally out of the experience of intersubjectivity. Intersubjectivity is the overreaching process that refers to the reciprocal influence of the conscious and unconscious subjectives of two individuals in a relationship.

Trevarthan and Hubbley (1978: 213) have provided a definition of intersubjectivity that can be effective in the analytic process: 'a deliberately sought sharing of experiences about events and things'.

Stern points out and investigates three mental states in infancy which give evidence of sharing, or at least of expecting the mother to share. These states are at a pre-verbal level. They are seen to be of great relevance to the interpersonal world and yet do not require translation into language:

• sharing joint attention
• sharing intentions
• sharing affective states.

Interaffectivity may be the first, most pervasive and most immediately important form of sharing subjective experiences. Research as well as psychoanalysis confirms that early in life affects are both the primary medium and the primary subject of communication. Trevarthan and Hubbley (1978) have commented that the sharing of affective moods and states appears before the sharing of mental states which reference objects, that is, things outside of the dyad. The sharing of affective states therefore seems of paramount importance during the first part of intersubjective relatedness.

There are a number of views as to why the infant adopts a subjective perspective about itself and others that opens the door to intersubjectivity. Shields, Newson and Vygotsky understand the achievement as the result of the mother's entrance into 'meaningful' exchange beginning at the infant's birth. Mother attributes meaning to her infant's behaviour. She provides the semantic element and gradually, as the infant is able, the framework of meaning becomes mutually created. This approach is referred to as the approach of interpersonal meanings.

Writers in France and Switzerland pushed the notion of maternal interpretation into richer clinical thinking. They assert that mother's 'meanings' reflect not only what she observes, but also her fantasies about who the infant is and is to become. For these thinkers, intersubjectivity ultimately involves interfantasy. This reciprocal fantasy interaction is a form of created interpersonal meaning at the covert level. It has been called 'interactions fantasmatique'.

Trevarthan (1974, 1978) stands relatively alone in maintaining that intersubjectivity is an innate, emergent human capacity. He points out that the other explanations for the appearance of intersubjectivity, especially the constructionist explanation, do not allow for any special awareness of humans or for the shared awareness that is so highly developed in humans. He sees this developmental leap as the differentiation of a coherent field of intentionality, and views intersubjectivity as a human capacity present in a primary form from the early months of life.

The capacity for a special form of awareness must come into play and this capacity must enfold maturationally; however, the capacity must have some tools to work with and the constructive approach has provided the tools in the form of rule structures, action formats, and discovery procedures. Finally, the capacity plus the tools would be operating in a vacuum without the addition of interpersonal meanings that are mutually created.

The more one conceives of intersubjective relatedness as a basic psychological need rather than only another autonomous ego-function, the closer one refashions clinical theory.

There is no question but that the reinforcing power of intersubjectivity is related to achieving security needs or attainment goals. Intersubjective success can result in feelings of enhanced security and minor failures can be interpreted, experienced and acted upon as total ruptures in a relationship. This is often seen in therapy.

Hegel (1952) showed how the self's wish for absolute independence conflicts with the self's need for recognition. In trying to establish itself as an independent unit, the self must yet recognise the other as a subject like itself in order to be recognised by it. Each self wants to be recognised and yet to maintain its absolute identity. Hegel's description of the absolute self is approximately the same as narcissism – Freud's conception of the earliest ego with its hostility to the outside, or its incorporation of everything good into itself.

Winnicott's thesis suggests a basic tension between denial and affirmation of the other (between omnipotence and recognition of reality) – destruction and survival. The collision Winnicott has in mind is the notion of 'aggression creating the quality of externality' (1971: 110), that is, when destructiveness does not succeed in damaging the parent or the self, externality comes into sharp view as a distinction from inner fantasy. A problem is created when there is a loss of balance between the intrapsychic and the intersubjective, between fantasy and reality. When destruction is not countered with survival, when the other reality does not come into view, a defensive process of internalisation takes place. What cannot be worked out in the domain of the intersubjective, shifts into the domain of the intrapsychic. Even though aggression might be dissipated, there is internalisation, since no process of destruction and survival is perfect. But when the other does not survive and aggression is not dissipated it becomes almost exclusively intrapsychic.

When mutual recognition is not restored, when shared reality does not survive destruction, the 'relating' to the inner object predominates.

Analytic theory and technique have undergone radical change over the past fifty years, becoming increasingly focused on the study of the interdependence of subject and object, and on transference and countertransference in human development and in the analytic process.

Klein's view of projective identification, elaborated by Bion, Heinmann and Rosenfeld, expanded the analytic understanding of the nature of the dialectical tension underlying the creation of the subject. The concept of projective identification introduced a conception of the subject constituted in the context of a complex system of psychological interpersonal focus. The idea of the interdependence of subject and object became fundamental to the analytic understanding of the development of subjectivity.

The analytic process which creates analyst and analysand, is one in which the analysand is not simply the subject of analytic inquiry; the analysand at the same time must be the subject in that inquiry (that is creating the inquiry) since his self-reflection is fundamental to the enterprise in psychoanalysis. Similarly, the analyst cannot simply be the observing subject of this endeavour since her subjective experience in this endeavour is the only possible avenue through which she gains knowledge of the relationship she is attempting to understand. The analyst and analysand are interdependent (as subjects creating and created, destroying and destroyed by one another).

Robert Young (1994: 61) says:

> in the traditional . . . approach the knowing subject is at one end of an investigative instrument . . . . What is essential about this way of representing the mind and the process of knowing is the spatial gap. The subject is at one end, while the object is at the other end, or 'out there'. The subject is the knower, the object is the known. The object is open to scrutiny, and the subject is not.

Young (ibid.: 62) goes on to make the point that interpersonal relationships are much richer and more multi-layered than the subject–object allows.

In an interaction, where things bounce back and forth, interpersonal space loses the quality of a simple subject–object picture with simple locations. Spaces are not simple in an expanded account of the interactive, or dialectical relationship. In a dialectical account, there are many layers, and reverberations (projections are taking place) – not along a one-way street, but in a two-way street – and are being internalised and re-projected.

O'Shaughnessy says:

> During the past half century psychoanalysts have changed their views of their own method. Instead of being about the patient's intrapsychic dynamics, it is now widely held that interpretation should be made about the interaction of patient and analyst at an intrapsychic level.
>
> (1983: 281–90)

Returning to the more personal origins of my interest in the intersubjective with which I began this paper, I want briefly to describe an aspect of my encounter with a colleague whom I supervised for a PhD at London University (Leal, 1975).

The broad subject proposed for the research was to do with the emotional development of the child. A particular query that preoccupied us had to do with the meaning of the expressive gesture of 'in-out-going' repetitive activities of the young child. I am referring to that compulsive-like quality of young children which has as a source or expression the use of any available container which may be filled and emptied alternately with water or other suitable objects conveniently lying around. Later we came to see this as symbolising the meaning-forming movement of the mind.

I say *later*, because our understanding arose out of the dynamic process of our interrelationship within the supervision in a seven-year struggle to identify the subjects and criteria which would constitute the content of the research; the struggle revolved around our need (intentionality) to make ourselves understood to each other. The problem for us was that, though we were dealing with emotional development, English was not the mother tongue of either of us – 'mother tongue' being the primary affective language of our original relationship with our caretakers. In addition, we in no way shared a cultural history, symbols, etc., that influenced our early development. We were two subjects, each with our own intrapsychic world, attempting to communicate without the common expressive affective symbols.

The content of our encounters was dialectical, that is, it was a continuous contradiction of opposites and resolutions. The urgency was the need to create a third object; a language, symbols, that were neither of us yet represented both of us.

The first created object arising out of our dialogue was the repeated figure of the number eight – which we drew on the blackboard in a repetitive motion repeated by the other as we tried to explain something. We had expressed the 'in-out-going' activity that was taking place between us, and recognised it as similar to the child's repetitive behaviour. We saw the figure eight, now drawn on its side, as a continuous, not polarised, simultaneous reaction/response to the *Other*. From this we postulated that the mother/infant responses, reactions, feelings, sensations, etc., to a stimulus/object were simultaneous – even though each subjectively responded to the stimulus in their own way. Hence, feeding and being fed is one event; cuddling and being cuddled is one event; the dialogue between supervisor and supervisee around an object or stimulus (for example, an idea) is one event; between analysand and analyst is one simultaneously experienced event – albeit the subjects of this intersubjective process are separate, involving continuous cross-projections. In my opinion, most of these cross-projections, like the Gordian Knot, cannot be unravelled. The only creative way is to attempt to define or clarify the subject around which the interplay takes place.

The conception of intersubjectivity places central emphasis on its dialectical nature and represents an elaboration of Winnicott's notion that 'there is no such thing as an infant (apart from maternal provision)' (1965: 179). In similar fashion, in an analytic context, there is no such thing as an analyst apart from the relationship with the analysand. Yet, as for the infant and mother who constitute separate physical and psychological entities, the analyst and analysand are separate, with their own thoughts, feelings, sensations, corporal and psychic reality, but co-exist in dynamic tension with each other in their separateness.

Neither the intersubjectivity of the separate psychological entities exist in pure form since 'each create, negate and preserve' the other through the process of projection, introjection and projective identification. . . .

The task, both in the mother–infant relationship or the relationship of analyst and analysand, is not to tease apart the elements to determine which belongs to each individual, but to attempt to describe as much as one can the specific nature of the experience of the interplay of individual subjectivity and intersubjectivity.

(Ogden, 1994: 64)

Andre Green (1975) coined the phrase the 'analytic object' and Ogden calls the intersubjective analytic third a product of a unique dialectic generated between the separate subjectives of analyst and analysand.

Psychoanalysis can thus be seen as an effort to experience, understand and describe the shifting nature of the dialectic generated in the confrontation of subjectivities in the analytic situation.

I believe it was T.S. Eliot who said: 'An immature poet imitates, a mature poet steals.' Whether in my case it is due to my maturity, my inadequacy, or my delinquency, I have begged, borrowed, stolen and internalised from so many people whose writings have stirred me that I am inclined to feel that my extensive References do not cover all those to whom I am indebted. At times, in writing this chapter, I have felt that all of its content should be in inverted commas.

Many years ago one of my patients was very fearful of where his innovative ideas came from, since they seemed to just pop into his mind. Indeed, in one of his well-known designs he had incorporated my uniquely shaped brass door knocker. Until I finally pointed it out, he had no idea from whence it had come – though he had been knocking at my door four times a week for seven years of analysis.

References

Baldwin, J.M. (1902) *Social and Ethical Interpretations in Mental Development*, New York: Macmillan.

Beebe, B. (1985) 'Mother–infant mutual influence & precursors of self and object representations', in J. Masling (ed.), *Empirical Studies of Psychoanalytic Theories*, vol. 2, Hillsdale, NJ: The Analytic Press.

—— and Lachmann, F. (1988) 'Mother–infant mutual influence and precursors of psychic structure', in A. Goldberg (ed.), *Frontiers in Self Psychology*, vol. 3, Hillsdale, NJ: The Analytic Press.

—— and Stern, D.N. (1977) 'Engagement–disengagement and early object experiences', in M. Freedman and S. Grand (eds), *Communicative Structures & Psychic Structures*, New York: Plenum Press.

Benjamin, J. (1990) 'An outline of intersubjectivity: The development of recognition', *Psychoanalytic Psychology*, 7, Supplement: 37–46.

Binswanger, L.H. (1956) 'Freud's Psychosentherapie', *Psyche*, 10: 257–66.

Bion, W.R. (1962) *Learning from experience*, New York: Basic Books.

—— (1967) *A Theory of Thinking. In Second Thoughts*, New York: Jason Aronson.

Boyer, L.B. (1967) *Die Psychoanalyticscher Berhandlung Schizophrener*, Munich: Kindler Verlag.

Fenichel, D. (1945) *The Psychoanalytic Theory of Neurosis*, New York: W. Norton.

Freud, S. (1912) 'The Dynamics of Transference', Standard Edition 12, pp. 97–108.

Gay, P. (1988) *Freud, a Life for Our Time*, New York: W. Norton.

Green, A. (1975) 'The analyst, symbolisation and absence in the analytic setting. (On changes in analytic practice and analytic experience)', *International Journal of Psychoanalysis*, 56: 1–22.

—— (1990) Interview following his invited address to the Division 39 Spring Meeting in New York, 8 April.

Grosskurth, P. (1985) *Melanie Klein: Her World and Her Work*, London: Hodder & Stoughton.

Grotstein, (1994) Foreword in T. Ogden, *Subjects of Analysis*, Northvale, NJ, and London: Jason Aronson.

Habermas, J. (1971a) *Knowledge and Human Interests*, Boston: Beacon.

—— (1971b) 'A theory of communicative competence', In H.P. Dreitzel (ed.), *Recent Sociology*, no. 2, New York: Macmillan.

Hann-Kende, F. (1933) 'On the role of transference and countertransference in psychoanalysis', in Devereux (ed.) (1953).

Hegel, G.W.F. (1952) *Phenomenologie des Geistes*, Hamburg: Felis Meiner Verlag. (Original work published 1807.)

Jung, C.G. (1946) 'The Psychology of the Transference', *Collected Works* 16.

Klein, M. (1946) 'Notes on some schizoid mechanisms', in *Envy and Gratitude and Other Works, 1946–1963*, pp. 1–24, New York: Delacorte (1975).

Laplanche, J. & Pontalis, J.-B. (1983) *The Language of Psycho-analysis*, trans. D. Nicholson-Smith, New York: W. Norton.

Leal, M.R.M. (1975) 'An enquiry into socialisation processes in the young child', PhD degree, London University.

Menzies-Lyth, I. (1988) 'Containing anxiety in institutions', *Selected Essays*, vol. 1, London: Free Association Books.

Ogden, T. (1994) *Subjects of Analysis*, Northvale, NJ, and London: Jason Aronson.

O'Shaughnessy, E. (1983) 'Words and working through', *International Journal of Psychoanalysis*, 64: 281–90.

Racker, H. (1968) *Transference and Countertransference*, New York: International Universities Press.

Sartre, J.P. (1956) *Being and Nothingness*, trans. H. Barnes, New York: Philosophical Library.

Sharpe, E. (1930) 'Technique of psychoanalysis', *International Journal of Psychoanalysis*, 2: 361–86.

Stern, D. (1974) 'The goal and structure of mother–infant play', *Journal of the American Academy of Child Psychiatry*, 13: 402–21.

—— (1977) *The First Relationship: Infant and Mother*, Cambridge, MA: Harvard University Press.

—— (1985) *The Interpersonal World of the Infant*, New York: Basic Books.

Symington, N. (1983) 'The analyst's act of freedom as agent of therapeutic change', *International Review of Psycho-Analysis*.

Trevarthan, C. and Hubbley, P. (1978) 'Secondary intersubjectivity: Confidence, confiders and acts of meaning in the first year', in A. Lock (ed.), *Action, Gesture and Symbol*, New York: Academic Press.

Winnicott, D.W. (1965) *The Maturational Processes and the Facilitating Environment: Studies in the Theory of Emotional Development*, London: Hogarth.

—— (1971) 'The Use of an Object and Relating Through Identification', in *Playing and Reality*, London: Tavistock.

Young, R. (1994) *Mental Space*, London: Process Press.

Transference and Countertransference
Historical and clinical developments in the Society of Analytical Psychology

Jean Knox

In this chapter I will discuss the evolution of Jungian theory and practice in relation to the transference and countertransference and illustrate the richness of the framework which forms the basis for the work of present-day Jungian analysts, with particular emphasis on analysts of the Developmental School. The model of deintegration and reintegration can, I think, be used as a metaphor for the way in which the core of Jungian theory has unfolded to meet ever-changing ideas within psychoanalysis, psychology and other fields, transforming and being transformed by them and then being reintegrated into the framework which we use in our thinking and in our daily work with our patients.

As Jung began to develop his own views on the nature of symbolism and of libido, his concept of the transference began to diverge from that of Freud. Initially Jung accepted Freud's argument that libido was always sexual in origin and that the images patients produced in analysis were always unconscious expressions of infantile sexual drives. He also shared Freud's view of the transference, seeing it as the unconscious expression of infantile incestuous fantasies towards the contrasexual parent, fantasies which needed to be worked through and resolved in the analysis. However, Jung's theoretical and personal conflicts with Freud became so profound that they finally severed their relationship (leaving their mutual transferences unresolved) in 1913 and Jung then felt freer to develop and expand his own model of psychological functioning.

In 'Two Essays on Analytical Psychology' he offers a theory of transference which goes beyond the personal projection of infantile sexual fantasy and draws on his evolving concept of the collective unconscious. He is careful to acknowledge the importance of reductive analysis of projected infantile fantasies which are founded on personal memories but he is clear that this forms only part of the analysis of the transference. Jung found that there is a further stage of treatment, when fantasies are produced which no longer rest on personal memories but which are 'manifestations of a deeper layer of the unconscious where the primordial images common to humanity lie sleeping' (Jung, 1953: para. 102). These are the archetypes of the collective unconscious which cannot be reduced to personal components; they form the basis of the archetypal transference and require a synthetic mode of treatment which integrates their powerful imagery into consciousness. As Jolande Jacobi describes it, 'a new bond is created between our personal unconscious and the primordial experience of mankind', and she argues that this accounts for the 'liberating effect that may result for a sick psyche, severed from its natural order, when it encounters and comes to grips with the archetypes' (Jacobi, 1959: 67). Jung called this process individuation, and said that at this point in an analysis 'we must follow nature as a guide and what the doctor does then is less a question of treatment than of developing the creative possibilities latent in the patient himself' (Jung, 1931: para. 82). In analysing the archetypal projections, the analyst helps to give their value back to the patient and 'the analysis is not finished until the patient has integrated the treasure' (1935: para. 352).

It seems to me that there were profound implications of this theoretical position on the role of the analyst in relation to the analysand; Jung saw that the archetypal processes activated in the analysis would influence the analyst as well as the patient, and he was one of the first analysts to recognise that the analyst's countertransference could provide useful information about unconscious archetypal processes. He realised that the analyst was as much in the analysis as the patient and must be as much available to change and transformation as the patient, 'for you can exert no influence if you are not susceptible to influence' (Jung, 1929: para. 163). It was this that led him to be the first to state that it was essential for the analyst to have been analysed himself before working with patients, in order to avoid falling into the same dark hole of unconsciousness as the patient, and to be able to maintain the delicate balance of remaining open to influence by unconscious processes without being overwhelmed by them.

I have always found the conceptual framework for the transference and countertransference which Jung developed to be more interactive, subtle and complex than Freud's view that countertransference, the analyst's emotional responses and reactions to the patient, was always indicative of pathology and inefficiency in the analyst. Many present-day psychoanalysts now share Jung's advanced insight, and agree with Bollas when he writes, 'I do not believe there is such a thing as interpretative neutrality' (Bollas, 1989: 58).

However this model of the analytic process was formed in part as a reaction against Freud's heavy emphasis on the central role of infantile sexual fantasy in analysis and Jung's statements on the value of transference are contradictory; in a detailed study of the historical evolution of Jung's ideas on transference, Steinberg (1988) draws the conclusion that Jung's negative comments about the transference, which devalue the central position of the transference in analytic work, are contaminated by an emotional extremism which arose directly out of Jung's conflict with Freud. One of the consequences of this conflict was that Jung's developing conceptual model was essentially concerned with the adult psyche and he did not develop an adequate and detailed account of maturation and individuation in infancy and childhood.

Michael Fordham, one of the founder members of the Society of Analytical Psychology, was not happy with Jung's view that individuation was a task undertaken in adult life only and not in childhood. His work with children at the London Child Guidance Clinic, before the Second World War, had shown him that children's dreams and paintings were rich in archetypal imagery and he was increasingly convinced that these dreams and paintings were not simply reflections of the parental unconscious expressed through the child (Fordham, 1993).

At about this time Dr Fordham read Melanie Klein's *The Psychoanalysis of Children* (1937); he was deeply impressed by her work and particularly encouraged in his own views by her clear opinion that children do develop a transference which involves projection of their own unconscious phantasy material and that the psyche of the child is separate from that of the parent. This supported Fordham's view that an infant should be considered as 'starting from being integrated – a person distinct from his mother' (Fordham, 1985: 50), and that there is a primary self which then comes into relation with its environment through the process of deintegration and reintegration. Individuation is thus seen as a continuous process throughout life, from the moment of birth or even before.

The implications of this discovery, which was increasingly supported by infant observation studies, were profound for the practice of Jungian analysis. It provided a theoretical framework for the emerging practice of Jungian child analysis involving analysis of the transference through the use of play techniques. However, it also affected the practice of adult analysis in that the transference, defined as the 'unconscious projection of the split-off or unintegrated parts of the patient on to or into the analyst' must therefore include infantile material and phantasy resulting from partial failures of the individuation process in childhood. The analytic setting would therefore need to provide a safe container in which regression could take place and this necessitated considerable changes from the practice of analysis as Jung described it and as it continued to be practised by Jungians trained in Zürich.

The changes introduced by analysts such as Michael Fordham were essentially the well-established techniques known to facilitate regression; they included an increase in the frequency of sessions from once or twice a week to four or more sessions a week, analysis with one analyst throughout an analysis, and an increase in the length of time an analysis would be expected to last. The patient would use the couch, with the analyst sitting in a chair by the patient and he or she would concentrate significantly more on interpreting the infantile projections and phantasies as they arose out of the patient's associations. The analyst would not herself introduce extraneous material in the form of myths or fairy tales to amplify the patient's unconscious material, whereas an analyst of the 'Classical' Jungian approach, rooted in the Zürich tradition, would attempt to elucidate the archetypal content of the unconscious by reference to such imagery, and so activate and resonate with the collective unconscious emerging in the patient's material. The assumption on which this Classical approach is based is that the activation and working through of archetypal imagery will eventually overcome any personal resistances to the individuation process.

Analysts of the Developmental School, based mainly at the Society of Analytical Psychology, increasingly diverged from this view as the need for analysis of infantile phantasy and therefore of infantile transference was recognised as fundamental. As Michael Fordham put it in his paper 'The importance of analysing childhood for the assimilation of the shadow', there is an 'urgent need for a genetic Jungian psychology if only because, if this gap in our analysis is not filled in, there is one certain result: the infantile material will augment the power of the shadow and often render it unmanageable' (Fordham, 1965). He pointed out that the psychic world of the adult patient's infancy is often reflected directly in pre-verbal manifestations acted out in the transference and that the analysis of these is only successful if they are recognised as re-enactions of mother–infant interactions. In a paper published in the first volume of the 'Library of Analytical Psychology', Mary Williams argued that the unconscious could not be divided into the collective and the personal, and that there are personal and collective aspects to all unconscious imagery and transference; analysis of the personal material allows 'humanisation' of the archetypal material and so its integration by the ego (Williams, 1963). An essential part of such work is always the analysis of the infantile transference. Freida Fordham felt that such infantile transference included the part-object relationships described by Melanie Klein, the 'breast, penis and faeces, to which I think we should also add eyes and mouth' and that archetypal imagery might begin with such part-objects; this illustrates the way in which analysts of the Developmental School began to integrate Kleinian concepts with Jungian theory, based on a model in which the polarised and simple internal objects of infantile unconscious phantasy resonate with and enrich the archetypal bipolar extremes which Jungians recognise in the unconscious material of their patients, including that of the transference (Fordham, 1969). However, more recent work by developmental psychologists such as Daniel Stern questions the bipolar nature of the earliest infant experiences, suggesting instead that babies are able to recognise and relate to whole objects in the earliest weeks of life (Stern, 1985). This research has given support to Michael Fordham's concept of an original self which is wholly integrated. In this model, the archetypal potential of the integrated original or primary self unfolds or deintegrates to meet the external world and to combine with it; the archetypal expectation and the experience of the response that meets it (usually the mother's response) are then reintegrated to form internalised objects, which are the first ego fragments. These gradually cohere to form the developing ego.

Just as this provides a theoretical framework for understanding psychological development in infancy, so it also shows how analysis offers a container and a relationship between analyst and patient in which the projection of split-off archetypal and infantile phantasies in the transference can be worked through, modified and reintegrated so that individuation and change can take place. The analyst is no longer related to unconsciously in a polarised way, but as projections are withdrawn, he or she can be seen as a whole separate person and no longer as a self-object, part of the patient's psyche in phantasy. The patient's perception of the analyst is initially determined mostly by the patient's unconscious projection of archetypal and personal phantasy, expectation and experience; as these unfold or deintegrate in the analytic work, they meet with the analyst's response which includes the capacity to carry the projections. As these are gradually worked through in analysis, so the patient reintegrates the projections, modified by the analyst's response. Kenneth Lambert emphasised how vital it is for the patient to be able to experience the analyst as a good and bad but reliably present parent–analyst; an analyst who does not enact the hostile internal objects projected on to him by the patient can be internalised and contribute to the formation of new 'good-enough' internal objects, whereas there is always a danger in analysis of the operation of the 'talion law', where the analyst responds to positive projections with positive counter-transference and to negative projections with negative counter-transference (Lambert, 1981: 152). Lambert is one of several Jungian analysts who have integrated some of Winnicott's concepts into Jungian theory and practice, particularly those of 'holding' and of the 'good-enough' parent/analyst. Rosemary Gordon gives an excellent and detailed discussion of the relationship between Winnicott's and Jung's work in various chapters of *Bridges. Metaphor for Psychic Processes* (Gordon, 1993).

The increasing integration of conscious and unconscious which is part of the larger process of individuation is an ego-transcending process rooted in the Self. Rosemary Gordon discusses this in terms of the transcendent function, the bridging process which is at the heart of the capacity to symbolise, that is, to link the known with the unknown, the conscious with the unconscious, the ego with the Self. This also resonates with Winnicott's notion of transitional relatedness, the development of the capacity to symbolise which originates in the infant's use of transitional objects as the first 'not-me' possessions (Winnicott, 1971). Impairment of the transcendent function emerges in the transference in the form of desperate unconscious resistance to the process of separation and differentiation and a need for omnipotent control of the analyst based on a phantasy of remaining in a regressive state of fusion with the analyst/ mother so that no change can take place and therefore the suffering and pain of loss can be avoided. Gordon points out that patients whose transcendent function is so impaired experience the world and therefore the analyst in terms of symbolic equivalence, citing Hannah Segal's famous example of the schizophrenic patient who completely equated his violin with his penis so that he could not touch the violin in public; for such patients the 'as if' quality of a true symbol has not yet been attained or has been attained but lost (Gordon, 1993: 199). Gordon highlights the fact that psychological functioning at the level of symbolic equivalence is usually accompanied by relationships characterised by projective identification, a term describing an unconscious process through which the individual 'insinuates himself into the psychosomatic world of the other', a similar process to that which Jung called states of 'primitive identity' or 'participation mystique'.

In both psychoanalysis and analytical psychology there has been an increasing recognition that the countertransference is the tool which the analyst can rely on most when working with a patient whose predominant transference mechanism is projective identification. Whilst Freud thought of countertransference as a hindrance and regarded it as arising from unanalysed parts of the analyst's psyche, Jung recognised the interactional aspects of the patient–analyst relationship and that the countertransference is evoked by the transference (Jung, 1931) but his views on whether it was a hurdle to be overcome or a valuable tool in analysis varied. Alchemical imagery provided a powerful metaphor for transference–countertransference interactions and in 'The Psychology of the Transference' (1946) Jung offers a detailed discussion of the alchemical treatise the *Rosarium Philosophorum*, first published in 1550 with a series of pictures which he felt anticipated the developments in the analytic process between analyst and patient. A summary of the stages described in the *Rosarium* and their relevance to analysis has been given by Andrew Samuels; the alchemical model has continued to provide vivid imagery for the analytic process, such as the mixing of two chemical substances as a symbol for the transformation of two people in the therapeutic relationship, the *vas* as the analytic container and the model of the 'wounded physician' as a basis for the countertransference (Samuels, 1985: 178).

Michael Fordham argued that with many patients analysts tend to 'introject their patients' unconscious phantasies or archaic objects', and are therefore in a position to study further their patients within themselves; he called this impact of patients on analysts the syntonic countertransference (Fordham, 1985: 141). Fordham stated that the roots of this concept can be found in Jung's observation that an analyst can introject his patient's psychopathology; this has therapeutic potential provided the analyst continues to analyse the projective and introjective forces at work and does not overly identify with the content of the introjection and act it out, thus perpetuating the patient's pathology. Although, as Plaut describes it, the analyst needs to allow himself or herself to 'incarnate an archetypal image', it is also vital that he or she can then work through that situation with the patient (Plaut, 1956). The analyst's central task is to 'hold' the personal and archetypal projections and by analysing instead of enacting them, gradually modify and metabolise them so that the patient can eventually take them back. Fordham contrasted this situation with the illusory countertransference which arises when the analyst's responses arise from splits within his or her own ego and reveal his or her own phantasies or complexes rather than those of the patient.

In my own practice, I have found that an increasing understanding of projective identification has extended my ability to use the information provided by the countertransference, particularly in relation to patients with narcissistic or borderline personalities. I have drawn on the writing of analysts who have described their work with such patients and who have recognised similar qualities in the nature of the transference such patients develop and in the countertransference responses this evacuative transference produces in the analyst. Fordham described some patients who develop a delusional rather than illusional transference, so that there is no 'as if' quality in the transference projections; such a patient places extreme unconscious pressure on the analyst, attempting to split the analyst and force his way into him, at the same time negating or doing away with the analysing function of the analyst; the unconscious purpose is to form an analyst–patient amalgam with the good but hidden 'real' analyst. These attempts to nullify the analytic procedure were identified by Fordham as 'defences of the self', total defences against the fear of annihilation by not-self objects which are split off and distorted deintegrates, evacuated by projective identification and then experienced in the delusional transference (Fordham, 1985: 160).

Other Jungian analysts such as Rushi Ledermann and Jane Bunster have described vividly the countertransference work with such patients who are extremely difficult to reach emotionally; the analyst finds herself experiencing, through projective identification, the patient's fragmented and split-off parts; she needs to identify with them in order to make sense of and return them to the patient in a more acceptable way so that they lose their terror and power. In her work with patients who seem so heavily defended and resistant that they seem to have an 'autistic core', Bunster describes her own powerful emotions of emptiness and despair through which she recognised the patient's fear of having nothing inside her; on other occasions she felt the anxiety and distress which the patient was unable to experience and had pushed into her instead (Bunster, 1993).

Ledermann also explores the transference and countertransference work with heavily defended patients, drawing on Fordham's model of defences of the self as the basis for a state of 'stagnation'; she describes this as a condition in which the patient's development has remained severely arrested for a long time so that deintegrative/reintegrative processes have been stunted from the beginning of life (Ledermann, 1991). She points out that in the case of the stagnated patient the analyst experiences a void, like an unbridgeable gap between them, perhaps because the stagnated patient has unconsciously abolished the analyst/mother and therefore cannot depend on, relate to, or demand of her. There is then no transference in that, by abolishing the analyst/mother, the patient avoids relating to her with either love or hate; there is instead a kind of limpet-like adhesion and a persistent need to dominate and control the analyst, rather than experiencing her as a separate person who can be related to erotically.

I think that Judith Hubback has made a particularly interesting contribution to the discussion of the countertransference when working with certain depressed patients who seem to have suffered from narcissistic deprivation in childhood because a depressed mother was unable to keep a psychological boundary between herself and her infant, and so 'ties the infant in a false closeness based on her unconsciously identifying with her own abandoned self that she has projected into the infant'. Hubback observes that with such patients, the introjected image of the depressed mother becomes much more amenable to analysis at times when the analyst herself either was or was believed by the patient to be depressed (Hubback, 1988: 127).

This observation seems to me to link with recent work by psychoanalysts such as Steiner who has suggested that with borderline patients it is necessary to focus on the patient's perception and phantasy as to what might be going on in the analyst's mind, because their pressing need is to be understood by the analyst rather than gaining understanding; what has to be understood is the patient's need to get rid of unwanted mental contents by projecting them into the analyst, and the fact that he is able to take very little back into his own mind (Steiner, 1993). In this state words are used primarily as actions having an effect on the analyst and likewise the analyst's words are felt as actions indicating something about the analyst's state of mind rather than offering insight to the patient. In this situation the analyst should accept and work with this pressure from the patient, using the countertransference to understand and articulate the patient's fears and phantasies about the analyst/parent's state of mind. This is part of the process of accepting the patient's projections, working with them as part of the analyst's psyche and, in so doing, modifying them until the patient can take them back and recognise them as his or her own.

A clinical example of this in my own practice concerns a patient with whom I increasingly felt that my interpretations were always wrong, being inadequate, mistimed or irrelevant. I became quite anxious, fearing her silent contempt for my stupidity, whereas she seemed to feel that all my remarks proved that she was the one who was always getting things wrong. In one session she described her despair when she felt that her partner wanted to hurt and damage her during an argument, and I suddenly realised that she unconsciously feared that my interpretations were malevolent attacks of the same kind. She feared that I hated her as she felt her mother hated her and her only defence was to communicate to me, through projective identification, how bad, useless and persecuted this made her feel. I said that I thought she was terrified that I hated her and so could only experience my interpretations as attacks to be kept out rather than insights which she could take in; she was then able to think about her fear of what might be in my mind and to go further to see that she had always felt that her mother's mind was full of malevolence towards her.

Another paper which has been helpful to me in my own practice was published by Roderick Peters; he questions the theoretical position which underpins most of the work that I have discussed, namely that the transference is only effectively analysed within the analytic relationship (Peters, 1991). He points out that with some patients a powerful transference relationship exists with other people in the patient's life and that a forced and artificial situation is created in the analysis if the analyst constantly tries to interpret all this in terms of the patient's unconscious projections on to the analyst alone. He emphasises the need to recognise external reality and transference where it actually is, a view which questions Fordham's position that interpretations are only those observations by the analyst which clarify the patient's state of mind specifically in relation to the analyst. Peters argues that this can become an omnipotent and defensive position on the part of the analyst, a position in which the analyst 'knows' that all communications need to be regarded as infantile transference material to the analyst alone, and so he or she becomes unable to be open to the actual unconscious pattern of projections which may be predominantly to other people. Such patients need to experience the analyst as a safe container able to recognise the real existence and real whereabouts of transferred projections.

A woman patient of mine described the rage she had felt when a car had been parked so as to block her own entry into her driveway; she was furious at being deprived of her space in her own home. As we explored this in the session she realised that her feelings of rage and deprivation were probably rooted in similar childhood feelings towards her younger sister, born two years after her, but at that point it was the driver of the car who had made her feel that way and not me. Another male patient formed an intense relationship with a woman with whom he needed to be constantly in a state of complete harmony; any conflict, disagreement or disapproval made him so anxious that he contemplated suicide and would do anything to regain her love. His infantile transference was directed towards his partner rather than to me.

So far I have outlined the ideas about transference and countertransference which have particularly influenced my own clinical practice, in which I am constantly made aware of the dynamic and shifting quality of the transference in analysis; it is like Proteus who could change his shape into a thousand different forms, but would finally reveal his secrets if the person holding him showed no fear. So, just when one feels one has understood one particular transference projection, it changes into something quite different with a new and unknown dynamic pattern between patient and analyst. Perhaps the concept of the complex best describes this constantly shifting dance of roles played out between the two participants in an analysis; sometimes I feel that I am being related to as though I were the patient's parent of childhood memory, and then on other occasions it seems as though I am being given the role of the child, with my patient needing me to feel directly and personally the kinds of anxieties and fears which it is intolerable at this moment for him or her to experience directly. At other times I feel as though I am being related to as an animate object, totally under the patient's control so that it is difficult to have any mind of my own; then the scene may change and my patient feels me to be an archetypal and terrifying magician who holds him or her as a victim of my abusive power. Magical powers of a benign kind may be attributed to me as though I am an omnipotent, almost God-like parent who can save the patient from a threatening world, and then there will be times when I am required to be a logical and impersonal thinking machine, devoid of all emotion. There are often occasions when a patient needs me to be able to recognise and identify accurately the projections which he or she experiences and describes in relationships outside the consulting room, as well as those which emerge within the analytic setting and this is particularly true when a patient is working through past experiences of trauma or abuse. For such patients, forced or inaccurate transference interpretations can become an added trauma because they are imposed and make the patient feel helpless, unable to influence the analyst's perception of him, an experience which re-enacts the helplessness he felt in the original trauma or abuse.

I have presented a personal view of some key concepts which contribute to a particular Jungian framework for understanding transference and countertransference. Shortage of space means that a great deal had had to be omitted; there are many psychoanalytic writers, such as Bion, whose work has been taken up and integrated into Jungian theory in the SAP, but a more detailed discussion of these would require a book in itself. I have made a very personal selection, tending to focus on more recent ideas about borderline patients because this is new and exciting territory in analytic work, territory in which the highly developed Jungian model of transference and countertransference can be a very reliable guide.

I would like to conclude by emphasising that effective analytic work is not based on the analyst's theoretical preconceptions but always arises out of the transference and countertransference which is the unconscious interchange between analyst and patient; this unconscious interchange takes many different forms, some of which are fairly easy to recognise, others of which are new and unfamiliar, so that as analysts we are constantly learning alongside our patients.

References

Bollas, C. (1989) 'Off the wall', in *Forces of Destiny*, London: Free Association.

Bunster, J. (1993) 'The patient difficult to reach: omnipotence, projective identification and the primary self', *Journal of Analytical Psychology*, 38, 1.

Fordham, F. (1969) 'Some views on individuation', in *Analytical Psychology. A Modern Science*, Library of Analytical Psychology, vol. 1, London: Heinemann.

Fordham, M. (1965) 'The importance of analysing childhood for the assimilation of the shadow', in *Analytical Psychology. A Modern Science*, Library of Analytical Psychology, vol. 1, London: Heinemann.

—— (1985) *Explorations into the Self*, Library of Analytical Psychology, vol. 7, London: Academic Press.

—— (1993) *The Making of an Analyst. A Memoir*, London: Free Association Books.

Gordon, R. (1993) *Bridges. Metaphor for Psychic Processes*, London: Karnac Books.

Hubback, J. (1988) *People Who Do Things to Each Other*, Wilmette, IL: Chiron Publications.

Jacobi, J. (1959) *Complex/Archetype/Symbol in the Psychology of C.G. Jung*, New York Bollingen Series lvii, New York: Pantheon Books.

Jung, C.G. (1929) 'Problems of modern psychotherapy'. *Collected Works* 16.

—— (1931) 'The aims of psychotherapy'. *Collected Works* 16.

—— (1935) 'The Tavistock Lectures'. *Collected Works* 18.

—— (1946) 'The Psychology of the Transference'. *Collected Works* 16.

—— (1953) 'Two Essays on Analytical Psychology'. *Collected Works* 7.

Klein, Melanie (1937) *The Psychoanalysis of Children*, London: Hogarth Press.

Lambert, K. (1981) *Analysis, Repair and Individuation*, Library of Analytical Psychology, vol. 5, London: Academic Press.

Ledermann, R. (1991) 'Regression and stagnation', *Journal of Analytical Psychology*, 36 (4): 483–504.

Peters, R. (1991) 'The therapist's expectations of the transference', *Journal of Analytical Psychology*, 36 (1).

Plaut, A. (1956) 'The transference in analytical psychology', in *Technique in Jungian Analysis*, Library of Analytical Psychology, vol. 2, London: Heinemann.

Samuels, A. (1985) *Jung and the Post-Jungians*, London and Boston: Routledge and Kegan Paul.

Steinberg, W. (1988) 'The evolution of Jung's ideas on the transference', *Journal of Analytical Psychology*, 33 (1).

Steiner, J. (1993) *Psychic Retreats. Pathological Organizations in Psychotic, Neurotic and Borderline Patients*, London/New York: Routledge.

Stern, D. (1985) *The Interpersonal World of the Infant*, New York: Basic Books.

Williams, M. (1963) 'The indivisibility of the personal and collective unconscious', in *Analytical Psychology. A Modern Science*, Library of Analytical Psychology, vol. 1, London: Heinemann.

Winnicott, D. (1971) *Playing and Reality*, London: Tavistock.

Chapter 4

Training and Supervision

Robert Fenton and Jane Knight write from their positions as the past and present Directors of Adult Training at the Society of Analytical Psychology. They explain the rigorous selection procedure for candidates and they emphasise how supervision of the trainees' clinical work is viewed as a core element. Although the development of an analyst proceeds individually, the authors draw attention to the way that the structure of training requirements can influence the analytic process. The work of C.G. Jung is the mainspring for the understanding of analytic work; however, in accord with Jung's empirical attitude, the knowledge of unconscious processes is supplemented with psychoanalytic theory and other perspectives. It is the trainee's ability to relate theory to clinical practice, and to have developed an analytic relationship with their analysands, which signals a readiness to apply for membership.

Complementing Fenton and Knight is a vibrant paper by Mary Addenbrooke – a contrasting view from the position of an analyst who has recently qualified. For her, the training functioned as a container with multiple layers within which profound changes could take place. This demanded stamina and an openness to uncertainties, but led to unforeseen aspects of herself coming into play which have continued to affect her, not only as an analyst, but in all aspects of life. Addenbrooke gives us an analogy of her experience in a painting by Uccello, which provides a backdrop to her succinct writing.

Training in Adult Analysis at the Society of Analytical Psychology

Robert Fenton and Jane Knight

Introduction

As a professional body of Jungian analysts the Society has provided a training programme since its foundation in 1946. This course is offered to those with the desire to become analysts who have the necessary personal qualities and experience. The programme has evolved and changed over the years since its inauguration. Originally trainee analysts attended one year of lectures followed by the supervised analysis of a patient and voluntary attendance at seminars.

In this chapter we describe the present state of the training, the stages through which the candidates pass, and the procedures for the assessment of candidates for acceptance as analysts and members of the Society. This also implies assessment of the course itself. In this connection, we should record that we have both served as Director of Training, Robert Fenton from 1987–91, followed by Jane Knight to the present, 1997.

Preparation for the practice of analysis originally took place only in Zürich where Jung himself supervised candidates and gave lectures and seminars. He was concerned that a training course within an organisation could lead to rigidity and that the relationship between patient and analyst would be replaced by technique or the application of pre-existing theories. Nevertheless he agreed to be the President of the Society when it was founded explicitly to be a training institute. Because of Jung's ethos it has always been a tenet of the Society's training philosophy that technique is the servant of that relationship. Vocation, however, is not inevitably destroyed by the study of theory and method.

By their investment – emotional, professional and financial – in the development of a training, the Society's members express their belief in the value of extending and deepening the practice of analysis. For the aspiring analyst the training provides a structure within which one may receive, discuss and integrate ideas and theories of psychological development and behaviour. There is time to pursue a deeper understanding of Jung and his work, to study the views of his followers and interpreters, to compare and augment them with those of other theorists in the realm of depth psychology, to risk controversy, to appraise and select.

In addition, at the clinical stage of the training, from the second year, the trainee analyst begins practice. The trainee's relative lack of experience is safeguarded by the Clinic Directors' assessment of patients and the enabling care of regular supervision.

Prospective patients are protected by the fact that members of the Society not only have experienced a lengthy training during which their work is rigorously examined, but are also held accountable for their professional conduct by virtue of their mandatory adherence to the Society's Code of Ethics. The contract between patient and analyst provides containment in the provision of regular times and length of sessions, agreed fees and boundaries of behaviour which are not over-stepped. This includes meticulous respect for confidentiality. Trainee analysts are expected to practise according to the Code.

From the perspective of the larger community the Society is a body of people with a shared knowledge base and shared principles of professional practice. As in medicine and law, each practitioner has a degree of experience and has been tested by fellow and senior practitioners regarding knowledge and skill, although what is involved in analytical psychology and psychotherapy is often far less understood by the public.

The core of the practice of analysis cannot be taught. Although a training is offered in which groups of trainee analysts attend seminars to discuss theory and clinical work, the intention is that each trainee develops individually, interacting with the experience rather than passively taking in what is taught. The trainees therefore bring understanding from within themselves. So the aim of the seminar leaders is to promote this understanding and learning. Trainee analysts learn, with the continued support of supervisors, to risk hearing and appreciating unconscious content and to accept the transference from patients, just as they come to value their own unconscious processes through their personal analysis.

Consequently understanding transference is a major component of the training. This implies containment of the projection and the strong affect accompanying the projection and also countertransference affects, without retaliation or enactment. Analysts have to learn to bear not knowing just as they have to learn to use their insights so that they time, shape and develop interventions and interpretations according to the needs of their patients.

To discuss the aims of a training in Jungian analysis implies a paradox. Analysis is not an intellectual procedure dependent on a body of knowledge, although there is a body of knowledge to be mastered and used. The effectiveness of analysis depends on the interaction between one specific patient and one specific analyst. The overview that we give addresses this paradox. The individual analyst combines study and experience with his or her own personality to inform and enhance the practice of the art of analysis. In Jung's words, 'The doctor [analyst] is as much in the analysis as the patient' (1931: para. 166). Analysts put to one side their learned theory while they are with the patients and hence allow themselves to take the risk of immersion in unconscious affects which may be very powerful. Training strengthens them in taking these risks, enabling them to meet patients with openness, empathy and imaginative receptivity. 'The real and effective treatment of neurosis is always individual, and for this reason the stubborn application of a particular theory or method must be characterised as basically wrong' (Jung, 1924: para. 203).

In a paper given in 1944 shortly before the Society was founded, Fordham pointed out a problem that had to be addressed when bringing organic growth within the framework of an organisation. 'We must not allow natural vitality to destroy the organising purpose, but, on the other hand, we must not allow the organisation to destroy the natural germinating vitality which springs from spontaneous impulse and reflection' (Fordham, 1958: 185). Hence we offer candidates a basis of both theory and clinical understanding which are essential and consensually agreed elements in becoming the particular analyst that only she or he is capable of becoming. If the desire to become an analyst arises from the developing personality and the Self, training enhances the process of individuation in the analyst.

Personal analysis

It was Jung who first insisted on the necessity of the personal analysis of the analyst. As a result he or she will have become aware of unconscious prejudices, conflicts and complexes and be enabled to recognise their effect on the relationship with the patient and their interference with the unfolding of the patient's material. This is why the first requirement for the Society's training is that the prospective candidate be in a well-established analysis with an experienced member of the Society.

Selection processes

In the selection of trainee analysts, previous life experience, breadth of interests and relationships are relevant as well as the more formal prerequisites. Applicants are expected to have a university degree or a recognised equivalent to demonstrate their capacity for thinking and ordering concepts. They are required to have experience of the practice of psychotherapy with supervision, to show some aptitude for the work and to have grasped an understanding of what is meant by professional attitude and vocational integrity. They will also need to have worked in a psychiatric clinic or hospital to observe and learn to recognise mental illness.

Selection for the training is a difficult and inexact procedure. Through the work of its Training Committee the Society takes great care to arrive at a fair assessment, but there is an infinite number of variables to be considered. The personality and mental health of the candidate are the most essential and yet the most problematic factors to assess. It is not necessarily the most conventionally sane person who makes a creative analyst. Candidates are asked to complete a searching application form with a brief essay about themselves and what has brought them to the wish to become an analyst. Each one is interviewed by two senior members of the Society and, if at that stage they are considered suitable, they also take part in a group selection procedure. Here they are asked to discuss two given themes in groups of three to six members. Each group is observed by two members of the Training Committee. The information gained from these contacts with each applicant is fully discussed in the Committee. Consideration is given to past achievement and evidence for future development towards becoming an analyst. Members of the Committee do not always agree and, after discussion, decisions are made by secret ballot.

This system of selection has evolved with the growth of the Society and its understanding of the demands of the practice of analysis. Formerly the applicant's personal analyst reported on the analysis to the Committee. Some have continued to support this practice on the grounds that the applicants' personal analysts know them better than can be ascertained by any selection method. However, a report from the analyst disturbs the patient's/applicant's transference to the analyst and it is also damaging to the closed vessel of the analysis. Nor is it always the case that an analyst can give an objective view of a patient because of the power of the relationship between them. Taking into account the advantages and disadvantages of a report from the personal analyst, the Committee decided in 1981 to suspend this requirement and to cover similar ground by a more searching selection procedure. Even so, selection may be affected by the development of transferences and countertransferences between applicants and interviewers which could give rise to over-positive or over-negative reactions.

Similarly, the group selection procedure has been criticised for giving an advantage to more extraverted applicants or those who have experience of working in small groups. One concern is that more weight might be given to the applicant's 'performance' on this occasion when the whole committee is present than to the interviewers' reports. This is an aspect which needs to be borne in mind. Then there may also be a tendency to weight the evidence in favour of the more introverted applicant because of the preponderance of introverts amongst Jungian analysts. We must consider the probability that like will favour like, so we need a system with inbuilt checks and balances.

The seminar programme

From the first seminar the trainee becomes a member of a small group. The Society has accepted up to ten trainee analysts in its adult department in any one year. This number may be augmented by the addition of trainees from the children's department during the pre-clinical year. After the first, pre-clinical year the training for child analysis follows a separate programme. This includes the analysis of children at various ages and stages of development. It is organised and administered by the Child Analytic Training Committee. This chapter is concerned with the training for the analysis of adults.

Seminars are held twice weekly in series of up to five meetings for each theme. They are led by members of the Society with a particular interest in the theme. The style of each leader is individual but we are concerned to facilitate learning through the participation of all group members; seminars are an opportunity for dialogue. In this approach learning is regarded as an interactional process bringing out a self-directing component in each trainee. Of course, direct teaching is very useful, for example when studying the history of how a particular concept has evolved, but we expect trainees to come with a budding point of view which will lead to each arriving at their own eventual integration. Trainees are encouraged to discuss and challenge theories presented by the seminar leader or in the reading material. Their previous experience is valued and they are supported in sharing it. They are thus enabled to contribute to the shape and content of the seminars. At the same time seminar leaders give consideration to the content of the contiguous series given by others and may consult on the progress of the seminar group.

The group has to accommodate to frequent changes of seminar leader so that it is the trainee group which holds the continuity. This is accepted as the group develops its own cohesion which we hope is established in the pre-clinical year before the impact of analysing the first patient is felt. Inevitably rivalry and competition arise within the group however much we may intend that each trainee work at his or her own pace. Apart from the jostling for place within the seminars, the timing of beginning work with the first patient, the capacity to hold and work with the patient, the presentation of case material and also, in due course, the application for membership, frequently induce intense anxiety, especially about failure or being left behind. Some trainees cope with this anxiety by remaining withdrawn from the group, but they are still affected by its dynamics. We are aware that this model is very challenging as both trainees and seminar leaders have to accept that there is no perfect theory to supply the answers. That is not to underplay the value of theory, to forget our Jungian identity or to substitute subjective preference for objective testing and validation. Rather it is to suggest that an urgency to regard a theory as final readily becomes persecutory in that it is a block to learning through one's own experience.

As well as the individual responses of its members, each group develops its own attitudes to the Society, seminar leaders and their idiosyncrasies, the sequence of themes, other training groups and 'the training'. It is the role of the Year Tutor to hear and respond to the group's conflicts and anxieties and, on occasion, to represent its views to the Director of Training and the Training Committee. Working on these issues is essentially task-centred rather than therapeutic, but inevitably the Year Tutor responds to some degree of necessary regression in the trainees. The Year Tutors have become increasingly active and the function more highly valued since the role was introduced in 1988. After attending the introductory meetings at the beginning of the pre-clinical year, the Year Tutor meets with the trainee group at the middle and end of each term and plays an important part in facilitating the progress of the training.

The pre-clinical year gives an overview of the substance of the course. It begins with Jung, an introduction to the man through his autobiography and letters and a discussion of his ideas in relation to his life and his work. We find that some trainees already have an intense acquaintance with him through their own experiences and have read many of his books and papers. Others find his style difficult and are bewildered by his mercurial associations. Analytical Psychology is placed within the context of depth psychology. Models of human development are explored in relation to evidence of archetypal activity. These models include those of Fordham, Klein and Winnicott. The work of recent psychologist researchers into infancy, such as Daniel Stern and A. Piontelli is also considered. The real child is distinguished from the mythological child and the child to be found in the adult patient. Infant observation is a requirement for the training in child analysis, but it is not mandatory for the training in adult analysis. However, many candidates for the adult training do take part in the regular observation of a mother and baby up to 2 years of age. They attend group discussions with a member of the Society. The aim of these sessions is the observation of behaviour as indication of emotion and inner mental activity, not the application of theory to explain the activity. In the third term of the pre-clinical year there are seminars on symbols and symbolisation and also on individuation at various stages of life.

Trainee analysts begin clinical work with the first patient during the first term of the second year, so the seminars are concerned with meeting the patient, the analytic attitude, transference and countertransference and unconscious defences.

Trainees have been allocated their supervisors, where possible according to their choice. Meanwhile the seminars continue, based on themes which may be theoretical but whose relevance to clinical practice is reinforced by the introduction of appropriate illustrative material. In addition the trainees are encouraged to bring examples from their own work. Subjects recur in a spiral of development. Thus there are seminars on dreams in both the second and third years of the seminar course. Work on complexes, myths and fairy tales in the second year are echoed in the third by seminars on amplification and active imagination. Attention is paid throughout to the analytic relationship, especially transference and countertransference.

A fourth year of workshops was introduced in 1992. Originally this served to meet the needs of trainees who had completed the formal seminars and were not yet ready to apply for membership of the Society. It has proved valuable in allowing for a deeper study of certain themes, for example through a concentrated course of Jung's works or focused case discussions. The fourth year also gives an opportunity to amend omissions in the formal course. The trainees are consulted about the content of these workshops and take an active part in the way they are structured.

Supervised clinical work

The clinical component of the course consists of analytic work with two patients, one man and one woman, both of whom attend four times a week. The work is supervised in regular weekly meetings with a different supervisor for each case. This continues until the trainee is accepted as a member of the Society. After the personal analysis, clinical work is the most significant element of the training. The supervisor is available as a consultant who stimulates and guides and who also has the task of overseeing and assessing the trainee's progress.

The supervisor has a complex role and several responsibilities which are usually complementary but which may conflict. Supervisors have a duty to trainees to further their progress in the application of theory, the development of skill and the analytic attitude and the use of themselves in relation to their patients. Supervisors have a responsibility also for the trainees' patients having as good and effective an analysis as possible and to the Society in maintaining a certain standard of practice. Hence each supervisor holds considerable power and this affects the development of a relationship of trust. If the supervisor conveys respect for the trainee as a colleague, albeit less experienced, then openness in reporting what has been happening in the analysis and discussion of it can be fostered. It is essential that trainees be enabled to express their personal responses towards their patients, for it is recognised that the analyst's emotional response is a vital factor in understanding the patient and that being emotionally involved is not a matter for criticism. Similarly, movement in the relationship between trainee and supervisor may lead to understanding of the relationship between the patient and the trainee analyst by what has become known as the reflection process, or, in the USA, as parallel process. For example, if the supervisor and the trainee disagree, this may sometimes be understood as stemming from the patient's ambivalence, or a sign of a split between the patient's internal parental figures. For these emotional nuances to be appreciated there must be a good enough mutual trust between trainee and supervisor. As the trainee analyst's unconscious processes and complexes may be activated by the patient's material, there is the risk that the supervisor will become a supplementary analyst to the trainee. This can be avoided by focusing on the patient and what is unconsciously stimulating an excessive or inappropriate response in the trainee.

Supervision is a delicate task. It includes guidance when the trainee is unfamiliar with the necessary process of establishing the conditions of analytic practice and clarifying theoretical concepts. Relevant reading may be suggested. The main focus, however, is on the close following of the process of the analysis. The supervisor demonstrates his or her style by the manner of listening and attention to the trainee as well as by focusing on particular elements of the patient's story. The task requires containment of the analytic pair, especially if the patient is very disturbed and likely to act out. It also demands openness to the impact of the patient's unconscious processes through the lens of the trainee's exposition. The supervisor's unanxious holding facilitates the continuity of the analysis through the crises which are very disturbing to a trainee analyst who is working with a borderline patient. So the supervisor presents as a model and occasionally as an antagonist to the trainee's protagonist, indicating a different viewpoint, if necessary standing for the patient. The aim is to help the trainee to discover and realise his or her own potential as an analyst.

A problem of management arises if unconscious processes in the trainee lead to a split transference so that, in extreme cases, either the personal analyst or the supervisor is idealised and the other experienced as persecuting, useless or interfering. Interpretation of such transference is the function of the personal analyst. It may take time before the impasse can be resolved so that supervision can be used appropriately.

Methods of supervision vary and are evolved by each supervisory pair. Many supervisors ask for very detailed reports, full verbatim records, as far as this is possible, of the trainee's sessions with the patient. Most trainees find this very difficult, but some supervisors consider that it is the means by which they pick up indications which have not been perceived by the trainee. However, such detailed reporting can be deadening and may be used to prevent the supervisor from participating. Spontaneous reporting is more alive, but issues may be avoided or overlooked. Over time there can be an evolution to a creative interchange and the manner of reporting may be varied according to the needs of the case.

Training patients are people who are referred or refer themselves to the C.G. Jung Clinic. They pay a reduced fee according to their circumstances and they commit to a full analysis of at least four sessions a week for a minimum period of two years. This distortion of the usual arrangement in private practice needs to be held in focus by trainees and supervisors because fantasies frequently centre around it. For example, the patient may secretly fear abandonment after the minimum period. This might be a shadow aspect of idealisation of the analyst. Or the patient might sense the trainee's need of him or her for training purposes and interpret this as being wanted and possibly exploited as a temporarily useful object. Alternatively, the patient may sense the trainee's anxiety about rejection and disruption of his or her training and proceed to play on this with unconscious relish. Then he or she would be frightened of an abandoning and exploiting retaliation from the trainee analyst when the minimum period had been completed. Unless brought into conscious containment this can lead to acting out by the patient, such as leaving just before the end of the minimum time with the unconscious purpose of both disrupting the trainee and actively bringing about the anticipated and feared rejection, rather than having to suffer it passively. A further complicating factor is the possibility that the patient is accurately sensing unconscious hatred from the trainee if the latter is feeling excessively at the mercy of the patient and resenting dependence on the patient. Some patients may feel constrained to attend for two years from a profoundly crippling sense of obligation. This may mean that the analysis, in one respect, cannot begin until after the minimum period has elapsed.

Individual supervision is very intensive, expensive and time-consuming. It gives the time and space for the experiencing and valuing of unconscious processes. Trainees learn to appreciate the positive aspects of the unconscious and to comprehend the interweaving of clinical process and symbolic understanding. In our experience it is the method of choice for the practice of such an intense undertaking as analysis. Having been well grounded in this method, qualified analysts may subsequently choose group or peer supervision in which there is a different kind of sharing of experience and response.

Trainee analysts are given the opportunity to communicate their choice of supervisor from among the training analysts of the Society, although the Director of Training holds the responsibility for the allocation. The training analysts are all currently practising analysts who have had at least ten years' membership of the Society since their own initial training. Appointment as a training analyst depends on a searching examination of the applicant's suitability by the existing panel of training analysts. Although trainees can rarely know who will help them most effectively, the supervisory pair usually develops a relationship in which the work is fruitful. On rare occasions a change of supervisor may be advisable because of incompatibility of style of practice or personality.

Assessing progress

Assessment of the trainee's work is a continuous process, but we allow that development of the trainee as a practitioner cannot follow a regular progression. Invariably in making personal space for the experience of the training and the ensuing subjective disruption, some phases of regression occur. We need to be sensitive to individual difficulties. Occasionally it may be advisable to delay beginning work with a new patient or to postpone undertaking the next year of seminars. Reports from seminar leaders and supervisors are used by the Director of Training to monitor individual needs. The six-monthly reports from the trainees on their analytic work are working documents for them and their supervisors to review the movement of the analysis over a longer span than the weekly detailed attention can provide. During the third year of the seminars each trainee discusses the work with the first patient with a group of his or her peers, the second-year group, the supervisor, the Clinic Director who originally assessed the case, and members of the Training Committee. This case discussion must take place before the application for membership and is considered in the assessment. In reports, clinical papers and case discussions the identity of the patient is stringently disguised for reasons of confidentiality.

The trainees are requested to send their comments on the seminars to the Director of Training. These are then passed on to the relevant seminar leader. This feedback may stimulate discussion about the content of the seminars or a review of their order. Individual seminar leaders use them to consider where their themes might be expanded or changed. In this way the trainees influence the future evolution of the course.

There is no strict sense in which we could claim a predictable quality assurance for the training of each group of trainee analysts. The process itself, however, is constantly observed through the engagement of seminar leaders, supervisors, the year tutors and the trainees themselves. Each year group is different in the personal qualities of its members and the experience that they bring. We endeavour to maintain standards while being sensitive to group and individual needs.

Membership of the Society

Trainees initiate application for membership of the Society when they have completed the formal requirements, attendance at the seminar course and the supervised analysis of two patients – one for at least a year and the other for a minimum of two years. Both supervisors must agree that the work is satisfactory and that the trainee is ready to practise analysis without regular supervision. In addition, the trainee should have submitted regular six-monthly reports on the work with each patient and have given a case presentation on one of them. The application must be accompanied by a thesis in the form of a lengthy clinical paper based on the work with one or both patients. Applications are considered by the Professional Development Committee. The supervisors and the Director of Training report to and inform the committee on the trainee's progress. This committee also has the task of subsequently facilitating the new member's further understanding of analysis.

Although there is no final written examination, the SAP training is an initiatory process with its own series of passages, thresholds and ordeals. The most testing experiences arise from the work with the patients when the trainee analyst is in a state of not-knowing, sometimes doubt, either feeling overwhelmed by the force of the other's affects and unconscious projections, or standing by the patient while unknown inner processes take place silently, which, in favourable circumstances, lead towards individuation. These are the real tests of the analyst's authenticity, the essential element without which theory, method and technique are empty.

The immediate goal, membership of the Society, is not the end of the candidate's endeavour. Continuing experience of the work and the study of new and conflicting ideas lead to the growth of perception and, in due course, the evolution of new theory. This is demonstrated by the work of those who have added to and modified the understanding of mental processes since Jung and Freud.

References

Fordham, M. (1958) *The Objective Psyche*, London: Routledge & Kegan Paul. Chapter XII, 'A suggested centre for analytical psychology', a paper originally read to the Analytical Club in April 1944.

Jung, C.G. (1924) 'Analytical Psychology and Education'. *Complete Works* 17.

Jung, C.G. (1931) 'Problems of Modern Psychotherapy'. *Complete Works* 16.

The Journal of Analytical Psychology (1961, 1962), Symposium on Training, vol. VI no. 2, vol. VII no. 1.

The Society of Analytical Psychology, 'Outline of Training in Adult Analysis' and 'Outline of Training in Child Analysis', both available from the Society of Analytical Psychology, 1, Daleham Gardens, London, NW3 5BY.

Training
A recent trainee's reflection

Mary Addenbrooke

Those who oversee a training programme must make plans in line with their philosophy of training in terms of elements, criteria and personnel. By contrast, arriving as a new trainee one comes with ideals and preconceptions but, basically, one is in the dark. I was no novice to theory and had already read and thought in detail about such matters as child development, pathology and projective identification, but what I found happening at the start of the training was a semi-involuntary letting go of preconceptions. I discovered that I needed to let myself be 'in the dark' once again and bring as fresh a mind as I could to what was happening.

In my study I have a reproduction of Uccello's painting *A Hunt in the Forest* painted around 1470. Here is a vibrant scene of mounted and unmounted huntsmen with their hounds, weapons and prey. Their clothes and accoutrements are brilliant reds and blues. The action is taking place virtually in the dark, for while the uppermost foliage of the trees is faintly touched with gold, little light penetrates to the forest floor. Uccello's passion was the exploration of perspective. It is said that he used to sit up all night wondering at the possibilities of this new concept. The central stag upon which the perspective of the painting is balanced is not visible in the painting.

I find this picture a convincing analogy for my experience of the training. A great deal of vigorous activity is going on, yet at the same time this is against a dark, shadowy background. There is plenty of instinctual life and a meeting of multicoloured facets of personality, but the object of the hunt is not visible. When our group of trainees met on the first evening, the object of training, though fantasised, was not visible. Each of us experienced the hunt quite differently, as we had our individual processes of change yet to accomplish. For while the overt aim was to prove oneself fit to be accepted as a member of the Society by taking the required steps and meeting the criteria laid down, this did not seem in any way like a measured progression. It seemed more like the exuberant and vigorous pattern of the huntsmen, some reining in their horses, others driving them forward. Once I had met people at the initial party I felt I was

Figure 1 Paolo Uccello, *A Hunt in the Forest*, c. 1470. Reproduced by permission of the Ashmolean Museum, University of Oxford.

part of the action and only a dire unforeseen accident would have dragged me out of it. 'Felt' is not a strong enough word, either. It was more a passionate sense of involvement, always slightly breathless due to the pace of the action, always attempting to be aware of where the other people and creatures were. Unlike the hounds in the painting, my own instincts were often on the timorous side; I was not at all sure that I could find a path, led on perhaps more by the scent than by any rational understanding. When I studied the reading material for the coming seminars, I was often struck by how I loved it or rejected it, rather than feeling neutral. It was presented, as it were, for us to taste, and some of it was not only nourishing but also rich and delicious. Other offerings seemed quite bland and said little to me. On the other hand I took issue quite violently with some, and then I came to the seminars in fighting (or regurgitating!) mode.

The hunt in the painting encapsulates a moment in the action. The point about a hunt is that it is time-bounded. It takes place and then it is over. Looking back, I realise that for me I needed some sense of bravado to take advantage of what was going on. I can hardly imagine anyone doing a training in a half-hearted way, but perhaps that is because I don't find groups particularly easy to belong to, so I need to ride in on the powerful horse of desire in order to participate imaginatively and to counter the exhaustion and discouragement which the struggle inevitably generates from time to time.

Within the temenos of the training group lies the possibility of regression in the service of the self. For the training group offers the opportunity for multiple transferences, as I have described elsewhere (Addenbrooke, 1997). Uncomfortable and even humiliating as these transference feelings may be, the regression permits the activation of those resources with which each of us long ago in childhood met the challenges of learning. Of these resources the most exciting is play. Watch any group of small children. Teachers will often comment that it is the time in the playground that is hardest for children just starting school. But the wonderful thing is that in play we discover creative solutions to our problems, and so we can start to cherish and value our creativity. The most difficult challenges we are called upon to face are those which demand our most imaginative and creative solutions.

I liken the training to the hunt because none of us knew quite what we might find in terms of changes we would be making or how they would come about. Intimate contact and intense interaction with new people would pose fresh questions. Unexpected aspects of the self were called into play in this complicated initiation. I think we each sustained some wounds and sometimes felt very frightened. A dark forest is dangerous. Who knows what may befall one there? From the relative security of the known (our families, our jobs and our relationships with our analysts) each of us set out on a personal trial of strength. What was at stake was not only what we could learn, but rather how we could bring our personal qualities, as well as our personal response to what we were learning, to bear on a new endeavour, namely, becoming an analyst. For me there was an enormous difference between seeing patients once or twice a week, as I had done as a psychotherapist for several years, and seeing them four or five times a week. It was not a matter of how much the technique varied, but how much of an impact it made upon my existence. Unlike the experience of my own analysis, I now had to carry the responsibility of working intensively with a patient, and find out what worked for me. Although each supervisor could be said to be supervising the work of analysis, I found I often thought of both of my supervisors as supervising me as an individual. With this shift in attitude changes could then happen.

Vigorous movement flows through the painting. This was certainly mirrored in the pattern of the days during training. Those of us who came from outside London especially, found ourselves either endlessly in transit or standing fuming at the cancellation of trains. Looking back, it is hard to believe that we fitted it in with so few hitches, but I realise that it was often friends or even mealtimes which were sacrificed. The train journey meant an hour in which I could either read a paper for the coming seminar, or grab some sleep, or neither – just let myself be swept along without thought or effort.

In contrast to the movement in the painting, the forest backdrop is quite still. It supplies a container for the action, albeit a shadowy and barely discernible one. Containment in the training, an essential part in any passage of initiation, came in different layers, rather like a Russian doll. Outside it all is the tradition of analysis as a whole, its structures and body of theory and the profession in all its guises. Within this is the Society itself, with which I guess most trainees have a relationship at the time both loving and fearful. A further 'outer' container is the pattern of the training in whatever form one chooses to create it in relation to a personal life and 'day job'.

Coming closer to home is the sense of being contained by supervisors. In my case, one had a room seemingly high up amongst the branches of a tree and evidence of feline occupants who returned when I was not there. The other had a guardian dog and a grey Mercedes which I much envied. In these two settings I was helped to struggle with my lack of confidence, my insecurity and my failures in a way which let me be me and led me to find new ways of being with my patients. Understanding and change came from being able to mull over my impressions of what I felt might be going on in the analyses with my patients with someone who would leave space for me to explore and who would sometimes say, 'Yes, go on, that sounds like it', or 'Have you thought about . . .?' In the week when I first took on one of my training patients, I had a dream of my supervisor graciously moving about a many-roomed ancient house ready to welcome guests. She looked extremely elegant and stately with glossy hair and a wonderful plain long navy dress. In the dream I arrived at her house wearing jeans and a sweatshirt, anxiously trying not to drop a large unwieldy parcel which for some unknown reason I was foolishly attempting to carry under my left arm. I felt rather small and scruffy and I didn't know what words to say.

Closest of all is the sense of containment provided by a four-times-a-week personal analysis which continues throughout and beyond the training. It is this requirement of the training which makes it so radically different from other types of training these days, such as that of counsellors, for example. While they too are offered the experience of becoming clients themselves, this is a far cry from a personal training analysis which lies at the heart of the endeavour of becoming an analyst and has to be well established before application for training. It is from the viewpoint of the relationship with one's own analyst that whatever changes take place in one's inner world can happen and be seen which makes such changes all the more radical as a result of this 'safety net'. Cross-currents of transference on to supervisors or indeed on to the training group may emerge, but benefit from being viewed from the more intimate perspective of one's own analysis. Even profound disturbance can be endured if there is secure enough containment, as can regression in the service of the self. Some degree of regression is inevitable if the learning process is to be at all radical, because of the need to become a 'beginner' all over again. Clinging to well-known certainties may be tempting, but is of little value in undertaking an enterprise which involves extending and deepening one's capacities. Analysis demands openness to uncertainties not only about the patients but within oneself.

Just how each trainee balances the demands made by the training against a personal need to develop his or her own inner life will be vastly different.

Jung himself had no personal analysis – he was on his own during the transformative phase after his break with Freud. In the troubled years that followed he battled alone in his struggle to accommodate the burgeoning but tumultuous sparks that were to form the basis for his future work. Nowadays, for us, whatever transformation takes place in our becoming analysts, this happens in relation to others. Closest of all is one's analyst, but there are the other crucial figures too – supervisors, one's seminar group and one's training patients. I have wondered to myself how much conformity training may tend to produce. Does fear of offending against some code, written or unwritten, force us into compliance, or, indeed, does longing for admiration and acceptance seduce us into it? Each trainee will meet the challenging task of deconstructing erstwhile ways of being and ways of understanding life in a unique way. The very influences which may result in a vivid clash of identities are those which fuel the process of change within us. This, I believe, is central to an analytic training.

Analytic training is an initiation which enables change at a profound level in the individual. It bears many of the hallmarks of more primitive initiatory experiences, for while it undoubtedly leaves symbolic scars which we may tend to decry, they can be honourable scars, gained in the painful process of giving up one's preconceived ideas and states of ignorance. Inevitably there is pain in the course of evolution into a more mature state and it involves the paradox of being on one's own, while also reflecting archetypal aspects of struggle in the emergence of the individual into membership of the group. It is existential, for it is one's being that is changed. Change brings in its wake loss of the prior 'state of naiveté' which has carried with it a certain freedom. This is lost forever. Such a training, grounded so firmly in the clinical work, is not limited to developing or enhancing technical skills in the consulting room nor yet again to an intellectual mastery of the analytic theory – the inevitable limitation of a more academic approach. It requires rather that the future analyst must dare a deeper commitment to life by allowing as yet undiscovered aspects of the self to come into play – while avoiding the perils of being inundated by the contents of the unconscious self. A new and different *coniunctio* between the ego and the self starts to unfold.

References

Addenbrooke, M. (1997) 'The creative potential of play and regression in analytic training. A personal reflection', *Journal of Analytical Psychology*, 42(3).

Beebe, J. (1995) 'Sustaining the potential analyst's morale', in P. Kugler (ed.), *Jungian Perspectives on Clinical Supervision*, Einsiedeln, Switzerland: Daimon Press.

Bruzzone, M., Casaula, E., Jiminez, J.P. and Jordan, J.F. (1985) 'Regression and persecution in analytic training: Reflections on experience', *International Review of Psycho-Analysis*, 12: 411–15.

Newton, K. (1961) 'Personal reflections on training', *Journal of Analytical Psychology*, 6(2).

Singer, J. (1982) 'The education of the analyst', in M. Stein, *Jungian Analysis*, La Salle and London: Open Court.

Chapter 5

Assessment, Diagnosis and Psychopathology

Jan Wiener focuses on the point that while assessors may have their own style and approach, the environment in which the assessment interview is carried out is likely to constellate unconscious personal and institutional shadow forces. These can subtly affect the assessor, the dynamic of the 'meeting' with the patient and the overall quality of the assessment. She uses the myth of Janus to illustrate the vicissitudes of the 'gate-keeping' process in four different assessment settings: a National Health Service psychotherapy clinic; in private practice; in a general medical practice; and in an analytic training organisation where patients are assessed for treatment with trainees.

In their paper, Clive Britten, Geoffrey Brown and Jenny Duckham concentrate on their collaboration in the assessment of applicants for analysis at the C.G. Jung Clinic, the low-cost scheme provided by members and trainees of the Society of Analytical Psychology. The authors emphasise how, in this intial session, care is taken to understand the client within the *vas* of a brief analytic encounter. The assessor uses the countertransference experience with the patient to predict how a journey of exploration and development of the self might proceed in a full analysis.

Tricky Beginnings
Assessment in context

Jan Wiener

Introduction

I would like to state from the beginning that I enjoy doing assessments. I am not sure whether or not we could postulate an archetype of curiosity as ubiquitous for all analysts, but in the course of my work, the *frisson* of anticipation is often heightened when seeing someone for an initial consultation. Patients' anxiety about revealing their 'story' to a stranger, often for the very first time in their lives, cannot but infuse the atmosphere in the room with a special tension.

Surveying some of the literature on assessment, I was struck by the quality of alert excitement which authors use to describe their personal responses to the assessment situation. Holmes (1995) compares his feelings before an assessment interview with the start of a theatrical performance: 'slight tension, pleasurable anticipation, anxiety about how I and the patient are going to perform'. Coltart (1993) refers to reading novels: 'I will be the privileged possessor of an entirely new story. It is as good as starting a new novel.'

As both a theatre-lover and a reader of novels, I was pleased to be invited to make a contribution to this book on the subject of assessment as, up to now, Jungian analysts do not seem to have been excited enough to write much on the subject. In my reflections on why this should be, I found myself wondering whether the rigours of assessment with their emphasis upon history-taking, psychodynamic formulation and diagnosis seem at first glance to be 'un-Jungian'. Discussions of psychopathology and symptoms which emphasise the need to place a patient firmly in a diagnostic category do not necessarily sit comfortably alongside the mysteries of potential 'individuation', which emphasise the unique 'self' of each person and the possibility that symptoms can be creative. This lack of interest may in part reflect our Jungian heritage as Jung himself seems to have been ambivalent and inconsistent in his views about the value of assessment for psychotherapy:

with growing experience, one even finds oneself at a loss in making a diagnosis . . . though we cannot do without such a nomenclature, we use it with the feeling that we have not said very much . . . because there are only individual illnesses, they practically never follow a typical course on which a specific diagnosis could be based.

(Jung, 1937: para. 540)

In another passage, he rather dramatically attacks any attempt at diagnosis:

the diagnosis is a highly irrelevant affair since, apart from affixing a more or less lucky label to a neurotic condition, nothing is gained by it, least of all as regards prognosis and therapy . . . it will profit the psychotherapist to know as little as possible about specific diagnoses.

(1945: paras 195–7)

I believe that an interest in assessment need not be 'un-Jungian' and is certainly not irrelevant. Today, we *do* need to know how borderline or psychotic a patient is if he/she is to start analysis or psychotherapy, as this has implications for the likelihood of a malignant regression and for potential management problems. Jung, writing fifty years ago, was addressing an audience of doctors about the special relationship of psychotherapy with medicine. He may have been exaggerating to make his point.

One paradox of our culture is that many more people are now seeking therapy but within an atmosphere of public scepticism and attack upon its benefits. The increasing number of different therapies from which to choose means that a careful assessment could be said to be even more relevant now than in the past as, with registration, the expectations of potential patients about what they may gain from psychotherapy are likely to increase. Moreover, our aetiological understanding of psychopathology has developed enormously over the past fifty years with increasing knowledge about the earliest stages of development.

The problem for analytical psychologists may be that the assessment situation is inevitably tense because two sometimes incompatible aims must be pursued simultaneously and within a short space of time. The assessor must try to create a safe enough containing atmosphere for sufficient unconscious material to emerge so that he/she may glean something of the internal world of the patient – a more receptive mode of being – while at the same time gathering relevant factual information – a more active, inquisitive mode of being.

We are always engaged with a number of different tasks during the assessment process and different therapists place a different emphasis on these various tasks. In this contribution, I shall concentrate mainly on the effect of the *context* on the assessment. I wish to make the point that, while assessors may have their own style and approach to an assessment interview, the environment in which the assessment is carried out is likely to constellate particular unconscious personal and institutional shadow forces which can subtly affect the assessor and the dynamics of the 'meeting' with the patient and the quality of the assessment.

The aims of assessment

Today, the term 'diagnosis' with its psychiatric overtones is rarely used. Psychotherapists and analysts who consider people for therapy or analysis are more inclined to talk of an 'assessment' or a 'consultation' or even an 'initial interview' and the search for a 'psychodynamic formulation' is more relevant. The word 'assessment' is generally used in the National Health Service. The *Shorter Oxford English Dictionary* defines an assessor as 'one who sits beside another', *or* 'a person who shares another's position'. The term 'consultation' is more usual in private practice and is defined as 'a meeting in which parties consult together, *or* one person consults another'. Whichever term is used, both definitions highlight the contrast between the more objective and distanced assessment of one person by another 'expert' with the greater mutuality of a meeting between two people where both will play a significant part in the outcome.

The literature on assessment also reflects these divisions. Some authors place more emphasis upon the medical approach, listing the characteristics of analysability (Malan, 1979; Coltart, 1992; Edwards, 1983; Kernberg, 1984). Others place more emphasis on the quality and atmosphere of the first 'meeting' and the interpersonal dynamics during the assessment process (Hinshelwood, 1995; Hobson, 1985; Steiner, 1993). Tensions between opposites, between the 'art' and the 'science' of assessment, between 'knowing' and 'not knowing', between 'empathy' and 'distance', between the 'objective' and the 'subjective' are of the essence at the time of an assessment interview and these are familiar to us, as analytical psychologists, of a continuing struggle for relationship. Samuels (1989) names these splits as the 'professional' and the 'poetic' analytic attitude to assessment today. Another way of putting it could be to say that the assessor must struggle to integrate the 'poetic' with the 'professional' through the smooth functioning of the *transcendent function*, that psychological function which mediates opposites and facilitates a transition from one psychological attitude or condition to another.

For me, the assessment process has three main aims. First, to find a way of engaging with the patient sitting with me that will allow a conversation to begin where feelings may emerge and access to unconscious material becomes possible. Second, at the end of our meeting(s), to emerge with a picture of the patient's relationships and inner world based on his/her life at present, in the past and through the relationship with me. I choose to express this as my attempt to gauge the present state of development of the patient's ego/self relationship which takes account of his/her strengths and difficulties. Third, I hope to be able to have a fairly open discussion with the patient about how to proceed and what kind of treatment plan we both think most appropriate.

I have noticed that with experience I have come to rely more heavily on my intuition and countertransference affects in the assessment situation than on the gathering of 'facts'. Sometimes, I find I form an impression of the patient within the first five minutes and spend the remaining time reflecting on and trying to falsify my hypotheses. However, the need to retain a capacity for thinking is essential. In her paper, 'The concentration of the body', Milner (1960) comes nearest to understanding what for me describes my own internal dialectical interplay during an assessment: 'the momentous meeting of the inner observer and the inner experience is also a meeting between mind and body'.

The context of assessment

> Assessment should be seen as an entity in its own right, with its own clinical technique.
>
> (Garelick, 1994)

> There is no difference between the analytic process in the first meeting and that in any other meeting: the analyst in the initial meeting is no more or less an analyst, the analysand is no more or less an analysand, the analysis is no more or less an analysis than in any other meeting.
>
> (Ogden, 1989)

Here are authors who make two contradictory statements about their beliefs about assessment. The differences between them can be explained if we attend to the context, the environment in which their ideas have emerged. Garelick is writing about assessments for psychotherapy in an NHS psychotherapy clinic, Ogden about the initial interview before taking a patient into analysis himself.

My personal interest in the context of assessment has developed through my work over a number of years in four different settings where I assess patients for psychotherapy or analysis. These settings are: an NHS psychotherapy clinic; privately in my own consulting room; in a GP practice; and for the C.G. Jung Clinic where patients are assessed for analysis by trainees. In all four settings, it is important to create an assessment environment where there can be therapeutic integrity. However, the assessor is always open to unconscious forces, partly as a result of the impact of the patient being assessed, but also I believe as a result of the impact of the vicissitudes of the setting in which the assessment is taking place, which impinge on the assessor in subtle ways.

Assessment: a gatekeeping process

The metaphor of assessment as a gatekeeping process can be helpful when trying to understand the impact of context on the assessor. While we are used to the dyadic model of the patient/analyst pair in our day-to-day work, in the assessment situation we are dealing with a triangular relationship. There is the *assessor/gatekeeper*, who inhabits a *place of work*/context and has the power to decide whether or not to admit a *potential patient* for psychotherapy or analysis. The assessor tries to create a protected space for himself and the patient so that the assessment process may proceed. This is not always easy, as the nature of the context, the place of work, may impinge upon this space.

I am reminded of Janus, the Roman god of beginnings who kept the gate of heaven and became the guardian of gates and doors. He is often portrayed as having two faces looking in different directions. His insignia is a *key* which opens and closes the door and a *stick* which porters employed to drive away those who had no right to cross the threshold. His two faces allowed him to observe both the exterior and the interior of the house and the entrance and exit of public buildings.

Frazer (1995) thinks it unlikely that Janus was nothing but the god of doors as a god so revered by the Romans would not have started life as a humble doorkeeper. He thinks it more likely that the door (*janua*) got its name from Janus. It therefore became customary to set up an image or symbol of Janus at the principal door of the house in order to place the entrance under the protection of the great god. It may well have been necessary to make this powerful god look both ways, before and behind at the same time, in order that nothing should escape his vigilant eye.

Like Janus, the assessor must always look in two different ways so that he may hold both the intellectual and the affective in some kind of dialectic during the assessment interview. To develop the metaphor further, the nature of the environment in which the assessment is carried out means that assessors must retain their capacity for vigilance along both a vertical and a horizontal axis. They require an internal sentry to guard against invasions from their unconscious arising from the influences of the setting (vertical) and an actual sentry who tries to find ways of looking around to gauge the outside pressures on the assessment process (horizontal). No wonder Graves (1975) referred to Janus as: 'the stout guardian of the oak door', as an assessor surely requires considerable strength and insight to hold his position with safety and confidence.

The following examples from four different assessment settings attempt to illustrate some of the powerful personal and institutional shadow forces with which the assessor must struggle in each environment.

Assessment in an NHS psychotherapy clinic

Patients thought suitable for psychotherapy are referred to the clinic by local general practitioners, psychiatric out-patient clinics and social services. The department is contracted to carry out a certain number of assessments per year. Patients often have to wait weeks, if not months, to be seen. Recent government policy to push mental health care out into the community has led to the introduction of industry-led strategies into the NHS which have forced clinics to make major adjustments to their style of work in order to avoid closure. Criticisms levelled at psychotherapists that they only treat the 'worried well' mean that assessors now have a political agenda to ensure that they assess a larger number of 'borderline' or 'psychotic' patients. The pressures to undertake brief therapy are strong, and freedom of choice to make psychotherapy contracts with patients according to their individual needs has been eroded. All this in a culture where resources are scarce.

In an NHS setting, assessors can easily become overwhelmed by external pressures. With limited resources, they may be required to take on a fairly active sentry function. The notion of triage, a term coined in wartime to refer to the process of discriminating amongst those wounded to decide who would most benefit from treatment, is relevant here and the assessor must develop a broader perspective than in private practice. The major institutional preoccupation may be: what is the least that I can do for this patient that will make a difference, or are there other resources available which I could use? A clinic may be forced to build defences for itself – to erect its own protected citadel, in order to deal with the vast numbers of referrals, political pressures etc. A protracted assessment procedure – three, four or five sessions spaced out appropriately (Garelick, 1994) – can be an effective way of containing not only the patient who after the assessment may have to sit on a waiting list for a period up to a year, but also the assessor, who is trying to maintain a 'good enough' space in which to work and reflect.

A woman in her thirties was referred to the clinic for an assessment. She had previously started to see a local psychologist for cognitive behavioural therapy following the birth of her first baby. She had left the psychologist prematurely saying that she would prefer individual psychodynamic psychotherapy. She had already had a considerable amount of analytical psychotherapy, including time as an in-patient in a therapeutic community. While this patient would clearly be able and motivated to use this style of approach, and might well have been taken on if assessed privately, limited resources in the clinic led the assessor to decide to refuse the patient's request. As Janus, she used her *stick* rather than a *key* as she thought that this patient might regress in a malign way as a way of avoiding the pain that motherhood and ongoing personal development would bring. The assessor explained to the patient that she thought that individual psychotherapy would be counter-productive at this stage and, despite the patient's protests, suggested that she and her husband return to the psychologist for support.

Assessment in private practice

Once they qualify, most analysts develop a network of colleagues who refer them private patients. By and large, if an analyst has a vacancy and receives a referral, the gate is likely to be left open. The sentry on duty is relatively passive, like the guards outside Buckingham Palace, and the assessment process in private practice is likely to involve a greater degree of mutuality than in other settings. However, the assessor's internal sentry may be more vulnerable to subtle and insidious attacks on his/her judgements. Assessment in private practice is the setting most likely to undermine the gate-keeping process and is one where both personal and institutional shadow forces may expose gatekeepers to their own pockets of 'madness' .

The analyst's need for work or money can colour his/her judgement about the suitability of a patient for analysis. The seductiveness of an interesting new patient can be a powerful influence on the analyst with a full practice to somehow find extra time to take the patient on him/herself. The relationship for the analyst between 'being in work' versus the valuation of 'space and leisure' is crucial here. Recently qualified analysts gain status and self-esteem from being fully employed at work, but later on they may come to place a greater value on out-of-work activity as contributing to their own personal development.

Referrals from friends or respected colleagues produce their own pitfalls and can also be seductive. Eisold (1994), in a paper about the intolerance of diversity within analytic institutions, writes refreshingly about the analyst's need to secure a place in the network of his colleagues:

> by and large, analysts work outside and quasi-independently of the organisations to which they belong, yet within strong systems of lineage, their membership of those organisations arouses particular ambiguities and anxieties. . . . for opportunities to supervise and teach, for referrals, for continuing self-esteem, as well as financial security, analysts are dependent upon maintaining their standing in their professional communities. . . . public deviance from established practices and beliefs is risky.
>
> (1994: 787, 790)

One aspect of this is the analyst's wish to preserve some idealisation of his/her own analyst. A recently qualified analyst told me of an unexpected referral from his ex-analyst who made the comment: 'This is a really interesting patient who should do very well in analysis.' At the assessment interview, the analyst, who had considerable previous experience of assessment, found himself unable to really 'see' the patient simply because of the pleasurable 'glow' at gaining the professional trust of his personal analyst. The continuing transference to an ex-analyst or supervisor is but one example of the way in which gatekeepers can be deflected away from their task by a conflict between personal wishes or needs and the imagined demands of their professional family.

Assessment in primary health care

A GP practice is usually a chaotic place in which to work. GPs lead busy lives, need to make quick decisions and are notoriously inefficient at creating and maintaining some space for reflecting about the work they do. As an environment for assessment, the surgery has particular characteristics. It is rather like a 'home' – a local place to which people come at many different times during their lives with a range of transferences projected on to the different medical personnel who work in the practice. Patients have close relationships with their GPs, often extending over many years. The structure of the system means that the therapist will often need to take more account of the circumstances of the referral, not just the patient. It is the practice as a whole which is the gatekeeper of resources and the image of a 'revolving door' through which patients pass at different times and for different reasons may be a more accurate image than a gate.

For the therapist who works on-site in the practice and comes from a training background where firm boundaries and structures are advocated, the adjustment to work in this particular setting can be slow and trying. The therapist is working inside the citadel, rather than at the gate and may need to be vigilant to forces from several different directions which can impinge on the assessment process. There are strong pressures to become like the GPs and the therapist may have to struggle to achieve a delicate balance between flexibility and firmness in terms of work style in order to maintain a space for the assessment process to evolve.

A GP referred a woman for an assessment to the therapist in the practice. The GP said that he 'wondered if she might benefit from psychotherapy'. The patient turned out to be a totally unsuitable referral. She was unapproachable, angry and, at times, psychotic and shouted at the therapist throughout the session. The therapist was puzzled by this referral from a doctor who seemed to be behaving out of character, as he usually referred patients thoughtfully after some preliminary groundwork. Because the therapist knew this particular GP quite well, she was able to discuss the referral with him. It emerged that this was a patient who had been asked to leave a number of practices in the area as GPs could not bear her. Unconsciously, the GP needed the therapist to know what a difficult time he was having. On realising this, the therapist could then offer the GP a service where she could support some of the 'difficult practice patients' for a time, as a way of relieving the over-burdened GP with a welcome rescue operation.

Assessment of training cases

The C.G. Jung Clinic was set up to provide analysis at reduced fees for patients with limited financial resources. Patients accepted are usually referred to trainees who are expected to analyse under supervision two clinic patients four times a week during their training.

The 1990s is a decade in which analysis is under scrutiny and attack. We are in a time of recession when the number of patients willing or able to attend four or five times a week for analysis is limited, and other training organisations who offer less frequent reduced-fee analysis or therapy sessions may be seen to be more attractive. In many cases, patients who refer themselves to our clinic, are likely to be 'borderline' or severely narcissistically damaged.

During my time as an Assistant to the Director of Training, my task was to select patients accepted as suitable for analysis by the clinic staff and place them with trainees. I had the opportunity to read and think about a considerable number of assessment reports written by the clinic staff and to talk to the assessors about these reports. Assessors who select patients for trainees sit at the gate as custodians. This is one of the few situations where the needs of the trainee come before the needs of the patient, and the Janus/assessor may only use his 'key' selectively. Trainees need patients who are sufficiently motivated to remain in four-times-a-week analysis for a minimum of two years. Patients need to have sufficient ego strength to survive the pain and turmoil of exploring their own inner processes within the intimate and intense relationship of analysis. The policy for SAP trainees is to look for patients who have had only a limited amount of previous therapy, and certainly no intensive analysis. This allows trainees an opportunity to 'start from scratch' with a patient. It is hoped that the prospective patient will be in employment, demonstrate some on-going capacity for relationships and have a personal history which shows no evidence of severe acting-out.

Pressures on the assessors may be considerable. First, trainees expect the institution to provide them with suitable training patients. During my time at this job, the supply just about met the demand, but this may not continue to be the case. The assessors will undoubtedly feel under pressure to accept patients rather than turn them away in order to 'keep the trainees happy' and thus ensure the smooth running of the system. Second, an assessment report is a candid and usually open account of one or more assessment interviews. It not only reveals much personal information about the patient, but also about the assessor. An assessment report is unlikely to undergo any 'narrative smoothing' (Spence, 1987) as might be found in a published paper in a book or journal where clinical material is carefully selected. In addition, assessors knows that their work will be seen and evaluated by a number of different people. Trainees may well question the standard of the assessment, and whether they have been referred a 'good' or 'difficult' patient. Any paranoia in the assessor may be activated by the knowledge that the trainee's supervisor, a training analyst of the Society, will also read the report. If assessors are relatively recently qualified members, they may be anxious about whether the quality of their assessments is likely to be used to evaluate their competence for advancement within the Society.

Eisold (1994) writes about the reasons for institutional fragility in psychoanalytic institutes which can lead to schisms. One source of anxiety which he identifies is the tension between analysts' need to belong to a particular school and their need to believe that they are fully open to the relationship with their individual patients. For analysts who assess patients for trainees within their own training institution, this delicate interface is likely to arouse anxieties of identity and divided loyalties – to the patient, to the trainee and to the assessor's lineage and professional family, the Society as a whole.

Conclusions

The assessment interviewing process may be described as a microcosm of the patient's life and probably also of any subsequent therapy or analysis he/ she may choose. Many patients are likely to remember the event for many years and the dynamics of the interview are usually a good predictor of the path of any future therapy. The responsibility of the assessor to get close enough to the patient to touch his/her unconscious processes while sustaining sufficient distance to think about what is happening, is considerable.

I have tried to illustrate how the excitement described by Holmes (1995) and Coltart (1993) confirms the emotional power of the assessment situation but can mask many of the difficulties inherent in the process itself. The principle of opposition was the foundation for much of Jung's most creative work and his ideas about duality are particularly relevant here as they present the assessor with the difficult task of living with the psychic disequilibrium that the different aims of the assessment process can arouse. Despite the paucity of literature, assessment is actually a particularly 'Jungian' activity.

When considering the setting in which an assessment takes place, the collision between inevitable opposing unconscious forces is likely to be strong and demands a Janus-like attention to a number of different perspectives simultaneously. For the assessor working in the NHS – in a psychotherapy clinic or a GP practice – pressures on the gatekeeping process are more likely to come from the outside in the form of excessive numbers of referrals, angry referrers whose patients have to wait to be seen, and political pressures in a time of change and diminishing resources. They are visible, however, the sentry can usually see them coming, and a vigilant external sentry function is crucial. Assessments which are connected with our own analytic institutions, either in private practice or of potential training patients, present the assessor with the possibility of more subtle and insidious attacks on his/her therapeutic integrity which are more likely to require a vigilant internal sentry function to stay in touch with both personal and institutional shadow forces.

References

Coltart, N. (1992) *Slouching Towards Bethlehem . . . and Further Psychoanalytic Explorations*, London: Free Association Books.
—— (1993) *How to Survive as a Psychotherapist*, London: Sheldon Press.
Edwards, A. (1983) 'Research studies in the problems of assessment', *Journal of Analytical Psychology*, 28 (4): 291–311.
Eisold, K. (1994) 'The intolerance of diversity in psychoanalytic institutes', *International Journal of Psycho-Analysis*, 75 (4).
Frazer, J.G. (1995) *The Golden Bough: The Classic Study in Magic and Religion*, London: Papermac.
Garelick, A. (1994) 'Psychotherapy assessment: theory and practice', *Psychoanalytic Psychotherapy*, 8 (2).
Graves, R. (1975) *The White Goddess*, London: Faber Paperbacks.
Hinshelwood, R.D. (1995) 'Psychodynamic formulation in assessment for psychoanalytic psychotherapy', in C. Mace (ed.), *The Art and Science of Assessment in Psychotherapy*, London: Routledge.
Hobson, R.F. (1985) *Forms of Feeling: The Heart of Psychotherapy*, London: Tavistock Publications Limited.
Holmes, J. (1995) 'How I assess for psychoanalytic psychotherapy', in C. Mace (ed.), *The Art and Science of Assessment in Psychotherapy*, London: Routledge.
Jung, C.G. (1937) 'The realities of practical psychotherapy'. *Collected Works* 16.
—— (1945) 'Medicine and psychotherapy'. *Collected Works* 16.
Kernberg, O. (1984) *Severe Personality Disorders: Therapeutic Strategies*, New Haven: Yale University Press.
Malan, D. (1979) *Individual Psychotherapy and the Science of Psychodynamics*, New York: Plenum.
Milner, M. (1960) 'The concentration of the body', in *The Suppressed Madness of Sane Men*, New Library of Psycho-Analysis, 3, London: Tavistock Publications.
Ogden, T. (1989) 'The initial analytic meeting', in *The Primitive Edge of Experience*, Northvale, NJ, and London: Jason Aronson Inc.
Samuels, A. (1989) 'Introduction', in *Psychopathology: Contemporary Jungian Perspectives*, London: Karnac Books.
Spence, D.P. (1987) 'The Sherlock Holmes tradition: the narrative metaphor',

in *The Freudian Metaphor: Toward Paradigm Change in Psychoanalysis*, New York and London: W.W. Norton and Company.

Steiner, J. (1993) 'Problems of psychoanalytic technique: patient centred and analyst centred interpretations', in *Psychic Retreats*, London: Routledge.

Reflections on Assessment at the C.G. Jung Clinic

Clive Britten, Geoffrey N. Brown and Jenny M. Duckham

Across the widening spectrum of mental health interventions, assessment for psychotherapy is being given greater emphasis. The past twenty-five years have seen the spawning of a great many new therapies. Some of these have evolved to a degree of maturation. In Britain the 'standing conference', after much labour, became the UKCP, established in1994 to register and define them. In the National Health Service, where psychoanalytically based psychotherapies used to play a minor role, the twentieth century will close with a range of therapists offering a wide diversity of practices. Brief focused therapy, cognitive and cognitive-behavioural therapies, family therapy, behaviour therapy, all deserve a mention. A number of others come under the heading Creative Therapies, and the importance in terms of numbers of practitioners and clients of 'Counselling' outweighs them all. In addition, those therapies once known as 'alternative' have slipped into the mainstream and even some National Health Service staff have training in these non-psychological therapies, such as aromatherapy or massage, that are derivatives of ancient ways of easing stress and providing comfort.

This plethora of styles and approaches, some old ideas in new presentations and some real developments, is in keeping with the post-modern *Zeitgeist*. It comes hand-in-hand with some now familiar values. Especially in state provisions the 'value for money' theme has been dominant and closely intertwined with a belief that shorter, faster solutions to problems are possible and preferred. Paradoxically, while using therapy or being a therapist is becoming commonplace, there has been an upturn in the level of critical comment about psychoanalysis. In part this is deserved and probably of value. The implications of the increased significance of traumatogenic external world factors have opened up some legitimate lines of criticism. Earlier the writing of people such as Masson (1984) took its toll. More recently issues such as 'false memory syndrome' have provided a further rationale for collective mistrust and attack.

In this context the task of assessment of suitability for analysis has inevitably needed redefinition. Psychiatric assessment for psychotherapy in the National Health Service has evolved along with the differentiation of therapies and therapists (Aveline, 1980). Clearly the most suitable approach to a particular patient or problem is likely to be the most efficient. A person seeking analysis has to work through criteria such as 'briefest', 'cheapest', 'most cost effective' or 'efficient', and arrive at another set of values. They will currently need to suspend belief over critical media comment. Somehow, through their own strivings and searchings or a chance encounter with a propitious suggestion, they will arrive at a wish for an idealised experience. Outside those few who seek analysis as part of their training and professional development, this current context provides a confusing and indistinct trail for potential analysands.

Those presenting themselves for assessment have changed over the years and these changes have influenced assessment criteria and process. While fewer in number, a greater diversity of ages, people and problems, arrive. Many have experience of other therapies and therapists, bringing preconceptions and additional transference issues both to the assessment process and to a possible subsequent analytic relationship. Increasingly, enduring life problems which have not yielded to simpler interventions are presented. The healthy neurotic patient with 'good ego strengths' seeking to enrich life is still to be found from time to time. More often, potential patients have serious difficulties and diagnostically have personality disorder features. Substantial numbers are now open about their abusive childhood experiences. Others may be seeking a setting in which they can be open. No longer is it ethically acceptable or intellectually tenable to exclude people if they are homosexual. Culture, race, gender, while perhaps never given as exclusion criteria, have become issues for therapists in training, demanding of them greater receptivity and skill.

This necessary diversity presents challenges to the analytic process. If potential patients are more likely to be damaged and disabled, then the question of effectiveness cannot be sidestepped. The anticipation of 'cure or healing' can be addressed. However, the analysis will be more likely to enable patients to whom the approach is suited. Thus diversity places greater demands on the assessment process. Rather than simply lowering the threshold for acceptance some greater focus on specific criteria is required.

Pioneering work in Europe and North America over the past fifty years by psychoanalysts and analytical psychologists has brought narcissistic and borderline personality disorders into the realm of treatable problems (Rosenfeld, 1987). Even psychosis, and especially psychotic phenomena outside a formal diagnosis of mental illness, have been subject to extensive experimental analytic treatment (Jackson, 1963; Searles, 1965). The slowly aggregated body of knowledge and technique derived from this work has permeated the analytic communities and trainings. No longer are analysts and therapists totally ill-equipped to help patients with such problems.

Hence, work with patients where ego function is immature and boundaries ill defined is not entirely uncharted territory.

In a discussion of the aims of assessment it is important to think about the aims of analytical psychology as practised in the Society of Analytical Psychology and also to consider how they figure in relation to other psychotherapeutic and psychoanalytic models. The aims go beyond elucidation of how the patient came to develop and persist in the psychological difficulties and ego defences with which he/she arrives in the consulting room.

Jung (1931a) described the first two activities undertaken in an analysis as catharsis and clarification, with education as the third. These encompass the same ideas as most other schools where the analysand is facilitated into a relationship in the analysis in which reconstruction and recapitulation of problems occur and where awareness develops utilizing transference, countertransference and projective processes. Beyond these Jung stressed a fourth activity which he termed 'transformation' or 'individuation', which was an extension of the task into ill-defined and uncertain realms which we struggle to put into words around the concept of development of the Jungian Self. In assessing applicants we have in mind a search for archetypal images that indicate a source of energy in the Self that might be used creatively to work in the synthetic region of an analytic journey where the patient becomes 'what he is and always was' (Jung, 1935).

Gordon (1979) takes up the relationship between ego processes and self processes and the concept of the ego–self axis. Ego integration is seen as the task of bringing into consciousness repressed, rejected and refused material, so extending and expanding the ego 'in the service of adaptation and of the experience of a personal and cohesive unity'. This is more aligned to the idea of cure, whereas healing is closer to the notion of a more comprehensive synthetic process which we call individuation. 'Individuation . . . is a process closely linked to the self and the functioning of the self.' It aims toward wholeness and the search for meaning in our lives, to life in general, in death, in the universe and the forging of links to creativity. It is in this sense that we have in mind the Jungian Self.

This concept seems to parallel Kohut's idea when he describes the possibility of restoration of the 'nuclear self' in an analysis which can penetrate beneath the organised layers of defences (Kohut, 1977). In this place the patient might re-experience what the self psychologists call pre-psychological chaos and primitive merger with an archaic self-object. The archaic self-object environment is recreated in the security of the analytic situation which includes the empathic responsiveness of the analyst.

In the 1930s Jung (1930) questioned the limitations of the analytical-reductive viewpoint of Freud which emphasised the use of regression to find the origins of neurotic behaviour and to illuminate fixation points. Object relations theory and more recent research-based developmental models (Stern, 1985) suggest that we should think more of repeated patterns of experience and relationship which build the self (variously defined) throughout our lives and can be developed and changed if the nature of past and present experience is available for examination and re-experience in an analysis. Sandler and Dreher (1996) have reviewed the historical development of the aims of psychoanalytic therapy among the differing schools of psychoanalysis including the ego psychologists, self psychologists, object relations theorists and Kleinians. No single description of aims becomes possible because each school has a different theoretical formulation. However, they conclude that when a modern clinical case is discussed there is less emphasis on transference neurosis, defence analysis and change in psychic structure and more on the synthetic potential of the self in relationship to the internal and external worlds. Further, there is more focus on the nature of the living interaction between the analyst and the patient, where the analyst is a vital contributor to the process and where both work towards a state of 'mental health' peculiar to that analysis.

Jung long ago emphasised a synthetic-anagogic attitude, that is, one with a spiritual or allegorical dimension, which seeks to find parts of the patient's personality which have remained under-developed, as if in an infantile state. Regression in a Jungian analysis is seen in the light of a journey of exploration accompanied by the analyst.

Fordham's application of Jung's ideas in his work on child development has provided a framework in which it is possible to view the interaction between innate characteristics (ego potentials) and the more or less responsive environment. This process, in a facilitating encounter between individual and environment, gives rise to the emergence and integration into the whole personality of innate potentials in the form of 'deintegrates' (Fordham, 1978).

As a child matures, and as a life unfolds, more and more of the archetypal core of Self becomes involved in this process and enters, in a phase-specific way, both the repertoire and consciousness of the individual.

Adults in assessment for analysis will provide the assessor with information about the status of this process. A detailed profile of deintegration and ego–Self integration is beyond the scope of an assessment interview. However, this perspective is of value, especially where incomplete or distorted development has left lacunae in the deintegration–integration process. These may be signalled by sudden areas of immaturity; primitive defences threatened by turmoil and archetypal material, often corresponding to information in the history where some failure of the environment can be identified. At times this failure is massive and the lacuna is more of a chasm. There may have been trauma and destruction as well as failure to facilitate as, for example, in child sex abuse.

Faced with an encounter with such a patient, someone for whom early and perhaps profound failure of interaction between child and mother has occurred, the assessor needs to operate on different levels in order to construct a psychodynamic formulation which looks toward the future potential relationship with the analyst. It is anticipated that the whole process will take place in the security of a new and vitally imbued container; the alchemical vessel of the analysis.

The applicant might reveal an image pertaining to his Self in a fantasy or dream. This can be very helpful toward an assessment of what may happen in an analysis. Jung felt that initial dreams were particularly significant in that in intangible ways they hold anticipations of the future. 'I do not mean that such dreams are necessarily prophetic, merely that they feel the way, they "reconnoitre"' (1931b: para. 89). The question we ask ourselves is to what extent these dreams are interpretable and to what extent they have a premonitory quality (Maduro, 1987).

As an example, a man brought a dream in which he is looking out to sea, with two guardian figures beside him. He walks down to the sea, and notices there are columns on the beach, between him and the water. At first the columns look like lugworm casts, then the ribs of a whale, and finally like the sides of a cave. He enters the cave which is dank and muddy; it continues to change its form, and he becomes trapped inside it, as the sea rises. In the event he was unable to use intensive therapy, feeling trapped by the boundaries, and becoming overwhelmed by his feelings.

We look for any evidence that indicates that the applicant may develop a malignant regression, that is, one in which there might be immobility in an intensely dependent relationship to the analyst. He/she may become stuck and unable to contact the archetypal image of an inner child. Such patients have severe difficulties making a creative relationship with the analyst and so have reduced chances even of beginning the process of repair. Lederman (1991) describes stagnated patients who can offer independent and omnipotently successful masks yet bring dreams of damaged, frozen, lost babies or children.

An example of such a patient presenting to the Clinic was an attractive narcissistic children's nurse in her mid-thirties. She complained of a long history of unsuccessful relationships with men who were often psychiatrically ill or married. She wished to understand why she still felt 'glued to her lifeless mother' who lived in another country. She recounted a dream where she gave birth to a limp and lifeless infant whom she repeatedly hit to try to force it to take a breath. In the analysis this image was dramatised in a recurrent stubborn refusal and dread of separation and independence. At a critical point she avoided actualising her potential and conceived a child with a passing lover. This trapped her as a lone parent entirely reliant on the welfare state. She herself had been conceived into a family lacking vitality; a desperate marriage between an older hypochondriacal woman unable to make warm or creative relationships and a passive-dependent widower. The initial dream and her history of repeatedly acting out her intense rageful dependency could have alerted the assessor (male) to the poor prognosis in analysis. However her presenting mask with its energetic oedipal demand for help, proved too seductive and blocked adequate processing of projected material and thought in the assessment.

A contrasting example is that of an unmarried woman of similar age who presented with a history of childhood deprivation and abuse. There appeared to be a picture of developmental distortion and arrest, with an adolescent period dominated by themes of escape and avoidance rather than autonomy. Later there was misuse of alcohol and a series of problem relationships. However, over some years she had become abstinent from alcohol, had taken on and succeeded in a field of study, tolerated painful depression and loneliness and requested analysis after progressing well. She presented with a coping adult persona while recognising she had unmet internal needs. The assessor experienced interest, warmth, and pleasure in the encounter and felt the patient exhibited evidence of a promising developmental process already begun which could be assisted by analysis.

In the physical and emotional space of the consulting room the prospective analysand is briefly offered a metaphorical alchemical vessel within which to use his/her ego capacities and to experience the Self in relationship with the assessor. This gives the opportunity for him/her to regress towards a reconstruction which seems similar to that described in Winnicott's model of the infant with the Mother who offers a holding relationship (Winnicott, 1960a and b). It might even evoke a glimpse, in Bion's model, of the patient using projective identification to seek linkage with the assessor as if an infant with a 'thinking breast' (Bion, 1962). These models arise from different structural theories but nevertheless seem familiar and useful in our work. Can the applicant take the initiative offered and how does this progress? We are asking ourselves what patterns assemble in our minds as we affectively experience the whole engagement.

Limentani (1972) discusses this in terms of assessment of ego strength with a view to the prospects of recovery and reintegration of lost parts of the self which might be used synthetically in the treatment alliance. We operate along similar lines in assessment, searching to discern and elucidate the desire, energy and means by which the patient gains relationship with us, or questioning whether relationship and empathic linking is unknown or blocked. We are not emotionally absent but quiet, listening, observing and noting the process, its pace and rhythm and the feelings generated inside and between us. We remark how, or if, or to what extent, the person affectively reaches, or touches us and with what material or activity. For example a silence might produce an image of a great stony impenetrable wall between us. Do we experience a desire in ourselves, or the applicant, to find a way through the wall or do we feel warned off? Could shame or paranoia be an issue? Alternatively, a sense of wordless pain, possibly experienced physically as the onset of backache or headache, and sympathetic connectedness might be created in the assessor. This experience of projective identification raises questions in the mind of the assessor. What is this telling us about the life patterns of the patient recapitulated in the room? This material is used to inform ourselves as to the potential for engagement in treatment for patients who fall into diagnostic categories such as neurotic depression or depressive personality structures, where we often feel quickly emotionally involved and yet the patient keeps us at a distance. A schizoid patient might feel unreal and not touch us affectively. We find ourselves wondering how this can be since we know that normally the content of the material raised would engage strong feelings. The communication may provoke us to feel manipulated, evoke in us a wish to retaliate in a covert (or overt) attack, or to suspect it as superficial or insubstantial. A narcissistic personality might block our affective engagement by eliciting in us boredom and an uncomfortable sense that we are being controlled and unable to gratify their desire. An observation or question (an *interpretation* in a broad definition) may be addressed to the patient to test how he/she responds to this developing formulation derived from countertransference awareness.

Having created the opportunity and given enough time for the patient to reveal himself spontaneously there usually comes an appropriate moment to begin asking questions (Edwards, 1983). These are geared to elicit essential information which may be missing, for example general health problems, suicide impulses, the use of addictive drugs, family psychiatric history and attitudes to the proposed analysis at home and work which could obstruct the maintenance of the contract.

Murray Jackson (1963) identified the need for analysts to be increasingly concerned about the treatment of borderline psychoses and personality disorders. He focused on the schizoid nucleus of these disorders, and on the therapeutic task of 'revealing and working through impulses of love and destruction, of body sensations and their associated fantasies'. Redfearn (1978) discusses some of the problems inherent in working with psychotic patients and elaborates similar themes. A consideration in clinic assessment is estimating the extent to which these mechanisms may exist in the patient and to gauge whether the analyst might be able to create a strong enough vessel to be 'able to contain and transform the large amounts of energy produced by the meeting of the opposites'. A predominance of paranoid defences and a paranoid way of relating does not augur well because of the risk of premature termination of therapy.

Naturally in one interview the scope and depth of the assessment has to be limited and the final image of the client in the assessor's mind and experience exists only from his particular perspective on that particular day in that particular setting. Surprisingly gaping holes may be apparent in the resulting picture. Did our complementary countertransference (Racker, 1968) blank out areas, or was it aroused in us to ignore or control the situation? What significance might accrue from that awareness, for example potential exposure and shame? Could it be an appropriate defence and what might we imagine if the defence was questioned or dismantled in analysis?

When the applicant for analysis departs from the consulting room the assessing analyst is left with what might be described as *embodied information*. The patient has begun to offer (and listen to) a verbal account of him/herself which to a varying extent has included a selective narrative of the events in his life plus a censored commentary. This is observed and received as objective material by the assessor who in turn makes a continuous internal commentary upon it and assembles it into patterns on the basis of his experience, including his knowledge. At the same time there has been an immensely important non-verbal, affective dimension to the encounter which leaves the assessor with identifications and countertransference material which also has to be brought to mind and assembled into patterns. This latter subjectively patterned image of the patient in the assessor is, as it were, laid alongside the objective picture and links between them are tested. We could say that we experiment with possible interpretations, as indeed we may have done verbally inside the session, to test the quality and potential of the dialogue.

Zinkin (1979) expands on this collective-personal dichotomy: 'The analytical psychologist, in his daily work, is combining his impersonal, collective knowledge with an activity best described in such terms as getting to know "the person."' The first activity involves observing and looking on and results in a sophisticated I–It statement. The second is described in terms of I–You where the exchange (or interpretation), frequently non-verbal, results from a reciprocal relatedness, a reaching out and emotional touching analogous to that between the infant with an available Mother. His hypothesis is that *the experience of the self comes gradually out of the mother's experience of him – which she communicates to him* and which exists from the beginning *before* I–It level communications. Perhaps the elucidation and education aspects of a Jungian analysis emerge from the I–It exchange but the healing transformative enterprise is related more to the potential for I–You relationship with the particular analyst.

The importance of this is that a potential analysis will involve both I–It and I–You communications. In an assessment we are trying to assemble in our minds, on the basis of the interview experience, how this might constellate in the prospective analysis, and to decide if there is sufficient hope for a creative dialogue. Inevitably this has a deeply personal dimension for the assessor who can only utilise himself or herself and cannot know with certainty how the patient will be with another analyst.

Arranging a series of assessment interviews poses problems if the assessment is intended to lead to onward referral to a colleague or trainee. It is not generally desirable, because a more intense transference relationship is more likely to be fostered which will obstruct or cause significant hindrance in the later analysis. A delicate balance must be recognised by all concerned in this work. A more relevant assessment is gained by accepting an incomplete psychiatric history in favour of the best psychodynamic formulation possible within the time constraints.

The assessor reviews a huge amount of information gleaned in the short time space of the interview. The attitude strives to be modest but influenced by knowledge, framed within the medical model, which emphasizes objective history, diagnosis, treatment protocol, prognosis and clinical experience plus long training and experience of analytical psychology. The assessor's ongoing self analysis reminds him/her of the propensity to view and experience the world and the patients in personal and archetypal terms. Our enthusiasm, energy and optimism may not be aroused in the analyst to whom we refer the client. Further we have in mind Jung's words:

> you must be able to put some trust in your intuition and to follow your feeling even at the risk of going wrong. To make a correct diagnosis, and to nod your head gravely at a bad prognosis, is the less important aspect of the medical art. It can even cripple your enthusiasm, and in psychotherapy, enthusiasm is the secret of success.
>
> (Jung, 1939: para. 539)

In conclusion, an assessment is an educated guess at what might happen when the analysand is given the opportunity to enter the metaphorical alchemical vessel formed together with and containing the companion analyst. The chemical results must always remain uncertain.

References

Aveline, M. (1980) 'Making a psychodynamic formulation', *Bulletin of the Royal College of Psychiatrists*, 192–3.
Bion, W.R. (1962) *Learning from Experience*, London: W. Heinemann.
Brown, G.N. (1993) 'Borderline states, incest and adolescence', *Journal of Analytical Psychology*, 38(1).
Edwards, A. (1983) 'Research studies in the problems of assessment', *Journal of Analytical Psychology*, 28(4): 299–311.
Fordham, M. (1978) *Jungian Psychotherapy: A Study in Analytical Psychology*, London: Maresfield Library.
Gordon, R. (1979) 'Reflections on curing and healing', *Journal of Analytical Psychology*, 24(3): 207–17.
Jackson, M. (1963) 'Technique and procedure in analytical practice with special reference to schizoid states', *Journal of Analytical Psychology*, 8(1): 51–64.
Jung, C.G. (1930) 'Some Aspects of Modern Psychotherapy'. *Collected Works* 16.
—— (1931a) 'Problems of Modern Psychotherapy'. *Collected Works 16.*
—— (1931b) 'The Aims of Psychotherapy'. *Collected Works 16.*
—— (1935) 'Principles of Practical Psychotherapy'. *Collected Works 16.*

Jung, C.G. (1939) 'On the Psychogenesis of Schizophrenia'. *Collected Works*.
—— (1946) 'The Psychology of the Transference'. *Collected Works 16*.
Kohut, H. (1977) *The Restoration of the Self*, New York: International Universities Press.
Ledermann, R. (1991) 'Regression and stagnation', *Journal of Analytical Psychology*, 36(4): 483–504.
Limentani, A. (1972) 'The assessment of analysability; A major hazard in selection for psychoanalysis', *International Journal of Psychoanalysis*, 53: 351–61.
Maduro, R.J. (1987) 'The initial dream and analysability', *Journal of Analytical Psychology*, 32(3): 199–226.
Masson, J.M. (1984) *The Assault on Truth: Freud's Suppression of the Seduction Theory*, New York: Farrar, Straus and Giroux.
Racker, H. (1968) *Transference and Countertransference*, New York: International Universities Press.
Redfearn, J.W.T. (1978) 'The energy of warring and combining opposites; Problems for the psychotic patient and the therapist in achieving the symbolic situation', *Journal of Analytical Psychology*, 23: 231–41.
Rosenfeld, H.A. (1987) *Impasse and Interpretation*, New Library of Psychoanalysis, No. 1, London and New York: Tavistock Publications.
Sandler, J. and Dreher, A.U. (1996) *What Do Psychoanalysts Want?* The New Library of Psychoanalysis, 24, ed. E. Bott Spillius, London: Routledge.
Searles, H.F. (1965) *Collected Papers on Schizophrenia and Related Subjects*, London: Hogarth Press.
Stern, D.N. (1985) *The Interpersonal World of the Infant*, New York: Basic Books.
Winnicott, D.W. (1960a) 'Ego distortion in terms of true and false self', reprinted in *The Maturational Processes and the Facilitating Environment*, London: Hogarth Press and the Institute of Psychoanalysis (1972).
—— (1960b) 'The theory of the parent–infant relationship', reprinted in *The Maturational Processes and the Facilitating Environment*, London: The Hogarth Press and the Institute of Psychoanalysis (1972).
Zinkin, L. (1979) 'The collective and the personal', *Journal of Analytical Psychology*, 24(3): 227–50.

Chapter 6

Dreams and Active Imagination

These two papers place some of Jung's most important concepts concerning the structure and function of the psyche in a clinical context. Roderick Peters gives examples which demonstrate the essential unity of the archetypal and the developmental perspectives. Peters regards this as Jung's own approach which has been widened to absorb the subsequent understandings of developmental psychology and the value of transference. Sheila Powell's paper engages with the notion that painting and writing and 'whichever media the unconscious prescribes' will, as Jung suggested, lower the threshold of consciousness and enhance understanding of the opposites in human nature. By linking the development of Jung's original concept of active imagination to the work of present-day depth psychologists – such as Winnicott and Bion – she is able to show how progress towards individuation through play and dreaming is assisted by the role of the transcendent function.

•

Dreams and Active Imagination

A Jungian's Approach to Dreams

Roderick Peters

Introduction

Freud said that dreams were 'the royal road to the unconscious'. Jung agreed with him, and although they were later to disagree on many things they both maintained the belief that dreams were of outstanding importance in the relationship between conscious and unconscious psyche.

I share this belief and most of my patients have clearly felt the same. No small part of this appreciation of dreams derives from their self-evident autonomy, their independence from waking consciousness: the dream is certainly a product of oneself in some way but not a product of the knowing centre of consciousness, the ego.

The enterprise of directing conscious attention upon one's own psyche is so beset with uncertainties, with maybe and perhaps, that both analyst and patient become more or less accustomed to the feeling of having no firm ground upon which to stand. Conscious material often turns out to be sturdier than doubt had made it seem, but a dream is, none the less, welcomed because it brings in material that one can be sure about in three ways: first, it belongs to the dreamer; second, it is unmistakably different from waking material; and third, the timing is the patient's – this dream has taken place, been remembered, and told at this time (N.B. the content of the dream, and how the patient relates to it, provide useful indicators for timing; the analyst's handling of the dream, and possible interpretation, however, remain as responsibilities.) Both patient and analyst often feel that a dream is a gift from some agency within the patient – even when no one can make head or tail of the dream itself!

It is not possible to give an account of a Jungian approach to dreams without referring, in however limited a way, to Jung's concepts about psychic functioning as a whole. In particular I shall refer to the division of the psyche into conscious and unconscious, ego as the centre of consciousness, the self as the totality of psyche–soma and the centre of that totality, the personal and collective unconscious, archetypes and archetypal images, complexes, transference, and individuation. I hope that my remarks, which will appear at various points, will complement rather than confuse or contradict what has been described elsewhere.

A Jungian approach to dreams implies a knowledge in the practitioner that dreams have communicative purpose: that dreams are a special form of linkage between conscious and unconscious by means of which consciousness becomes altered by a creative system which exists beyond the ego and yet within oneself. To come to know this is often profoundly moving for the ego. Even to have it silently embodied by one's analyst may be a comfort and a hope.

Jung conceived that within the totality of the psyche–soma there exist patterning or ordering archetypes which influence the development of consciousness and the personality, but which consciousness may only apprehend indirectly. The existence of the pure archetype is an inference and an assumption and cannot be known directly. The influence of the archetype, however, can be known through a variety of ways such as patterns of behaviour, emotional states, systems of ideas, and, most relevantly for dreams, through the dramatized and ego-participating experiences and images that constitute the phenomenon of dreaming.

The ego, our so familiar 'I', is of course present in dreams, at least the ones we remember. Almost always it is somewhat different from our waking ego, often less sure, more lost, and sometimes very different – even a different sex or species. Things happen to it, and it does things; it strives, it struggles, and most of the time it is trying to understand. Then one wakes, and remembers the dream, or more often parts of it. At first, and especially if it has been a powerful dream, one is still more in it than out of it; it still feels almost real. Then, as the waking ego gathers itself, the dream becomes more encapsulated and distinctly unreal. At this point it may be forgotten or, with some effort, worked upon with some objectivity.

The framework for thinking

A dream has been remembered; waking consciousness is in possession of this encapsulated dramatic experience. With a slight effort one can still get back into the feeling reality of it, while at the same time one can observe it objectively. But how can one handle it? What can one do with it? Jung's general concepts about the psyche as a whole, and dreams in particular, provide a framework within which to think and also certain tools for practical use.

Archetypes

Jung's theory of archetypes provides a valuable framework for understanding dreams. The seemingly limitless profusion of dream images and types of experience can be organised; that is to say, one can perceive or determine a number of differing and characteristic patterns of image and experience. In Jung's terms, a number of more or less characteristic canons of archetypal images can be recognised, and these are the basis for assuming the existence of corresponding archetypes. There is, for instance, the child, the mother, the father, the opposite sex (anima/animus), the shadow (which was Jung's name for the components of the personality rejected because of their conflict with individual and collective ego ideals), and the self (which Jung conceived as both the entirety of the psyche–soma system, and, simultaneously, the organising centre of that entirety). The ego, therefore, is a part of the self; Jung spoke of it as 'the proponent of the self in consciousness'. It enables knowing to be added as a dimension of being.

Dreams, then, are a particularly convincing and rich connection between the ego and the autonomous unconscious with its streaming archetypal influences. In our dream-life, far more nakedly than in our waking life, our less confident, less sufficient-unto-itself ego is bathed, as it were, in vivid portrayals of all those archetypal influences which are shaping our consciousness and developing us in our individual destiny. Dreams play a major role in individuation, as Jung called it – that lifelong and natural phenomenon of the human psyche in the course of which 'I' ever know and become 'myself' more fully.

As Jung saw it, the most constantly recurring experiences of evolving life have left their imprint in the psyche no less than the body. These imprints are the archetypes, and their influence, coming from a time frame so vast as to be virtually eternal in quality, tends to compensate or complement the often one-sided and limited attitudes of consciousness, attached as they are to time's arrow.

Jung understood the archetypes to be common to all people. They are collectively human and thus constitute the collective unconscious. The image-specificity of the various canons of archetypal images is less common. The images evolve through time, vary among cultures and within cultures, and are to some extent uniquely specified by individual experience. This, as it were, provides the combination of percept and experience which gives shape to archetypes, much as atoms of a salt aggregate and form the immanent shape of the crystal particular to that salt.

Collective and personal unconscious

There are many different levels of 'collective unconscious', like ever-widening rings, from the family to mankind as a whole, if not beyond. Between this multi-layered collective unconscious and ego consciousness lies an indeterminate region which Jung called the 'personal unconscious'. (This conceptual topography of the psyche should not be taken to mean neat separations between the realities referred to by the terms; the terms are conceptually useful, no more.) The personal unconscious, within which I think Jung embraced the family collective, is, as it were, closest to consciousness and hence most accessible. But on its other side it is actually indivisible from the remoter collectivities of the unconscious, which naturally flow through it in such a way that the influence of the archetypes can almost always be perceived in the material of the personal unconscious. This is an important point because there exists a tendency to think of archetypes and archetypal images only when the material is grand or strange, and not when it is composed of the stuff of the personal unconscious with its relatively familiar components.

Complexes

Jung's term 'complexes' (which was an earlier concept than the archetypes, and grew out of his word-association studies) is also relevant here. Complexes are conflicts in the psyche which attract to themselves much associated material and manifest in psycho-physical disturbances whenever anything touches upon their exquisite sensitivities. An example is someone who repressed the wish to kill her father and in whom, many years later now, any mention of death, murder, men and death, instantly evokes anxious feelings, thumping of the heart, constriction in breathing, cessation of or interference with thoughts, and numerous other disturbances of the system.

Complexes are similar to the personal unconscious (within which they anyway have a substantial part of their structure) in that they are an interface between ego consciousness and the archetypes. Just as one may expect to see the dramas of the personal unconscious brought to light in dreams, so one may expect to see the same with complexes; in both one will find the vicissitudes of personal history woven together with the archetypal influences which shape us all.

Illustration

The foregoing has provided something of an overview of a Jungian approach to dreams. At this point I would like to offer an illustration. Some personal details have been omitted for reasons of confidentiality.

1   I'm with my son; we go into a church; there is a sermon going on; I
    do not want to hear the sermon but I think I would like to return for
    the mass; we leave; later I return but mass has finished. I have missed
    it. Then I am recognised by a couple I see at a café; the woman talks
    to me; then we are all in an old-type racing car; everyone else is sitting
    but because we are cramped for space I am standing in the back; the
    man drives us straight towards a cliff face; it seems we may crash into
    it; just as we are about to hit it I see a small opening, a cave-like

tunnel, but it is far too small for the car; nevertheless he drives forward and somehow the long front of the car gets in; now I am frightened; it seems certain that because I am standing and cannot sit down, the top of the entrance will chop me off.

2   I am in Israel; I am standing in a crowd among whom there are six people who, I know and we know, are to be executed; they are to be executed by drowning; I feel upset, frightened; in some way I am identified with them. There is a bank behind them; beyond that is the water in which they will be drowned; they are led off towards it.

3   I am to meet some people with whom I am to journey; suddenly I realise I'm standing there with only my upper clothes and my under-pants on; I feel acutely embarrassed but I do not know the way home to get dressed properly. Then I'm with them on the journey (not aware of clothing now); we rest somewhere, and I have brought coffee but realise I'm carrying only one; I must go back to the café to get more, but do not know the way; someone tells me it's over a shoe shop. I begin to feel exhausted, terribly weary; now I'm lost and so weary I can hardly drag myself over the road and fear being run over; I see, sandwiched between modern buildings, a very old one; I go in; it's like a museum/church; my analyst is standing in there looking at something on a wall, I do not see what; the place seems quiet, empty, peaceful, beautiful; I go up to him and ask him to help me, then go to the entrance and wait for him; after some moments he comes to join me and we go together.

[I am not providing the associations for the third dream. I have included it so that you may form some impression for yourself of the development of the themes already introduced.]

These three dreams were in the order given and were dreamed within the space of a week by someone who had just returned from a visit abroad. While away he had not slept well and had, almost wilfully, not remembered any dreams. There was a sense of being scared to know them and of wanting to keep them away until back in analysis. This person had been raised as a Catholic, and in former years both the faith and the contain-ment by the Church had been very important. In recent years, however, while the Catholic faith had continued to be a part of his life, in church-going and as an area of unsureness which was nevertheless important, he had ceased to believe in the way he had and did not quite know where he stood in relation to it.

His associations to the first dream were, first, of missing a mass he had wished to attend while abroad; second, that there was an old love interest with one of the couple in the café; third, that the car had a phallic shape, and the tunnel was vagina-like; fourth, of caves and holes in hillsides that featured in the life and death of Christ, especially the connection with the resurrection.

His associations to the second dream were that the water behind the bank was the river Jordan or the sea of Galilee; and there was a strong awareness of baptism and St John the Baptist. The association of baptism of course led into the very extensive body of ready-made associative material that are the Christian doctrines about this ritual mystery and its meanings. I would say this person was unusually well-informed in this respect.

These two dreams were worked upon together. In both there is the theme of having to go completely inside a different element, first earth, then water. In both the entry is strongly linked with the fear of death. In both there are associations to transformation mysteries, resurrection and baptism. Meanwhile there is the mass within the Church that is missed. These were the first dreams he allowed himself to remember and they came after his return to the UK and immediately before re-entering analysis after the break. They were, therefore, his first consciously remembered immersion in his own unconscious for some time, and this, as we know, was something he had felt scared about and it was at least one of the reasons why he had slept so poorly. The phallic car and the vaginal hole into the mountain which the car surprisingly manages to enter evidently alludes to sexual intercourse; to which is attached the fear of death.

These dreams, together with their associations, and the few remarks I am able to make about the individual concerned, show unconscious material, obviously charged with compelling interest, made available to consciousness. They show conscious and unconscious in active relationship. They show (and would do so more if I could say more) how the individual's current situation and personal history are woven together with archetypal themes, how the personal and collective unconscious stream through each other. Possibilities for insight, understanding and meaning have been brought to consciousness with these dreams, and one can sense how they complement and compensate an attitude of consciousness that is limited by an anxious defensiveness.

In speaking of archetypal themes I am referring to the 'entering the cave/ death' and the 'baptism/death'. These themes, both within the dreams and through the associations, directly involve the relation of man to God. They therefore reveal the influence of the archetype of the self. The archetype of the *coniunctio*, the marriage of opposites, is similarly recognisable. These elements of the collective unconscious are involved and from their presence one may understand that there is a very active process going on in this person's psyche to do with the ego–self relationship: the ego is evidently afraid of the self in its wild or elemental state (earth and water), but is no longer satisfied with the tamed and conventional versions of union which are safely available (the mass in the church).

Sexuality is conspicuously involved: this person seeks the union of man and God that is offered in the Church by way of the mass; but that way has not worked for him, and furthermore his own soul presents images to consciousness of a sexual union between ego and self. This verges upon the pagan mysteries, which both frighten and excite a late twentieth-century consciousness that has been raised as a Christian in a Christian culture.

At this point we must consider that this person, unsatisfied by the Church, has entered analysis; in other words, embarked upon a different way, involving a relationship with an analyst who is an exponent of this different way. Is it safe? The ambivalence is clear in the dreams: the 'analysis' is evidently a safe place because the dreaming is held back until the person is once more in their analysis. The analyst, too, seems safe, to judge from the third dream, and is to be found in a building that is characterized as 'old', 'church', and 'museum'. But entering into the wild psyche is experienced by the ego as very unsafe, and of course the analyst is the exponent of precisely that way.

Why should it seem so unsafe to this person? This inquiry points the way into his personal history, the development of his psyche from the earliest days, and into the vast realm of the transference as it brings alive in the consulting room the vicissitudes of the earliest human relationships with the family. The Church is, of course, *Mother* Church, and so we may perceive all of the above story now in the light of developmental psychology. Hence a yearning, a fear, an ambivalence in relation to the mother, in whom the wild nature was apparently experienced as forbidden – only the established and conventional formula was available. Because this untamed part of himself could not be experienced as contained by the mother he was left unable to contain it for himself. In outline, though not in detail, I hope I have demonstrated how personal unconscious and collective unconscious, developmental traces and archetypal traces, are differing perspectives upon the one continuum.

Tools for dreamwork

I spoke above of a Jungian approach to dreams as offering both a framework within which to think and certain tools for practical use. In the remaining space I shall say something of the tools.

The differentness of dreams, while valued, is also why they are problematical and may seem senseless. Why aren't dreams more straightforward in what they mean?

Dreams as natural phenomena

Freud addressed this question in *The Interpretation of Dreams*. He decided that dreams were playing out wishes that the ego and/or superego could not allow and he proposed the existence of a 'dream censor' which, through various devices, disguised the true wishes sufficiently for consciousness not to reject the dream. Hence the difficulty in making sense of it.

Jung came to view things differently. He decided that dreams were natural phenomena appearing in a natural way and the difficulty experienced by consciousness in understanding them arose because of certain limitations in consciousness itself. These limitations are, first, that the compensatory nature of dreams means that they are presenting to consciousness the very aspects of some situation that have been consciously ignored, repressed, or are as yet unknown, and are therefore bound to be hard to grasp or understand; and second, that the mode of unconscious psychic functioning is different from the rationally trained habits of conscious thought. It is often true that the more one can look at one's dreams with a simple and more childlike vision, the easier they are to understand.

I find that both these explanations may be true sometimes. I think that the commonest form of dream censorship operates by influencing which dreams are remembered. But I can see that a dream ego, uncomfortably writhing in the grip of a dream dealing with some forbidden desire, may do what it can to disguise what is going on. As a working rule of thumb, however, I find it most fruitful to accept the dream as it appears, and to pay meticulous attention to both feeling my way into and understanding every nuance of the dream-ego's experience of all that transpires in the dream. This is an art and requires some measure of gift for it, to which must be added a great deal of practice and experience. The art consists of participating emotionally and imaginatively in the dream while simultaneously remembering and noting every part of it (or often them), together with all the thoughts and associations which arise in the process.

Associations

Freud asked his patients to free-associate to the material in their dreams. For some time Jung did the same, but he came to feel that free-associating ran the risk of getting too far away from the dream material and ending up with the conflicts already known to ego consciousness. He therefore advocated a more focused form of associating in which one endeavours to keep the associations always in touch with the dream material itself. My experience has confirmed that this approach works best.

Amplification

Jung coined the term 'amplification' to refer to a particular way of working with dreams. The basic idea is that dreams often contain some image or happening that may make patient or analyst, or both, think of a correspondence with already known material. If this correspondence is with the patient's own material, then this is a simple association. If, however, it is to some form of collectively known material, then the patient's personal dream content can be 'amplified' by considering what meaning it had and what part it played in this already established wider context. Typical amplifying contexts would be fairy tales, legends, myths, astrology, religions, doctrines, and theories (including all forms of scientific knowledge).

An example of this is apparent in the dreams I have quoted: both the patient and I thought immediately of baptism in connection with the second dream, and this led into the very extensive doctrines concerning baptism and so placed the individual dream meaning within an already established and much worked-upon wider context, thus amplifying it.

Whenever amplification is performed by the patient, using knowledge already in their possession, it is of course as safe as any other association and usually valuable. The difficult decisions arise only when the analyst finds a potentially amplifying association within himself which is evidently unknown to the patient. What is safe, and best practice in this circumstance, has to be weighed up carefully and is best not subjected to rules. Doing nothing, as in most therapeutic endeavours, is of course generally safer than doing something!

Since all complex and systematised bodies of learning available to the analyst may be used to amplify a patient's material, it is important to bear in mind that developmental theory should be treated with the same caution as fairy tales or alchemical theory. In all matters involving the question of amplification I keep in mind the bed of Procrustes.

Knowing/not knowing what dreams mean

Jung actively reminded himself that he 'did not know what this dream meant'. Since he was very intuitive, very knowledgable, and clearly had a strong tendency to know what things meant, he perhaps had more to hold back than most of us. Reading him, one is left with the impression that he has not entirely lived up to his own ideal injunction. It is a difficult dilemma: any analyst possessing something of a gift for understanding dreams *will* often feel an immediate understanding, but in fact he or she may be quite wrong. One does have actively to remind oneself that this is someone else's dream and remain as open to their associations as one has been to the dream itself. Not always, but often enough a different meaning or a significantly different aspect of the meaning will gradually appear; this will be truly shaped to the personal experience of the dreamer.

Naturally, this tendency to feel that one understands is greater when the dream contains a greater proportion of impersonal archetypal images, rather than material drawn directly from the dreamer's personal life. As images move deeper, away from the personal and further into the collective, they do acquire more fixed meanings. A volcano, for instance, means much the same to all of us, whereas *my father* has, in addition to the collective archetypal meaning, a dimension of uniquely personal meaning that no one else could know unless they knew me very well. An experienced analyst will have encountered a wide range of archetypal images many times over with many people. It simply is the case that they will have formed a fairly definite sense of what these things mean – the sea, the journey, the snake, the mountain, etc. Their understanding may be helpful for their patient, or it may not; it may seem wrong at the time, but right later; or vice versa. Many of the difficult choices poised between knowing and not knowing are the same as those considered above in amplification.

The relationship with the patient contains the dreams

It is worth remembering that Jung was rather more explorer and theory-maker than therapist. He had as much of an eye upon the development of a comprehensive model of the psyche as he did upon the specific area of psychotherapy itself, which also served as a field for research.

I and most, but not all, contemporary Jungians approach dreams far more as a component *within* the context of the psychotherapeutic relationship than appears explicitly in Jung's written work. In part this is because recent decades have brought a deeper understanding of transference, but also because much of what Jung had to say about dreams was written from the perspective of dreams as part of the life of everyman, and their place within his model of the psyche.

Within a specifically psychotherapeutic context, a dream is an event taking place between the conscious and unconscious, or the ego and the self, of the patient. It is then told, or not told, or half told, within the relationship of the analyst and patient, in which some version of that same relationship between conscious and unconscious, ego and self, will exist in a living form between patient and analyst. Clearly, this is a complex situation which raises a number of subtle and important questions concerning the elements of transference within dreams, as well as the manifold ways in which transference is involved in how the dreams are told, whether they are told, and why they are told, and how they might be handled. These questions I regard as belonging properly to the subject of transference and its management, rather than to a Jungian approach to dreams as such. The fact that I have addressed this matter briefly should not be taken to indicate that my approach does not give primacy to the analyst–patient relationship: the work with the patient contains the work with dreams.

Acknowledgement

I thank the person concerned for permission to use his material, and his endorsement of its essential accuracy.

Active Imagination
Dreaming with open eyes

Sheila Powell

We are all unwittingly affected by our ancestry whether we have suffered openly in the great movement of populations across Europe, in private recesses of the soul or in the inevitable alchemical mixtures of human life. Psychotherapists have learned to communicate with those lost pains in the spectrum of a language which is highly sophisticated. However they have also attempted to discover another communication through the psychological process in non-verbal communications.

Over the years I have been using active imagination with patients, and teaching Jung's views about it. I have realised that it is not a suitable method of work for everyone, although it has many forms which arise spontaneously out of the work. Since time immemorial we have known the importance of the message of our dreams and imagination. We have only to look at the dreams of Nebuchadnezzar, Daniel and Joseph to realise that the portents of their dreams needed to be taken seriously. Even earlier, Neolithic men had inscribed paintings on the walls of their caves, perhaps hoping to express their wish to control and manage their needs for a fruitful hunt and to contain their fear of the frightening creatures outside who were needed for food. Jung realised that there might be some serious misunderstanding of his work with active imagination for he wanted to put on record 'that there are certain cases where development can occur not because I force anyone to do it but because it springs from inner necessity' (Jung, 1953: 223). I would agree with Jung, for this has also been my experience. The analysis in these cases may proceed in the usual way, working through words with the transference and countertransference of our relationship and analysing the defences. During an analysis, of course, we are always mindful of the need to personalise and mediate any archetypal responses and perceptions of the patients. Later on in the paper we can see from my illustration from patients' work that archetypal images can occur and that these are striking and spontaneous, leaving room for further understanding. Patients who communicate through active imagination have often suffered for many years in deep depressions or anxiety states. They may use the vivid processes of dreams to begin to understand their inner worlds, which might otherwise be obscure and unknown. They might write their fantasies and stories down so that the sequence can be analysed.

When Jung conceptualised the idea of active imagination in Volume 8 of his *Collected Works* he was giving us a revision of a paper 'The Transcendent Function' (Jung, 1958) which he had written in 1916. He was introducing us to his ideas of working with the conscious and the unconscious as the opposites in our nature. In the paper he described the process in the patient by encouraging the patient to relax and concentrate on the inner world of imagination. As he suggested in his method of dream interpretation, it is important to keep relatively close to the original image, fantasy or dream so that the 'whole procedure' is a kind of enrichment, amplification and clarification of the affect and the contents are brought nearer to consciousness. They become more impressive and understandable. Jung felt that depression is an unwelcome intrusion from the unconscious, an elaboration of the mood which is, as it were, a picture of the contents of the unconscious. In other words the unconscious in the depression can produce an image or a story, an inner situation which could be expressed by some people more easily in images in paint, in writing, and so on. In his paper on 'The transcendent function' it was clear that it was his contention that by struggling with these images something new would emerge. For, as we integrate the understanding of the contents of the unconscious into our understanding, another aspect of the self would be reached on the way to development and change in the psyche.

Psychotherapists have learned to communicate with lost pains through language and spoken discussion. However, they have also attempted to discover other forms of communication, which are non-verbal. By engaging in different ways of expressing themselves, some patients may learn to share with us deep realities which few may wish to own until they are in considerable distress. It was mainly because of his discovery of the collective unconscious or the deepest layer of the psyche that Jung realised the importance of confronting images appearing on this level. (See his *'Memories, Dreams, Reflections'* and his meeting with Philemon – Jung, 1980: 207, 208, 209, 261). Certainly Jung demonstrates in his work with Miss X (1950: 290) that if we can hear what the psyche is telling us, then we can begin to discover that there are other intense unconscious forces through which we may be helped to develop and grow. As therapists we can hope to enhance the imaginative potential of our patients and enable further individuation through understanding and meaning. We endeavour to connect two worlds, the unconscious and conscious.

As others before him, Jung was very aware that the process of becoming oneself could be held up. Jung saw that at times the interaction between the conscious and the unconscious does not function satisfactorily. Help is needed to move the person from stagnation and depression to regain a living, internal, psychic process. Sometimes we have a dream, or our lives are interrupted by an unaccountable occurrence. Perhaps we look for signs and symbols which might help us to understand our dilemma. Jung felt that this process was spontaneous and natural and could be encouraged through the process of psychotherapy. A neurosis he saw as a temporary blockage in the path of individuation and development through transformation and he discusses this idea in his work with Miss X (Jung, 1950). Active imagination is a process in which, as Jung said, we dream with 'open eyes'. By concentrating on a mood or a picture and by paying attention to them the images begin to have a life of their own. They develop according to their own logic. Psychologically this creates a new situation for the individual, feeling is raised and the conscious ego is stimulated to react more immediately.

Jung later developed his ideas on active imagination throughout what was for him a time of profound disturbance after his separation from his involvement and friendship with Freud. This had been an important relationship for them both. At that moment in his life he was in a deep encounter with his own unconscious. He was ill, but his illness was a creative one and put him in a sensitive and emotional place where he could explore his fearful experiences. He had been critical of Freud's reductive method because he felt that the full meaning of the symbol is not easily known and the function of the symbol may be lost. He needed to know its meaning and its purpose. Jung realised that his poem 'VII Sermones ad Mortuos' (1967), written during this period, was searching out his relation to his past history. In the poem he was deeply engrossed with the importance of members of his family now long dead. Indeed he was undergoing a profound mourning process. He writes about that episode in *Memories, Dreams, Reflections* (1980: 215–17):

> for since the questions and demands which my destiny required of me to answer did not come to me from outside, they must have come from the inner world. These conversations with the dead formed a kind of prelude to what I had to communicate to the world about the unconscious, a kind of pattern of order and interpretation of its general contents.

This was a pointer for his life's work. Jung gradually began to appreciate that while he always examined his dreams and fantasies with great intensity, it was particularly at times of great stress that he felt he needed to re-establish contact with the unconscious, to see where it led him. In his biography *Memories, Dreams, Reflections* (1980) he talked about the importance for himself of his mandala drawings during World War I which kept him in touch with the subtle changes in his psyche at times of inner turmoil. In the drawings he felt that the configuration of the boudary was important in itself, to create a container for his disparate feelings. He could see that while he might be striving to manage his inner turbulence, the frame of the mandala could act as a symbolic container. His own remarkable ability to contain these emotions was important for sailing so close to the boundary of the psyche but for others such a journey could be profoundly dangerous. Michael Fordham (1967: 51) too emphasised that active imagination was useful only for those patients who were able to use a strong ego function to attempt to understand and resist the powerful pull of the unconscious processes. Fordham felt that active imagination could otherwise lead to disintegration rather than reintegration.

While Jung was striking out again on his own journey he realised that he had come to a feeling of impasse. To discover how to proceed he began to play with stones by the lake as he had as a child. He remembered his despair when as a child he had felt hurt and had carved the little wooden manikin at the end of his ruler, which he then left secretly in the loft. Whenever he felt upset he would visit it and experience a sense of security. Later he found a special black stone from the river to keep the manikin company, and he made tiny scrolls for him to read. It was only when he was 35 that Jung recalled this episode. He thought deeply about the links between symbolic childhood play and later adult imagination. It seemed a vital understanding to realise the links between meaning and image. While play is a spontaneous activity of the psyche Jung could see that it also served individuation processes. He could begin to understand that if he gave in to his impulses and followed what happened, a stream of fantasies would result. This was only a beginning and he could see that the contents of old experiences belong to our living being. By discovering which images lay at the heart of intense emotions there was a chance of being released from the emotional state. In *Memories, Dreams, Reflections* he wrote that

> if an image is charged with numinosity, that is with psychic energy, then it becomes dynamic and will produce consequences. It is a great mistake in practice to treat an archetype as if it were a mere name, word or concept. It is far more, it is a piece of life, an image con- nected with a living individual by the bridge of emotion. Emotion is like a bridge between instinct and archetype, body and psyche . . . it is the alchemical fire whose warmth brings everything into existence and burns all that is superfluous to ashes . . . steel meets flint and a spark is struck . . . emotion is the chief subject.
>
> (1980: 253)

The crux of the concept of active imagination lies in how far the individual is clearly and feelingly involved. There may be many levels to the process.

An instance is the illustration painted and modelled by a patient (see Figure 2, p. 150). The painting is dominated by a clay head, in front of which is a deep space; on the other side of the space is a worm. The patient felt dominated and denigrated by a mother who was sometimes severe and crushing. Here we can see an image of an archetypal terrible mother. The patient's unconscious perception of her mother became embodied in the clay model and symbolically showed her deeply felt experience. We can see that it is necessary to let ourselves, as Jung did, sink into the unconscious, allowing it to take charge of the process whether it is writing, painting or dancing or indeed any expression which the unconscious prescribes. For while it is the self which can suggest the creative medium of expression, all these processes may engage the unconscious in that category of the imagination which is beyond the ego. Rix Weaver (1964), an experienced Australian practitioner of active imagination, says what comes into play are those 'things which have always "been" and have a universal underlay of mythological and religious motifs', in other words the collective unconscious comes to the fore.

Let me give you an illustration of the power of the imagination. Recently I took part in a group which was discussing fairy tales. I found myself engaged in the story and in my imagination identified with the youngest son in the story. Brambles caught at my clothes as I rushed breathlessly through the forest in my journey to find the fountain of life to collect some healing water to restore the king, my father, to health. It was exhilarating and transcended the everyday reality experience with my group of colleagues sitting quietly together in a library. I was participating in a timeless fairy-tale world. The intense concentration of my inner world produced an incredibly vivid and involving fantasy. There was a keen perception of the ride through the forest, the trees and brambles, the smell of fresh vegetation and the crashing noise of the horse pounding through the undergrowth. I was amazed by the immense energy and concentration of the experience. It is this attention and concentration which I feel characterises active imagination.

Although a new situation is created when unconscious contents are exposed in a waking state and conscious work is needed to understand them, the fantasy image has everything it needs for its subsequent development. The active and creative participation of active imagination, as I said earlier, requires us to sink into the unconscious, whose contents are then observed or painted, modelled in clay, and sometimes danced or written as in a fairy story. Jung used Janet's term 'abaissement de niveau mental' as a starting point for the mode of affect when the ego disengages to induce an altered state of consciousness. The patient may subsequently explore the painting and associate to it if possible.

One important issue for the analyst is to help the patient to find words to express his experiences. Words themselves may not be sufficient for the intense feeling, and I think that active imagination in some form such as painting, drawing or writing is a step towards communication and understanding. Although Jung thought of his own productions as a means of enhancing understanding he believed that spontaneous art work produced therapeutically could not be viewed as 'art' if it were also to be used as an analytic communication. He thought that there might be considerable inflation and distortion arising in the patient if the aesthetic quality were taken into consideration. I believe that he was taking this point of view from his own struggles, recorded in *Memories, Dreams, Reflections* (1980: 212), and that defining a product as art is separate from its role in analysis. The risk of inflation may be great but none the less I do regard art as a communication. The paintings, or other imaginative forms, produced in an analysis are only part of the opus and are encompassed and entwined with deeper dynamic processes within the patient (and the analysis) over a long period of time. The patient and the analyst working together in a relationship will create a container which will help to transcend the forms and shapes in the picture or image. This will promote further understanding of the inner world of the patient and will enhance the psychological progress. The work creates a bridge between the conscious and unconscious and in this way the therapy mediates the creative and understanding modes of active imagination itself. In warning us that we should not undertake the work of active imagination lightly, Jung reminds us of its power so that we can protect patient and therapist from eruptions of unconscious processes. For where the ego is weak or the patient is close to psychotic disintegration this may be a signal for breakdown rather than deintegration and reintegration. In analysis it is the analyst who keeps the container and the setting safe with a regular and predictable time frame. In this way too the analyst can keep a close watch for any risk of inflation.

In Jung's day active imagination was practised in the way Jung describes. Today I think that there have been various developments and we have extended our work in this area of practice. In London, for instance, we feel that the very use of transference and countertransference involves the analyst in an imaginative process, as three SAP members demonstrate. Dorothy Davidson was clear about this in her work (1966: 135) while Fred Plaut (1966: 113) has commented that the early relationship is important for the development of basic trust to allow the symbolic use of the imaginative illusion of transference/countertransference. In my own paper (Powell, 1985: 45) I show the use of the analyst's transcendent function as a bridge to understanding.

The psychoanalyst Marion Milner has written an important paper on 'The role of illusion in symbol formation' (1987) showing us how we use ourselves as analysts and how our imaginative illusion can promote understanding. Unless the patients can use their capacity for symbolic realisation it is not easy to use the analytic process. This may develop during the course of analytic work through the analyst taking on the ego role until the patient matures sufficiently to take over. We know too that we can use our countertransference experience of projective identification and our imaginative function to understand the patient's dilemma.

Joyce MacDougall, the French psychoanalyst, has called our primitive experience of emotions prototype language (1989). It is here that we can link our body sensations with our understanding of the patient. For example, I had a fantasy with one patient in a session, that I had a mouth and genitals but no other connecting inner body links. After listening carefully to the patient I began to realise that I was experiencing something of how she experienced herself when as a tiny baby she felt she was inadequately held, both physically and mentally in her mother's mind. Adequate holding would have enabled her to manage the frightening sensations of the immature little body and its functioning.

Today we are usually more familiar with our responses as analysts in the transference and countertransference of the analytic relationship than Jung was when he wrote about his work with Miss X. Her paintings were part of a study in the process of individuation:

> The paintings are, as it were, self delineations of dimly sensed changes going on in the background, which are perceived by the reversed eye and are rendered visible with pencil and brush, just as they are, uncomprehended and unknown. The pictures represent a kind of ideogram of the unconscious contents. I have naturally used this method myself too and can affirm that one can paint a very complicated picture without the least idea of their real meaning while painting them. The picture seems to develop out of itself and often in opposition to one's own conscious intentions. It is interesting to observe how the execution of the picture thwarts one's expectations in the most surprising way.
>
> (1950: 290)

We can have another view of this through Marion Milner's book *On Not Being Able to Paint* (1971), in which painting was for her a form of therapy.

Katherine Killick, an art psychotherapist in training with the SAP, has written a beautiful paper on working with psychotic processes in art therapy (1993: 25–38). She cites Bion's idea about the problems for recovering psychotic patients who, when attempting to think, seem to regress to pre-verbal states where the inner world splits and sinks defensively to projective identification. Within this early world is involved initially what Bion describes as 'an agglomeration of objects' prior to the capacity to bring the splits together and to symbolise. Using other terms, Jung comments in his paper on 'The Transcendent Function' (1958) that this process towards seeing how opposites can form symbolic wholes, allows affect that has all been clustered in one place, often to find expression through imagery before it can be described in words. Art therapists have found considerable encouragement in Jung's writing for their work in mental hospitals, or with those suffering life-threatening illnesses in hospices and hospitals.

Kalff's writing about sandplay (1980) has influenced Jungian analysts in Italy and America to play with toys and models in sandboxes to produce inner-world pictures in their therapy sessions. In England, Joel Ryce Menuhin (1992) has led in the world of sandplay with adults as well as with children. It seems that the element of play is important, and together with the interpretation of the adult patient's childhood, enables the patient to assimilate the shadow through the use of transference and countertransference. For it is through this work that the patient can picture the people from his or her inner world and can see that they are projected into the analytic relationship. It seems to me that when a patient spontaneously brings his or her own painting, drawing or whatever is felt to come out of their own encounters with the unconscious, then this can validly be incorporated into the analysis.

I thought it might be of added interest to the reader to include some drawings and pictures of models from my own work with patients. Because of confidentiality I can, with their permission, only tell you briefly how the pictures arose and give you some idea of the work which we did together. Although the ensuing work was intense I can leave it to the reader to imagine how the pictures convey something of the inner dilemma of the patients.

Emma was preoccupied with drawing spiders' webs and tangles and we were soon able to get into the relationship she had had with her mother and of course with me. She had spent many years in deep depression. Although she had been a skilled artist herself, she found it hard to get back into painting or drawing in a serious way. Later in the therapy she made a picture of her mother and herself. Her mother looks like a witch, although I thought I could discern a slight amused smile on her face. The patient depicts herself as a worm separated from her mother by a dark hole into which she fears she will fall if she approaches closer to her mother or to me. Our work had encompassed many of the pains which the patient had endured over the years, fearing the retaliation of the witch-mother. In the picture the archetypal core complex with the mother was constellated, embodying the relationship between the patient and the analyst within the analysis. The imaginative portrayal of the mother who could frustrate and withhold was experienced within our work together and so we were gradually able to work through the projected images contained in the picture. At our first meeting the patient had been deeply depressed and angry. Her first analysis had come to nought but she was determined to find some way through the webs she had endured. Gradually she struggled through

Figure 2 The Witch Mother.

different and changing phases of her life and its changing relationships. Emma attempted different creative work to lead her back into what she considered to be her creative life again. During our relationship we began the deep process of exposing the persecutory pain she was feeling. Gradually she found her way into what she considered to be her self before 'she was murdered', a symbolic expression for the murder of her self. Through a growing capacity for verbal symbolisation, she found her way into a sense of a true, alive self. It was a painful journey, but one which she could value and use to further her life in a meaningful way. Our relationship eventually felt more appropriately warm rather than cold and empty. Throughout her analysis she painted; the process gripped her and she explored her feelings and fantasies more intensely. Increasingly she was able to put them into expressive words. The webs unravelled as she began to understand her own experience and how she had been emotionally stuck and quite unable to move forward.

Another patient, Petra, felt betrayed by God and man. She painted extensively and it seemed as though it was a symbolic way of getting into touch with a desperate situation during her childhood hospitalisation. Through this and her analytic work she discovered that her frozen feminine self had been released and the ice in her soul had been thawed. In many ways her journey seemed to mirror the journey of Gerda in the fairy tale

'The snow queen', which was a guide for the analyst in understanding the trials of her frozen experiences when she had felt devoid of human relationship. Her paintings were unfortunately lost in a house move, but there were many, mostly depicting screaming mouths. At that time she was preoccupied with the painting 'Anxiety' by the Norwegian painter Edvard Munch. Life began to unfold and she was able to use her creative self more appropriately. It is interesting to reflect that the analyst was experienced as cold, icy and out of touch. Here the opposites were enacted through the transference/countertransference and the analyst could take the full weight of the painful dislocation of the patient until she was able to experience the thaw.

Rosamund, a woman of intellect, brought a drawing to the second session of her analysis. The drawing was of a man and woman facing each other across a desert. I wondered whether this was the inner situation of her contrasexual dilemma. She seemed out of touch with her painful emotions as her long marriage disintegrated. At first she could only draw stick figures. Her pain seemed locked inside her and she was fearful of falling into the unconscious. As her dreams gradually showed that she was struggling with her problems in relationship to her baby self and her inner rages, the colours in her collages changed and paints began to be used more extensively. Where previously the work had been dark and simple, now warmer, brighter colours began to appear. The colours deepened as her feelings became more available to her. Life began to be more complex and so did her relationships. The anger which she had been unable to reach now appeared in her dreams as monsters from the deep. However, they slipped out of her grasp as she was about to confront them. Gradually the anger began to reach the surface and be confronted. Her experience of herself as a profoundly intellectual woman led by cognitive thought moved into a warmer and more sensuous experience of herself as the feminine in her moved into the foreground of her life.

For the purpose of this paper and the limitations of print I can only show a few illustrations of pictures she made as part of the analytic process. Suffice it to say that the whole experience led her to find a life which felt more authentic to her. In spite of her fears of the unconscious and her resistance to the process, once she had allowed herself to confront her unconscious through her dreams, her paintings and our relationship, her experience was transforming. She found the child she was searching for in her dreams.

All the patients had suffered deep psychological wounds which could, through the course of therapy, be released and some transformations could be lived through to new beginnings. The task of the opus was brought about through elaborations or the development of the fantasy by giving full rein to it. The images of the archetypes could be depicted and by allowing the ego to form a relationship with them during the process, they could be

Figure 3 Girl with Pain Locked Inside.

Figure 4 Hello the Lost Child.

experienced and worked through within the analytic relationship, so that the paradox of the *coniunctio* of the unconscious and conscious could be acknowledged. This led on to further transformations and new energy was released to engage with life afresh.

Summary

I have attempted in this chapter to define and describe the development of active imagination in my practice. I have used Jung's ideas and linked them with the practice of Analytical Psychology in London. In this way I have attempted a synthesis with reductive analysis to bridge the creative processes within the individual. When using active imagination we must take full care to elucidate the negative transference using the reductive techniques which clarify the complex inner structures and so give infantile needs full expression. We can see that the analytic space can be used as a creative imaginal space (Cwik, 1991) to bridge early needs with play in the symbolic form of active imagination in a facilitating environment.

Acknowledgement

I am indebted to my colleague Mary Lister for our discussions on active imagination, and for introducing me to the work of Katherine Killick.

References

Cwik, August, J. (1991) 'Active imagination as imaginal play space', *Liminality and Transitional Phenomena*, Wilmette, IL: Chiron Clinical Series, p. 99.
Davidson, Dorothy (1966) 'Transference as a form of active imagination', *Journal of Analytical Psychology*, 11 (2).
Fordham, M. (1967) 'Active imagination – deintegration or disintegration', *Journal of Analytical Psychology*, 12 (1).
Jung, C.G. (1931) 'The Structure of the Psyche', *Collected Works* 8.
—— (1950) 'The Archetypes and the Collective Unconscious', *Collected Works* 9, Part I.
—— (1953) 'Two Essays on Analytical Psychology', *Collected Works* 7.
—— (1958) 'The Transcendent Function', *Collected Works* 8.
—— (1961) 'The Symbolic Life. Healing the Split', *Collected Works* 18.
—— (1967) 'VII Sermones ad Mortuos', trans. H.G. Baynes, Robinson and Watkins.
—— (1980) *Memories, Dreams, Reflections*, London: Fount.
Kalff, D.M. (1980) *Sandplay. A Psychotherapeutic Approach to the Psyche*, Sigo Press.
Killick, K. (1993) 'Working with psychotic processes in art therapy', *Psychoanalytic Psychotherapy*, 7 (1).
MacDougall, J. (1989) *Theatres of the Body*, London: Free Association Books.

Milner, M. (1971) *On Not Being Able to Paint*, London: Heinemann Educational Books.
—— (1987) '1952: The role of illusion in symbol formation', in *The Suppressed Madness of Sane Men*, London: Tavistock Publications.
Plaut, A. (1966) 'Reflections on not being able to imagine', *Journal of Analytical Psychology*, 11 (2).
Powell, S. (1985) 'The transcendent function in the analyst as a bridge to understanding', *Journal of Analytical Psychology*, 30 (1).
Ryce-Menuhin, J. (1992) *Jungian Sandplay. The Wonderful Therapy*, London: Routledge.
Weaver, R. (1964) *The Wise Old Woman*, London: Vincent Smart Ltd.

Chapter 7

Religion and Spirituality

Jung saw Gnostic and alchemical systems of belief and practice as the precursors of analytic psychology. Peggy Jones explores these systems as expressions of the religious function, and as demonstrating the central tenets of Jungian psychology. The unconscious is first encountered in projection and not only is the realm in which these projections are realised 'the intermediate realm of subtle reality . . . expressed by the symbol', but also the work of psychotherapy and the alchemical *opus* depend on the 'Third' for their outcome. This principle is enshrined in the alchemical formula *Deo concedente*.

Margaret Clark builds her paper around an understanding of traditional Christian symbolism. Through a series of clinical examples, she shows the importance of patients becoming aware that the psyche is not a simple unity and that it is difficult to integrate opposing aspects of the self. She uses Jung's theory of opposites in maintaining that psychic conflict, unconscious or conscious, is necessary and inevitable. She considers his view that the Christian story – God incarnated in Jesus, the battle with Satan, the coming of the Holy Spirit, the Assumption of the Virgin Mary – is a projection of our own essential psychic process. These symbols convey the tremendous power and danger of the process of individuation – consciously becoming who we are.

Processes of Transformation

Peggy Jones

Introduction

In his commentary on the alchemical treatise, *De Sulphure*, Jung writes, 'the psyche is only partly identical with our empirical conscious being; for the rest it is projected and in this state it imagines or realises those greater things which the body cannot grasp, i.e., cannot bring into reality.' He continues:

> That this activity of the soul 'outside the body' refers to the alchemical *opus* is evident from the remark that the soul has the greatest power over the body. . . .' 'Thou canst conceive the greater', says our author; therefore your body can bring it into reality – with the help of the art and with God's permission (*Deo concedente*), this being a fixed formula in alchemy.
>
> (Jung, 1944: para. 399)

This quote, and my title, may not seem at first glance to represent adequately the day-to-day work (or 'art') of psychotherapy, the painstakingly slow pace with which understanding and consciousness evolve, the all-too-familiar feelings of frustration and fatigue. It may not even seem to represent a particularly 'religious' standpoint. Yet the two basic principles which it encapsulates reflect all that is most essentially 'Jungian' for me, in my practice and in the theoretical background to that practice, namely:

1 The central tenet of not just Jungian, but all depth-psychological systems, that we encounter what is unconscious first in projection, on to an image, a person or a situation. This means that the Other, and our relationship to it (or her, or him, or them), is central to the integration of those unconscious contents and thus the realisation of the Self. This is the basis of the psychotherapeutic '*opus*'.

2 The central tenet of alchemy that the alchemical *opus* can only succeed

'God willing', if God 'gives the nod' to it, this phrase reflecting the Latin derivation of *numen*, 'nod'; that is, it is an intrinsically 'religious' process.

Body and soul, or psyche, are thus inextricably interlinked, the Seen and the Unseen, the Known and the Unknown, interdependent but, more importantly, mutually dependent on the transforming and bridging power of the symbol, the product of 'this activity of the soul "outside the body"'', which both creates and is itself dependent upon what Jung called 'that intermediate realm of subtle reality which can be adequately only expressed by the symbol' (ibid.: para. 400).

This paper explores two different expressions of 'this activity of the soul "outside the body"'', alchemy and Gnosticism, the two fields which Jung considered to be the precursors of his 'analytical psychology'. In the paragraphs which follow I have chosen only to sketch out what I see as some of the fundamental themes to emerge from the Gnostic and alchemical quests for meaning. The answers discovered are inseparable from the questions asked and reflect equally the nature of the questioner and that of the intermediate realm in which both question and answer reside. I begin with a brief investigation of what Jung termed the 'religious function' because it seems to me to be the instinctive 'motor' which drives the process of self-realisation and transformation.

The religious function

' . . . the religious function is an essential component of the psyche and is found always and everywhere, however undifferentiated it may be' (Jung, 1960: para. 529). For the purposes of this paper, I consider the religious function as an innate readiness to discover or create meaning, although the word 'religious', according to Jung's own definitions, has at least two possible etymologies, *religare*, meaning to 'bind to' and *relegere*, meaning 'a careful observation and taking account of the numinous' (Jung, 1949: xxviii). The search for meaning expresses itself in the question 'why?' Such questions are religious questions, not religious in terms of a particular church or credo or organised religion, but rather in terms of reflecting the search for meaning, for a different sort of 'knowledge', which wins our assent because it finds an inner resonance. Religious questions are not looking for a linear or causal answer; they are seeking an imaginative response which encourages dialogue and circularity. In itself, the question 'why?' reflects only half of an impulse towards meaning, an impulse which is, by its nature, antiphonal, that is, there are two 'voices', question and response, which create a whole. 'Why?' is like an anchor thrown out into the depths of the unknown against which, when it has caught, we can pull ourselves – towards the unknown – by the use of our imagination.

As Jung reflected on his experiences, he concluded that not only have we at all times and in all places been asking these 'religious' questions, but that we have also been engaged in answering them, projecting our imagination into the world and 'finding' the answer, or the echo, apparently outside us. Recognising the central role of imagination in alchemy, he wrote: 'The *Imaginatio* . . . is in truth a key that opens the door to the secret of the *opus*' (1944: para. 400). In symbols and stories, art and myth, ritual and education, in the sciences and in philosophies and theologies of all sorts we have found – and created – this antiphonal response.

Jung's ideas have always resonated for some with their own experience, while others have found them mystifying or alien. While he was, personally, convinced of the universality of the collective unconscious and the religious function, he none the less needed and sought validation for his conclusions. In a candid and poignant expression of his self-doubt and insecurity he speaks in his memoirs of his continuing need for recognition: 'it was clear to me from the start that I could find contact with the outer world and with people only if I succeeded in showing . . . that the contents of psychic experience are real, and real not only as my own personal experiences, but as collective experiences which others also have. . . . I knew that if I did not succeed, I would be condemned to absolute isolation' (1963: 220). Jung felt he found confirmation for his conclusions when he discovered the early Gnostic writings and the extensive work of the alchemists. Here were intelligent and dedicated men and women, seeking to penetrate and understand the hidden nature of matter and of its relationship to the spirit. As they struggled to express their experiences and discoveries, the language they employed was that of symbol and paradox, of myth and allegory, the same vocabulary and images which Jung had found occurring not only in fairy tales and the religions of antiquity, but also in his own dreams and experiences and those of his patients. 'I had stumbled upon the historical counterpart of my psychology of the unconscious. The possibility of a comparison with alchemy, and the uninterrupted intellectual chain back to Gnosticism, gave substance to my psychology. When I pored over these old texts everything fell into place' (ibid.: 231).

Gnosticism and alchemy – redemption and transformation

Gnosticism

Background

'Jesus called for a full reversal of values', writes James Robinson, General Editor of *The Nag Hammadi Library in English*,

advocating the end of the world as we have known it and its replacement by a quite new, utopian kind of life in which the ideal would be
real. He took a stand quite independent of the authorities of his day
. . . and did not last very long before they eliminated him. Yet his
followers reaffirmed his stand – for them he came to personify the
ultimate goal. . . . Christian Gnosticism thus emerged as a reaffirma-
tion, though in somewhat different terms, of the original stance of
transcendence central to the very beginnings of Christianity.

(Robinson, 1988: 3–4)

What Robinson identifies as 'somewhat different' was, in fact, radically
different in terms of both social structure and shared belief. In the early
centuries of the Christian era the establishment of a central teaching and
authority was of prime importance if the new faith was not to be defeated by
distance and diversity. The loose structuring of Gnostic groups and their
emphasis on the individual's personal experience and expression of revelation was at odds with the need the church fathers perceived for consolida-
tion and conformity. But a more fundamental difference of view and – in its
implications – a more far-reaching one, centred on the nature of good and
evil and its application to the perennial question of the relationship of spirit
to matter. Whereas the early church was formulating a creed which envi-
sioned a loving Creator God, the Father who had incarnated Himself in His
only Son, and who gave in addition the gift of Himself as Holy Spirit, the
Gnostic view was of an original God who was wholly outside of and alien to
the cosmos, which was instead the creation of the demiurge. Matter, rather
than manifesting God's love, was viewed as worthless and even evil, whereas
in orthodox Christianity evil was only the absence of good, of God, not a
force in its own right. This is a bald statement of the dualism for which
Gnosticism is well known, and it does not do justice to the creativity, beauty
and subtlety of Gnostic mythology and belief. It seems characteristic of
Gnosticism that it both enchants and alienates. Gnosticism is a general term
which includes non-Christian, pre-Christian and early Christian systems of
religious belief and practice. Stephan Hoeller writes:

Most of them probably would not have called themselves by the name
Gnostic but would have considered themselves Christians, or more
rarely Jews, or as belonging to the traditions of the ancient cults of
Egypt, Babylon, Greece and Rome. . . . People who shared with each
other a certain attitude toward life. This attitude may be said to
consist of the conviction that direct, personal and absolute knowledge
of the authentic truths of existence is accessible to human beings, and,
moreover, that the attainment of such knowledge must always constitute the supreme achievement of human life.

(Hoeller, 1982: 11)

Central themes

The following notes summarise elements common to most Gnostic sects. Individuality of expression was, however, encouraged and the 'flesh' which covered these 'bones' produced a multitude of different forms.

The revelatory experience of 'gnosis' – of both knowing and being known – was immediate, compelling and numinous. The 'call', when it came, may have been facilitated by the transmission of esoteric knowledge, but the 'knowledge' which was gained through the experience of 'gnosis' was personal and life-changing. Once awakened by the 'call', man's alienated soul, separated from the true God in the original pre-cosmic 'fall', experienced 'homesickness' and came to long for and lament its lost home. The 'rulers' of this world, the archons, seduced and bound man to and within the created systems and powers to prevent him from 'waking up' and remembering his original 'home' and the true God. 'Gnosis' frees man from his thraldom to these powers and systems.

The cause of the 'fall' was the subject of many beautiful myths and speculations; the effect of it was that 'sparks', particles of the original Unity or Pleroma, became separated and entrapped within matter. Thus the One was dispersed into the Many. Redemption of this divine 'spark' was the primary goal for the Gnostic, undertaken through the pursuit of self-knowledge and requiring the recognition of both the base and the divine within each individual. Elaine Pagels summarises: 'Whoever comes to experience his own nature – human nature – as itself the "source of all things", the primary reality, will receive enlightenment' (1982: 149). The doctrine of the Valentinians, Jonas notes, 'justified the equating of individual unification with the reuniting of the Universe with God' (1992: 61).

Relevance

Gnosticism was a system of belief which attempted, as all religions do, to answer fundamental questions. In the face of what was seen and known, that life was full of suffering, persecution and inequality, questions were asked about the Unseen and the Unknown and thus, as we have seen above, the intermediate realm of the symbol was opened. The 'activity of the soul "outside the body"' took the form in Gnosticism of elaborate and beautiful myths of redemption and transformation which demonstrated and affirmed the Gnostic intuition that the 'empirical conscious being' was only a partial and illusory representation of reality. Through experiences of revelation and 'gnosis' the individual's need for a sense of coherence and agency was satisfied.

Not everybody experiences a life-defining 'call', but the discovery of an inner 'voice' which seems to reflect and speak from an authentic centre of the personality, capable not only of sustaining the individual through times of conflict, when seemingly impossible choices must be made, but also of challenging one's assumptions – this discovery can be life-changing. 'Integrity' ceases to be solely a concept and becomes a continuous challenge, experienced by the whole person, to live creatively connected to this centre.

In his Afterword to *The Nag Hammadi Library*, Richard Smith writes:

> If cultures define themselves not at their calm centers but at their peripheral conflicts of inclusion and exclusion, then Gnosticism, whatever we mean by it, is more than an antiquarian curiosity. It stands as a continuing testament to difference in the face of our cultural tendencies toward closed homogeneity.
>
> (Smith, 1988: 549)

Difference is always disturbing for the individual and for society. Our sense of identity and security is largely dependent upon the experience of 'belonging', and when an individual is unable to identify with traditional collectivities, s/he may come to feel an 'outsider', to herself and to the group. Existentialism provided and still provides a 'home' for many in the twentieth century who have found themselves alienated in this way. This experience brings many to analysis and perhaps makes others avoid it for fear of being 'shrunk' to fit into a world unable to contain their difference. The comparison with the early Gnostics is apposite. It is important, however, to recognise the potential nihilism which lies at the heart of Gnostic belief: if matter and spirit are not seen as indissolubly linked, then there may be little motive to value sacrifice, suffering, joy, love or life itself.

Patience and imagination are necessary if one wishes to 'understand' Gnostic or alchemical material; both speak in a language of symbol and paradox. In his book *The Redress of Poetry*, Seamus Heaney explores 'the way consciousness can be alive to two different and contradictory dimensions of reality and still find a way of negotiating between them' (Heaney, 1995: xiii). The untitled poem with which Heaney concludes his book seems an appropriate if paradoxical note on which to conclude this section (ibid.: 203):

The annals say: when the monks of Clonmacnoise
Were all at prayers inside the oratory
A ship appeared above them in the air.

The anchor dragged along behind so deep
It hooked itself into the altar rails
And then, as the big hull rocked to a standstill,

A crewman shinned and grappled down the rope
And struggled to release it. But in vain.
'This man can't bear our life here and will drown,'

The abbot said, 'unless we help him.' So
They did, the freed ship sailed, and the man climbed back
Out of the marvellous as he had known it.

Alchemy

Unlike Gnostic texts . . . Jungian psychology does not see salvation as
a separation of [the] divine fragment from the mundane and its
removal to the divine. Rather, Jung takes the entire dualist myth
and locates it within the psyche.

(Smith, 1988: 540–1)

Although Jung admired the Gnostics' intelligence, individuality and intuitive grasp on the vital work of self-knowledge, his concern was always that
mankind should face the eternal conflict of the opposites within and
address the Gnostic demiurge as the inner Shadow. He stressed what he
saw as our moral and ethical duty to become aware not only of the inner
dark and light, but also our proclivity to project the dark and identify with
the light. Jung never underestimated the demands which disciplined work
towards greater consciousness and the development of moral integrity
imposed. Like the alchemical '*opus*', this endeavour was '*contra naturam*',
in opposition to mankind's preference for unconsciousness.

One of the reasons why the work of the alchemists was of such great
importance to Jung lay in the fact that their observations and interpretations – the 'activity of the soul outside the body' – were made not only
scrupulously but also innocently. Marie-Louise von Franz writes:

They believed that they were studying the unknown phenomenon of
matter . . . and they just observed what came up and interpreted that
somehow, but without any specific plan. There would be a lump of
some strange matter, but as they did not know what it was they
conjectured something or other, which of course would be unconscious projection, but there was no definite intention or tradition.
Therefore one could say that in alchemy, projections were made
most naively and unprogrammatically, and completely uncorrected.
. . . Thus there exists in alchemy an astonishing amount of material
from the unconscious, produced in a situation where the conscious
mind did not follow a definite program, but only searched.

(von Franz, 1980: 21–2)

As we have seen above, the result of this concentration of energy and
observation is that the embedded, unseen and unknown contents of the
psyche are projected and 'discovered' in the intermediate realm of the
symbol. Within the tightly boundaried space of the alchemist's laboratory,

the observer both effected and was affected by his or her participation in and interpretation of what was 'seen'. This circularity of transformational processes – projection, combination, transformation, reintegration – reflects the *Circulatio* of the alchemical fountain, one of the great images of alchemy.

Jung devoted volumes to the study of this ancient art, philosophy and discipline. His essay, 'The Psychology of the Transference' discovers and weaves the process of psychotherapy within the alchemical *opus* as imaged in the text and ten plates of the *Rosarium Philosophorum*, offering an unparalleled vision of the interpersonal and intrapsychic dynamics underlying the analytic relationship. Edward Edinger's *Anatomy of the Psyche* (1993) explores and amplifies the seven alchemical operations of *Calcinatio, Solutio, Coagulatio, Sublimatio, Mortificatio, Separatio* and *Coniunctio*, his sensitive approach making these great processes both accessible and recognisable. Marie-Louise von Franz explores other manifestations of alchemy in her book, *Alchemy* (1980), where, using the format of a lecture followed by questions and answers, she devotes three lectures each to Old Greek, Arabic and later European alchemy. What follows is an approach to the subject based on personal discovery and experience. I hope it will serve as an example of the living reality of the processes described by Jung and all those who preceded and followed him.

Alchemy is a term describing an activity which seems to extend backwards in time, in various guises, as far as human records go, sharing with the equally ancient practice of shamanism, a common vision of a spiritual process of continuing transformation through recognisable states of integration followed by disintegration, of death and rebirth, of growth and stagnation. It addresses the living relationship between the visible and the invisible, the world of matter and that of the spirit. It came alive for me when, ten or fifteen years (or more) after I had dreamt or experienced them, I returned to a series of waking and sleeping experiences with the intention of gathering them up, seeing if there was a common thread or a process I could recognise at work. I was highly motivated at this time by a sense of urgency which I did not understand but which was compelling, and the period of recalling, painting (for that was how I decided to gather up these parts of me) and reflecting – about eighteen months – was characterised by a single-mindedness of energy and focus which is best described by the word 'driven'. I chose to consult weekly with a Jungian colleague during this period; however, although I showed him the paintings, we did not discuss them. He offered me support at a time when I felt I was in danger of being almost overwhelmed by the process which was 'driving' me.

These dreams and experiences had not formed part of my original analysis and, until I went back over journals and notebooks, many, indeed most, had been forgotten. The image that occurred to me in reflecting on this process at a later date was that of the Möbius strip which may be constructed by taking a thin strip of paper, giving it one turn and connecting the ends. The result is an endless surface which turns back upon itself over and over again; there is no top or bottom, just a continuity. The original dreams and experiences had been one movement on this continuum which was turned back on itself when I re-collected and re-covered the material, some of which went back almost fifty years, a living experience of the *Circulatio*. In reflecting on it, painting it and further reflecting on the order in which I 'chose' to paint the experiences – an order which was neither chronological nor consciously systematic in any way – it seemed that further 'turns' in the spiral were occurring 'naturally' and I felt a continuity emerging between the past and the present, the known and the unknown and, most dramatically, between my personal images and words and what I found later in exploring the images and language of alchemy. In fact, Jung's memorable image of the alchemist as one 'who no longer knew whether he was melting the mysterious amalgam in the crucible or whether he was the salamander glowing in the fire' (1954: para. 399), reflects my experience; it was often more as if I were being recollected and recovered by the material than vice versa. And here again, the spiral turns as I bring the material forward into this chapter.

My paintings were primitive and lack of skill frustrated and limited my efforts constantly, but the experience of attempting to translate the impact of a dream or an ineffable experience into a single image was intense and exhilarating; it felt dangerous, incomprehensible and incredibly satisfying when a finished picture somehow captured what remained, none the less, elusive and deeply mysterious. I will list some of the images: the inside of a massive tower where layers of air and water slowed or sped my own descent as I tried to catch a falling scrap of blanket, with the knowledge that if it fell beyond the reach of light we were both doomed; a skinned man, bound on a wheel, being roasted; an image of four birds, first growing blindly out of the soil, then unfledged and fighting, then defeated by an eagle, then transformed into what I called a 'Missal' Thrush; an image of a sort of 'crucifixion' taking place on a massive stone globe while I watched and then, shockingly, when I wondered what my face looked like as I observed this scene, I turned to look at myself and my face *was* the stone globe, alight and alive. One image which felt almost more dangerous than I dared attempt was that of a descent into the underworld down a receding spiral staircase with the certain knowledge that dismemberment and death lay at the bottom and no promise at all of return. A recurring and violent earthquake heralded by astonishingly beautiful and massive cloud movements was relatively straightforward, whereas some dreams – for example, one at a crossroads where a composite animal ran from the left and disappeared into the right quadrant – seemed impossible to depict, mainly, I believe, because I did not understand or grasp the symbol.

Altogether I did about forty small paintings and then, it seemed, I had completed what I needed to do and the 'grip' of the process lessened. The experience was one of being 'operated' upon by forces beyond my conscious perception. Vividly and arrestingly I 'saw' a process at work during the course of my life, during the period of most intense dreaming and experiencing, during the period of recalling and painting, and later, when I worked to find words to describe those experiences. It was and is a process of change and growth, of disintegration and transformation, of well-nigh unbearable conflict and oppositional tensions, of learning about alchemy from the inside, feeling and learning about the terrifying power and depths of the unconscious and, most of all, being incredibly moved by what felt like a silent and invisible 'partner' whom I had not attended to or sufficiently respected in spite of many, many 'taps on the shoulder' indicating an active, living presence with, within and with-out me.

Concluding remarks

Responding to a question about the Mass, Jung said, 'The heart of the Mass contains a living mystery, and that is the thing that works. When I say "a living mystery", I mean nothing mysterious; I mean mystery in that sense which the word has always had – a *mysterium tremendum*' (1939: para. 615). If I have conveyed nothing else I hope to have communicated a sense of this *mysterium* around which questions of meaning and experiences of transformation have always centred. At the heart of existence, as at the heart of matter, there is a *mysterium tremendum*. We may well be touched by it in the course of psychotherapeutic work and call it 'grace'. My emphasis in this chapter has been on the projected psyche, the 'activity of the soul outside the body', the search for meaning which, as Jung wrote, 'makes a great many things endurable – perhaps everything' (1963: 373). But that is only half the picture, which is why I want to close with the famous inscription above the door at Küsnacht: 'Vocatus atque non vocatus deus aderit' – 'Called and not called God will be there.'

References

Edinger, Edward F. (1993) *Anatomy of the Psyche*. Peru, IL: Open Court Publishing Company.
Heaney, Seamus (1995) *The Redress of Poetry*. London: Faber and Faber.
Hoeller, Stephan A. (1982) *The Gnostic Jung and the Seven Sermons to the Dead*. Wheaton, IL: Theosophical Publishing House.
Jonas, Hans (1992) *The Gnostic Religion*. London: Routledge.
Jung, C.G. (1939) *The Symbolic Life. Collected Works* 18.
—— (1944) *Psychology and Alchemy. Collected Works* 12.
—— (1949) Foreword to *I Ching*, trans. Richard Wilhelm, London: Arkana.

—— (1954) *The Practice of Psychotherapy. Collected Works* 16.
—— (1960) *Psychological Types. Collected Works* 6.
—— (1963) *Memories, Dreams, Reflections.* London: Routledge and Kegan Paul/ Collins.
Pagels, Elaine (1982) *The Gnostic Gospels.* Harmondsworth: Penguin.
Robinson, James M. (ed.) (1988) *The Nag Hammadi Library in English.* Netherlands: E.J. Brill.
Smith, Richard (1988) 'Afterword', in *The Nag Hammadi Library in English.* Netherlands: E.J. Brill.
von Franz, Marie-Louise (1980) *Alchemy.* Toronto: Inner City Books.

'God Could Be Something Terrible'

Margaret Clark

'I regard the psyche as *real*'
(Jung, 1952: para. 751)

> As kingfishers catch fire, dragonflies draw flame;
> As tumbled over rim in roundy wells
> Stones ring; like each tucked string tells, each hung bell's
> Bow swung finds tongue to fling out broad its name;
> Each mortal thing does one thing and the same:
> Deals out that being indoors each one dwells;
> Selves – goes itself; *myself* it speaks and spells,
> Crying *What I do is me: for that I came.*
>
> I say more: the just man justices;
> Keeps grace: that keeps all his goings graces;
> Acts in God's eye what in God's eye he is –
> Christ – for Christ plays in ten thousand places,
> Lovely in limbs, and lovely in eyes not his
> To the Father through the features of men's faces.
>
> (G.M. Hopkins)

For Jung, as for Hopkins, 'Each mortal [person] does one thing and the same: / Deals out that being indoors each one dwells; . . . / Crying *What I do is me: for that I came.*' This 'being' that dwells indoors us Jung calls our self, and he writes: 'the urge and compulsion to *self-realisation* is a law of nature and thus of invincible power' (1940: para. 289; my italics). This self is at first unconscious. So we project it – as from infancy we project our unconscious feelings, 'seeing' them first outside us, in another person, situation or story. Our self is so huge that we need a huge symbol as a container to project it into – such as a circle, a tree, a jewel, an egg, a god. Such projections are inevitable. They are also useful, enabling us to understand in depth our affective responses, first to our symbol and then, if we can take back our projections, to our own self: we realise in consciousness that the mystery, power and terror formerly attributed to God (and the devil) belong to our own self and are our responsibility. Thus we come to see other people, objects and ideas more objectively, less distorted by our projections into them. Only then can we be just and act justly: 'the just man justices'. This process Jung calls individuation; its effects are not confined to internal psychic development.

Analysis/therapy is for me about accepting as much as we can of our own reality. Internal reality, to Jung, is as real as external reality. So an apparently universal belief in God is a psychic fact which needs to be taken seriously, understood as a projection of our self and not as establishing (or denying) a metaphysical truth (Jung, 1938: paras 166–8).

Because, like Jung, I have a background in traditional Christianity, I'm focusing here on Jung's interpretation of Christian, rather than of Gnostic or alchemical imagery, following his injunction to 'give a little thought to what the symbols really mean' (Jung, 1948: para. 293). The Christian story, of God incarnated in Jesus and of Jesus' struggle with Satan, exemplifies in powerful symbols the process of our self coming into our consciousness, including our struggle with our shadow. So we can use this story to explore, in a projected form, our internal reality. I find these symbols have immediate relevance in very ordinary clinical situations.

God and Satan

In the traditional Christian story, evil is split off from good. Satan has been expelled from Heaven; then, on earth, either on the Cross or in a final battle at the end of time, Jesus defeats Satan, who is bound for ever. And the 'new Jerusalem, coming down from God out of heaven', offers us a place solely spiritual and with no pain or sorrow (Rev. 21. 1–4). Satan – and matter – have been eliminated.

Jung sees this as no solution: it represents an idealised view of the self based on denial of our shadow and our bodies. In fact, we live in matter – in our bodies, and in a material world – and our struggle with our shadow is never ended. This struggle is essential as, for Jung, the psyche is essentially structured through a tension between opposites: we can know 'above' only in contrast to 'below'. So for good to be 'real' and known, evil also must be 'real' and known. Jung consistently attacks the view which implies that good is the norm and evil only a lack of good, and which thus minimises the power of evil (1948: para. 247). He reinterprets the story that God created Satan, to emphasise that Satan stays part of God.

Even as a child, Jung knew that 'God could be something terrible' (Jung 1983: 25, 56f.). And in his 70s, in six tremendous essays published between 1946 and 1956, he writes that God is terrible because Satan is an integral and inevitable part of God. God is originally 'a unity unclouded by criticism' who then 'begets' Jesus – and thereby, also, inevitably, Satan: 'the opposites latent in the Deity flew apart when the Son was begotten'; we can recognise Jesus 'only by virtue of something else that is *not* Jesus', i.e. Satan (1948, paras 201, 254, 259).

This account is an archetypal image of individual development, in the separating of the baby's ego out of her primary self (c.f. chapter 1 in this volume), of consciousness out of unconsciousness, of mind from body, and of the baby from her parents. Each separation inevitably 'begets' a shadow, because consciousness brings awareness of difference, which means, inevitably, awareness of loss, frustration, anxiety. So the regressive pull not to become conscious is powerful.

Earlier in his analysis, my patient, Andrew, kept his 'unity', in unconsciousness, by projecting into his wife his envy and hatred of me for what he perceived as my power over him – his wife, he said, didn't want him to have analysis. He himself felt only gratitude to me. Now he realises, after struggling with his shame, that the envy and hatred are also his. When someone loses the 'semblance of unity. . . realises that he himself has a shadow, that his enemy is in his own heart, then the conflict begins and one becomes two' (1946: para. 399).

The shadow: Satan within

The shadow is therefore not a metaphysical but an eminently practical problem. And 'one of the toughest roots of all evil is unconsciousness' (1948: para. 291). So, when Andrew's wish to dominate was unconscious, he projected it into his workmates, experienced them as dominating him, and was therefore abusive to them. Similarly, in society, we project our collective shadow – for instance, into nuclear weapons (c.f. Redfearn, 1992).

When Caroline came to therapy, she was suffering from depression, panic attacks and feeling 'unreal'. She was totally unconscious of her shadow, totally identified with her persona, seeing herself solely as a loving wife and mother and assuming a pseudo-independence based on omnipotence. She's now gradually accepting that she's an ordinary woman, who gets tired and cross, wants to control people and be dependent, feels insecure, and would sometimes like to leave her husband and children.

These feelings are now irreversibly conscious, and Caroline feels more 'real'; as Jung says, 'My shadow. . . gives me substance and mass' (1929b: para. 134). But Caroline isn't sure what is her shadow, what's right or wrong for her to do, as in the dream Jung reports of a black magician confusingly clad in white and a white magician clad in black (1928: para. 287). She knows only that her wish to stay and her wish to leave are both inextricably part of her self; 'Satan' is inextricably part of 'God'. She's caught in 'a conflict of duties, whose solution requires us to understand that our "counter-will" is also an aspect of God's will' (1948: para. 292). Through her now conscious tension between these opposites, she may find her own 'life-form'. I certainly can't find it for her. As Jung says: 'the shoe that fits one person pinches another; there is no universal recipe for living. Each of us carries his own life-form within him – an irrational form which no other can outbid' (1929a: para. 81).

What we've met of Caroline's shadow so far isn't satanic, 'merely somewhat inferior, primitive, unadapted, and awkward; not wholly bad' (1938: para. 134). But other people in my consulting room can experience their shadow as an evil power like Satan: a man realises he wants to punch me to pulp; a woman discovers she wants to murder her husband. It's the death of our previous partial view of ourselves – which brings the possibility of resurrection or of re-birth, as 'a new man' (1938: para. 56). It also brings the possibility of the ego being overwhelmed by the shadow, as with the patient who's becoming aware of her sadism, her depression, and the hollowness of her omnipotence, and is finding it hard to keep going. The patient may even identify with the emerging shadow, as in psychosis, when the devil or the tiger in them may act out murderous attacks. The risks are real; God (our whole self) can be terrible.

In his late teens, Jung had a dream about the shadow and consciousness:

> It was night in some unknown place, and I was making slow and painful headway against a mighty wind. Dense fog was flying along everywhere. I had my hands cupped around a tiny light which threatened to go out at any moment. Everything depended on my keeping this little light alive. Suddenly I had the feeling that something was coming up behind me. I looked back, and saw a gigantic black figure following me. But at the same moment I was conscious, in spite of my terror, that I must keep my little light going through night and wind, regardless of all dangers. When I awoke I realised at once that the figure was a 'spectre of the Brocken', *my own shadow* on the swirling mists, *brought into being by the little light I was carrying.* I knew, too, that this little light was my consciousness, the only light I have. My own understanding is the sole treasure I possess, and the greatest. Though infinitely small and fragile in comparison with the powers of darkness, it is still a light, my only light.
>
> (1983: 107f.; my italics)

Although our shadow is there all the time, it seems to us that we bring it into being by the light of our consciousness – because that's when we become aware of it. Quite early in our work together, Anna, a white woman, dreamed of her shadow wanting to become conscious. She dreamed of having to tie a black girl of fifteen on to a bed. This girl was pleading to be allowed to get up, with just her hands tied. The dreamer decided she could tame her, that it would be all right and that the judge had been wrong in saying she should be tied up for life because she'd stabbed her elder sister and perhaps her mother.

Through our discussion, Anna found it safe to untie her shadow, to allow into consciousness her hostile feelings to her sister and mother, and her wish to kill her internal sister and mother. In place of the clarity of splitting and denial, where the shadow remains unconscious (in the Christian story, Satan is bound for ever and Christ rules in triumph), Anna, like Caroline, meets her shadow, in confusion and compromise, in consciousness (c.f. Dourley, 1995: 186f.).

The Incarnation

This coming of unconscious contents (the self) into consciousness is symbolised in Christianity by the story of the Incarnation of God in the man Jesus, his crucifixion and resurrection. The dangers attending his birth, for instance, symbolise the difficult and uncertain beginnings of the individuation process, with Herod as that part of ourselves which feels threatened by change and tries to eliminate it (see Edinger, 1987). Jesus, Jung writes, 'must suffer the terrible torture of having to endure the world in all its reality. This is the cross he has to bear' (1948: para. 265). As our self comes more into consciousness, we become more conscious of reality, of the inevitability of limitation, failure, separation, conflict, loss.

But, without this limitation, there can be no Incarnation at all. The only channel for a realisation of any part of my self is the consciousness and actions of my ego and my body, which have to exist and act in particular time and particular space – as Jesus lived when he did, chose his apostles from the people he met – and one of them betrayed him. Equally, I can live only one of the many lives potentially in my self: if I choose to be an analyst, I can't also be an accountant. For some people, having thus to relinquish anything of their selves is so painful that they can't choose anything: they stay suspended, unable to commit themselves to this partner, this job, because of the loss this entails of all the other potential partners and jobs. So there is no incarnation, no action, no life.

Jung sees Christ, crucified between a good and a bad thief, as experiencing the agony of uniting opposite experiences – of the choices and limitations of life, of good and bad, of horizontal and vertical held together in the structure of the cross (Jung, 1951: para. 123). Early in her work with me, Brenda used this symbolism to express her sense of herself. Excruciatingly stuck in her depression, she brought me a 'picture' – with nails and fragments of wood and leather embedded in plaster, all in white except for a streak of red dripping off a nail. It represented for her a broken cross, and this was how she experienced herself. The opposites, symbolised in the structure of the cross as held together, were for her fragmented, and she had no sense of her self as able to unite them – there is here no Christ being crucified. After some six months, she began to dream of opposite states which didn't meet – literally 'states' in the case of the heavily guarded border between France and Germany, metaphorically in dreams of the beach and the sea, or of the walls of a house which didn't quite meet the floor. She was becoming aware of the opposites she was carrying inside herself – such as her passive depressed mother and her active manic father.

Jung writes frequently that 'Christ exemplifies the archetype of the self'. But sometimes he thinks of God as symbolising the self – a God who can beget both Christ and Satan – and Christ as lacking 'a nocturnal side' and so realising only part of the archetype of the self, because the self is 'by definition a *complexio oppositorum*'. In this view, Jesus isn't fully man, as he was born 'perfect', without Original Sin (1948: paras 232, 283; 1951: paras 70, 123; cf. 1954: para. 414).

Jung writes, 'What happens in the life of Christ happens always and everywhere' (1938: para. 146) – and the Christ stories help us understand what is happening, always and everywhere in our human psyches. When we read these stories as an enactment in projection of our own psychic processes, then they are invaluable, as symbols which represent for us what is, without a symbol, irrepresentable. But when we take the stories literally, as if they are about someone else, we stay unconscious of our own rich potential and of the ethical imperative this brings. We then remain as little children, dependent on God, instead of taking responsibility for our own 'child' and our own 'God'. Jung says, 'The Christ Child . . . is a religious necessity only so long as the majority of men are incapable of giving *psychological* reality to the saying: "Except ye become as little children . . ."' (1940: para. 287; my italics).

The coming of the Holy Spirit: Christ within

Viewing the whole Christian story, including the coming of the Holy Spirit at Pentecost, as 'psychological reality', we understand as symbols Jung's statements that 'the future indwelling of the Holy Ghost in man amounts to a continuing incarnation of God', and that we are now 'the stable in which the Lord is born' (1952: para. 693; 1948: para. 267). This develops the Christian mystical tradition of the 'God within', which the Church has emphasised less than the historical Jesus, in order to preserve continuity and the Church's own authority, and to prevent the dangers of heresy and inflation (c.f. 1954: para. 446).

Inflation occurs when 'God dwells in me' becomes 'therefore I am God'. As Jung points out, Jesus himself says that 'you are gods, sons of the Most High, all of you' (1952: para. 692) (echoing the Serpent's temptation in Genesis (3: 5): 'Ye shall be as gods'): but how are we to integrate into our consciousness the powerful aspects of our self previously projected into

God? Jung writes movingly of how, when Nietzsche proclaimed that 'God is dead' (i.e. withdrew his projections into an external God), his ego was overwhelmed by the returning archetypal contents, and he became mad (1938: para. 142).

One safeguard is to try to control the rate at which the archetypal contents of the self enter the ego – but the Holy Spirit at Pentecost entered the apostles like wind and fire (Acts 2: 1–4), at a rate of its choosing, not of theirs. A patient may need the help, especially during breaks, of a container for these forces other than the analytic relationship – a new relationship, or a hospital.

But with some people, their 'own psychic constitution' seems to 'know' (in Jung's phrase) what to do, if the analyst will 'take deep-seated resistances seriously at first' (1929a: para. 76). David, although desperate for relief from his stomach pains and asthma, stayed bright and cheerful for more than a year of analysis. I think he was internalising sufficient of me as a good object so that 'I' (and so 'he') would survive his subsequent searing attacks. Janet, on the other hand, chose to leave after two years of twice-weekly therapy, before she would experience her negative feelings towards me: for her, enough of her self had become conscious.

For incarnating more of our self reveals to us our shadow. 'Ye shall be as gods' has its price; it involves 'knowing good and evil' – about ourselves. And this is not only about internal psychic development. As Hopkins says, 'The just man *justices* . . . *Acts* in God's eye what in God's eye he is – Christ' (my italics). But how about the *unjust* (wo)man that I also am? This realisation – of what I may, and do, enact – is another safeguard against an inflated identification with the God within.

The bodily assumption of the Virgin Mary into heaven

Jung welcomed a new dogma of the Roman Catholic church, proclaimed in 1950 – 'the Assumption of the Blessed Virgin Mary, that is, the taking up of Mary's soul into heaven *with her body*'. He understands it as symbolising a far-reaching change in our collective psyche – an acknowledgement that our self, previously projected into a masculine, spiritual God, also includes the feminine and the body (and thereby includes sexuality); with the body, it includes all matter, and so also the aggressive Satan, who is 'the Prince of this [material] world'. The dogma recognises symbolically our need to include and co-operate with, rather than to deny and exclude, much of what we call our shadow. Jung writes powerfully, 'The dark weight of the earth must enter into the picture of the whole' (1948: paras 251, 264; cf. Dourley, 1995: 187).

And, slowly, it is entering. Forty-five years later, we're more aware of when we damage our bodies, nature, matter, the feminine; we sometimes attempt to respect and co-operate with, rather than dominate or deny, them. A Roman Catholic retreat offered 'to explore massage within the context of a spirituality which finds God in *all* things and which redeems the body from the context of sin and temptation into which previous unhelpful spiritualities had cast it' (Noddfa Retreat Centre, 1995; cf. also Cotter, 1988: 18, 43). Movements such as Friends of the Earth work for 'sustainable development' rather than exploitation of the earth's resources; Lovelock (1979) writes of the co-operation between all organisms necessary for life to exist on our planet. A greater equality and co-operation between men and women has often become possible, partly through feminism. Some educational, religious, medical and philosophical schemes respect right-brain functioning and a more holistic approach to life (cf. Stevens, 1982; Jaffe, 1990). Zohar writes from the perspective of quantum physics of the indivisibility of mind and matter (Zohar, 1991: 20f., 58–88).

Jung says it's 'fairly probable' that 'psyche and matter are two different aspects of one and the same thing' (1947: para. 418; cf. Bohm, 1983: 11), and that our unconscious psyche affects matter in 'synchronous' events, which occur with a meaningful, but not a causal, connection, as if they were dream images experienced in the external world. He thinks that 'the symbols of the self arise in the depths of the body' (Jung, 1940: para. 291). Out of the original unconscious psychosomatic unity of infancy, psyche and soma separate. In this dogma, we see in projection the developmental achievement of their coming together again in consciousness, the body welcomed and honoured by the psyche.

But the most important symbolic implication of this dogma is in the provision of a heavenly bride (Mary) for Christ, which brings sexual activity into Heaven and the possibility of a child, 'a saviour', born in 'the natural man who [unlike the perfect Jesus] is tainted with original sin' (1952: paras 741, 746). This, for Jung, is a symbol of the possibility of individuation.

The process of individuation

Jung acknowledges that for most people individuation is an unconscious process, with the self still experienced mainly in projection: then, 'it means no more than that the acorn becomes an oak, the calf a cow, and the child an adult.' But this is not necessarily a smooth process: in this unconscious individuation 'we become its victims and are dragged along by fate towards that inescapable goal'. We may project our self into other members of a group, 'within the framework of an existing credo – including a political credo'. Or we may rely on a super-ego, as 'a necessary and unavoidable substitute for the experience of the self'. Or we may meet God mediated through religious rituals, and so be 'effectively protected against [the] immediate religious experience' of meeting our own self. In all these cases, 'that should be enough for the doctor' (1952: paras 755, 746; 1935: para. 21; 1954: para. 394; 1938: para. 75).

But when we withdraw the projection of our self, from God or the social collective, 'then one is truly one's own yea and nay' (1954: para. 396). This rarely feels like a conscious choice: 'Nobody ever feels himself as the subject of such a process, but always as its object. *He* does not perceive holiness, *it* takes him captive and overwhelms him' (1948: para. 225), as Mary is overshadowed by the Holy Ghost (Luke 1: 35). The self (God) is still 'something terrible'.

As analysis continues, a patient may realise, in a Copernican revolution, that her ego is not the centre of her psyche, but that the ego revolves round the self, like the earth round the sun, and that the self, like the sun, is by far the greater and is the source of life and sustenance. Yet also 'the position of the ego must be maintained as being of equal value to the counter-position of the unconscious' (1929a: para. 107; 1957: para. 183). Ego and self are in dialogue: each is both its own subject and the object to the subjectivity of the other. The dialogue continues our life long, because our unconscious contents are boundless and we constantly meet new external situations. I become at the same time more like my self, more individual, and also more aware of the ways in which I am like other people. My psychic experiences, like my body, are both uniquely mine and recognisably like everyone else's.

People get impatient with the process of life, as they do with the process of analysis – the man who didn't want to progress from A to B but to jump from A to Z, the woman who saw me, to her horror, as 'a boring old woman' because she wanted only excitement. But, for analysis as for individuation, 'the goal is important only as an idea; the essential thing is the *opus* which leads to the goal: *that* is the goal of a lifetime' (1946: para. 400). The purpose of life becomes living itself.

Attacks on therapy as inward-looking and selfish miss the point of individuation. For Jung, 'individuation has two principal aspects: in the first place it is an internal and subjective process of integration, and in the second it is an *equally indispensable* process of objective relationship' (1946: para. 448; my italics). The two go together. Giving up the fantasy of the ego's omnipotent control over the psyche goes in parallel with giving up the omnipotent fantasy of controlling other people. As I know more fully my own 'other', my self, so I project less of my self into 'other' people – and so I relate to them more objectively.

Jung sees the social, enacted work of the individual as a necessary – and inevitable – part of the whole individuation process. 'One cannot individuate with mere words' (1948: para. 292). And in his own prolific writings, in his involvement with the varying development of analytical psychology, its trainings and rivalries, and in the many Prefaces he wrote to others' books, we see the realisation in intellectual, social and cultural action of his own individuating self. It is a useful counter-measure to our picture of him alone at Bollingen and to his emphasis in *Memories, Dreams, Reflections* on his 'inner happenings' (1983: 19).

Individuation is the 'myth' Jung lived by (1983: 195, 224). He sees it as 'the spiritual adventure of our time' (1938: para. 168), and as a development from Christianity in three particular ways: that we understand the Christian story as describing in symbols our own psychic processes; that we understand our own self as a numinous power rather than projecting this into God; and that in our self we understand the power of our shadow. We could then, Jung hopes, take more responsibility for ourselves and perhaps integrate what Christianity has often excluded – our sexual and aggressive instincts. We could become less 'perfect', but more 'complete'.

References

The Bible. Authorised Version, 1611.

Bohm, D. (1983) *Wholeness and the Implicate Order*, London: Routledge (first published 1980).

Cotter, J. (1988) *Pleasure, Pain and Passion*, Sheffield: Cairns Publications.

Dourley, J.P. (1995) 'The religious implications of Jung's psychology', *Journal of Analytical Psychology*, 40(2): 177–203.

Edinger, E.F. (1987) *The Christian Archetype*, Toronto: Inner City Books.

Hopkins, G.M. (1953) *A Selection of his Poetry and Prose*, ed. W.H. Gardner, London: Penguin Books.

Jaffe, L.W. (1990) *Liberating the Heart*, Toronto: Inner City Books.

Jung, C.G. (1928) 'The relations between the ego and the unconscious', *Collected Works* 7.

—— (1929a) 'The aims of psychotherapy', *Collected Works* 16.

—— (1929b) 'Problems of modern psychotherapy', *Collected Works* 16.

—— (1930) 'The stages of life', *Collected Works* 8.

—— (1935) 'Principles of practical psychotherapy', *Collected Works* 16.

—— (1938) 'Psychology and religion', *Collected Works* 11.

—— (1940) 'The psychology of the child archetype', *Collected Works* 9.i.

—— (1946) 'The psychology of the transference', *Collected Works* 16.

—— (1947) 'On the nature of the psyche', *Collected Works* 8.

—— (1948) 'A psychological approach to the dogma of the Trinity', *Collected Works* 11.

—— (1951) *Aion, C.W.* 9.ii.

—— (1952) 'Answer to Job', *Collected Works* 11.

—— (1954) 'Transformation symbolism in the Mass', *Collected Works* 11.

—— (1957) 'The transcendent function', *Collected Works* 8.

—— (1983) *Memories, Dreams, Reflections*, London: Fontana (first published by Collins and Routledge & Kegan Paul, 1963).

Lovelock, J.E. (1979) *Gaia*, Oxford: Oxford University Press.

Redfearn, J.W.T. (1992) *The Exploding Self*, Wilmette, IL: Chiron Publications.

Stevens, A. (1982) *Archetype*, London: Routledge & Kegan Paul.

Zohar, D. (1991) *The Quantum Self*, London: HarperCollins (first published by Bloomsbury Publishing, 1990).

Chapter 8

Gender and Sexuality

Wendy Bratherton uses clinical examples to show how powerful emotions within, and between, men and women which affect personal relationships may be traced to deep damage within the psyche. Writing from a point of view that is acknowledging the interplay between collective culture and the individual, Wendy Bratherton finds Jung's concept of anima and animus provides a dynamic model by which to witness not only the movement of masculine and feminine energies within the psyche, but also the relationship of these to dominating cultural norms. For example, Bratherton comments on how, within patriarchal western societies, the valuing of the thinking function over the feeling function can lead to a serious split in how men and women experience themselves and the world.

In his paper entitled 'Contrasexuality and the unknown soul', Warren Coleman notes how Jung's conception of contrasexuality has become controversial because of an over-rigid equation between anima and animus, on the one hand, and the so-called masculine and feminine principles, on the other. His paper distinguishes this restricting aspect of Jung's thought from Jung's deeper concern with the contrasexual as an archetypal image of the soul. In this more 'contingent' view, the nature of the soul image is dependent on those aspects of the personality which have been relegated to the unconscious 'otherworld' and need to be reclaimed in order to further the quest for wholeness. The longing for union with this 'unknown soul' may be represented by sexual desire for the other gender, and, in addition to clinical vignettes, Warren Colman uses the lyrics of Bob Dylan to illustrate this numinous process vividly.

The Collective Unconscious and Primordial Influences in Gender Identity

W.J. Bratherton

Introduction

One day in the autumn, while wandering along a Devon beach pondering upon the vast and important topic of sex and gender, which touches everyone and can stir such deep emotions, various pebbles caught my eye. I picked them up. Each one had a hole through it. They reminded me of sculptures of Henry Moore and Barbara Hepworth. I recalled standing below some of their sculptures set on a hillside and experiencing powerful sensations which connected me to nearly overwhelming archetypal images of the primordial great mother – in both her destructive and creative aspects. I thought how difficult it can be to conceptualise these archetypal images in order to write about them, except through metaphor and myth. The beach, I mused, might be compared to society and the pebbles to individuals – each one shaped by the same elemental forces but each one different. My awareness shifted into considering the power of opposites, the tension of holding them, and especially of Jung's description of the alchemy of the transference.

Just as my thoughts navigated around the subject of sex and gender identity so I intend, in this chapter, to present glimpses of its different aspects. The main theme will be to show what a struggle it can be to come to terms, both culturally and individually, with aspects of the personal and collective unconscious. How can Jungian analysis and Jungian ideas, especially of anima and animus, can illuminate debate on this topic. This theme inevitably focuses on the interplay between the culture and the individual. Jung was interested in this interplay, suggesting that if people came to terms with the inner conflicts in their psyches it would have an effect on the culture. Conversely, individuals growing up in a culture imbibe its norms and values which remain unconscious unless thrown on to the shore of consciousness by, say, conflict or depression. Here the experiences and struggles of the women's movement have much to offer as they challenge the preconceptions of what is taken culturally to be innately masculine and innately feminine.

Children growing up in a society assimilate and absorb its ideas and norms. Collective beliefs about what it is to be male or female filter through to the child through families and the education system, as well as through the media and other social institutions. As such beliefs about how girls and boys should behave appear to be 'the norm', they remain unquestioned and unconscious. In this way people aquire their gender identities. On the basis of anthropological research, Oakley states that 'gender has no biological origin, that the connections between sex and gender are not really "natural" at all' (1972). Sex, that is, to be male or female, is biological, whereas gender is cultural or psychological, in that it encompasses ideas of masculinity and femininity. Elements of both masculinity and femininity exist in both sexes 'but the male has a preponderance of masculinity and the female a preponderance of femininity' (Stoller, 1968: 9). Gender identity therefore grows through the interaction of biological and environmental factors.

In this chapter I have particularly focused on the inner journey a person might take, bearing in mind the interplay of such inner and outer influences. I intend to show that correcting the imbalances of the masculine and the feminine elements in both the individual or society, is not a matter of making the feminine dominant nor of simply giving greater emphasis to the feminine. Rather, the masculine and feminine are in dynamic relationship and the development of both needs to take place. Out of this 'mix' a new element is conceived, bringing a change in the whole individual. Jung describes this in his writing on the alchemy of the transference (1946). It is part of the individuation process. I suggest, moreover, that issues which are, at first, felt to be about masculine and feminine – for example the hating of 'all men' or 'all women' – may lead back to early damage within the psyche. It is just these elements of the psyche which are unmet in infancy which get pushed into the shadow and projected on to the 'other' and which may cause such difficulties in relationships. There is a complex interplay of inner and outer influences, between the inner journey and society and it is upon this aspect that many feminist writers focus.

The main wound of modern society

In my wanderings on the beach some holes in the pebbles appeared to me as wounds. I reflected on what many consider to be the main wound of modern western society, namely the pursuit of scientific objectivity and logic with the consequent devaluing of subjectivity and the world of feeling. It could be said that in western culture the Apollonian approach is valued over the Dionysian one. This is not to deny in any way the great benefits that the scientific approach has brought to modern society, but to recognise that it is achieved at a cost and other aspects may be denigrated. In the case of western society it has been the feeling aspects which have been traditionally cast into the shadow. In this chapter I am asking the reader to enter, to some extent, a more Dionysian frame of mind which is more non-linear and non-rational, more empathic and intuitive as a balance to the Apollonian, causal, logical approach.

It may be worth pausing here to consider the way the word 'feeling' is used. In everyday English language the word 'feeling' is frequently used imprecisely and interchangeably to describe a whole gamut of human experience, emotions, intuitions and sensations. The *Oxford English Dictionary*, for instance, includes in the definition of feeling 'the sense of touch, emotion, sentiment, conviction not based solely on reason, intuitive belief'. Here, I understand 'feeling' to mean that faculty which enables us to evaluate experiences (as described by Jung when he defines the four functions – feeling, thinking, intuition and sensation). Feeling, as the act of valuing an experience, can be distinguished from mood which is described by Johnson as being 'like a small psychosis, or possession. A man's mood comes from being overpowered by the feminine part of his nature' (1974: 35). The feeling function may be differentiated from emotion, affect or mood in as much as these do not share the quality of evaluation. Emotion, then, can be all-consuming and is described by Johnson as 'a sum of energy that occurs, or is set off, in a person by a meaningful experience. Its chief characteristic is its energy' (ibid.: 34).

In the clinical examples I hope to show how some patients may struggle with immensely powerful emotions and experience elemental forces which have to be held in the analysis and not acted out, until they change. When some of the archetypal forces have been modified and projections withdrawn, then patients find there can be feeling in the evaluative sense.

Anima and animus

Before giving the clinical examples, it would seem pertinent to examine Jung's concepts of anima and animus. The inner figure of man which a woman has in her psyche and the inner figure of woman which a man has in his psyche, are the animus and anima respectively. Jung suggests the anima and animus are archetypal structures which are universally experienced and unchangeable. The archetypes are known through archetypal images and it is these which may alter. 'The anima can be defined as the image or archetype or deposit of all the "experiences of man with woman"' (1938: para. 58).

Anima and animus are images which represent that aspect of the person which is 'other' and different from the way they behave consciously; so there is a contrasexual emphasis. The 'other' side may appear in projection on to a real man or woman. This may spark the seed of attraction or understanding, or indeed the opposite. However, as Hillman argues in his book on anima – *Anima: An Anatomy of a Personified Notion* (1985) – it is not just a projection of anima on to the woman and animus on to the man. Both women and men have an anima and an animus in some kind of relationship within their psyche. One side may be more dominant than the other depending on the individual, the society and the culture. A woman, for instance, who feels empty inside and that life has no meaning, as does Annette in the clinical example below, may be seen to have a similar problem to a man in the same state. Both suffer from loss of soul and an imaginal space internally. Jung stresses the importance of this inner relatedness – the relationship to aspects of oneself which if not related to may be projected out on to another and cause loss of soul. Alternatively the person may be taken over or possessed by the elements of the self which have been cast into shadow, causing a loss of ego.

The archetypes of anima and animus are present from the start of an individual's life, in the form of inherited patterns (as distinct from inherited characteristics), and contain all previous experiences of women with men and men with women. The archetypal images are initially given form and content by experience of the relationship with the personal mother and father. However, Humbert, in his book *C.G. Jung*, stresses that 'the feminine element within the man's psyche does not appear by internalising the mother's image, nor does the animus come about by having the woman internalize the father's image' (1988: 56). Rather, the archetype may be modified by the personal experiences with mother and father. It is necessary to realise that anima and animus are not *just* internalised parents, although the relationship with the parents will shape the archetypal *images* and the ways in which they work together in the psyche. The anima and animus form the link between the ego and the inner world. Jung saw this capacity for mediation between the unconscious and the conscious which the anima and animus performed, as being essentially sexual in nature. Animus and anima are the 'organisers' of everything which relates to the sexual identity of the person including oral and anal eroticism, oedipal relationships, fantasies of the opposite sex. Hence they are more than the projected image of the opposite sex. Animus and anima as mediators may appear in dreams, mythology and in the emotional life of the subject. They may also operate as autonomous complexes (that is, a law unto themselves) and, while they remain unconscious, their effect is mostly negative (Humbert, 1988: 56). However, if anima and animus are made more conscious their effect can become creative. The effect of the anima's influence and power is explored by Jung: 'the unconscious anima is a creature without relationships, an autoerotic being whose aim is to take total possession of the individual' (Jung, 1953: paras 329 and 331). 'When this happens to a man he becomes strangely womanish in the worst sense, with a moody and uncontrolled disposition which, in time, has a deleterious effect even on the hitherto reliable functions – e.g., his intellect' (1946: 504).

Animus is associated with men and, in our western society which values the rational, has become linked to logic. Anima, on the other hand, which is associated with women, has come to be equated with eros, the connecting and relating principle. In *Memories, Dreams, Reflections* (1983: 210–12) Jung describes how his anima emerged in an image through which he could feel more in touch with his unconscious. She emerged as a feminine voice telling him that what he was doing, which was writing down his fantasies, was art. This voice came from deep within him and felt fascinating and strange. He began to relate to her and he describes the need to personify these unconscious contents, at least until it is possible to relate to them easily. It must be remembered that it is not only men who may develop their masculine side at the expense of their feminine side; women too may do so and the masculine side of a woman (in its negative form) may exert a tyrannical control of the feminine. Marion Woodman in her introduction to *Addiction to Perfection: The Still Unravished Bride* graphically describes how Lady Macbeth personifies the masculine divorced from the feminine, and the way in which this leads to a cutting off of inner psychic life and meaning (1982: 19).

The clinical examples I will now present show that it can take great courage, for both sexes, to face the rage and conflict engendered by anima and animus projection or possession.

Clinical examples

Annette

The first example concerns a woman who was, at the outset of therapy, a very angry feminist. She started analysis at a point in her life when, after attending consciousness-raising groups and some counselling, she was on the verge of a breakdown. Annette was in her early thirties, the mother of two young children. She was having difficulties in her relationship with her husband and both were having affairs. In the course of her analysis she discovered that her driving force was the masculine side of her nature (her animus) which made her strident, bossy and opinionated in relationships and behind which she felt non-existent.

When Annette was a small child her mother had been extremely depressed and agoraphobic, to the extent that she was unable to go out without her husband and at times could not walk across a room without incapacitating palpitations. Annette had been cared for by *au pairs*. She became a clinging child and was frightened of leaving her mother, even when she desperately wanted to play with other children. Attending school was a terrifying ordeal, especially as she was frightened of what would happen to mother. During the course of her analysis it was discovered that, in Annette's mind, mother had become equated with death. When Annette was small, her mother frequently had to stay in hospital for treatment for her depression and no one explained to Annette what was going on – for her, mother just disappeared. Moreover, the 'emotionally dead' mother was not able to respond to the little girl in her daily interaction in an alive, interested way. As a teenager Annette felt ashamed of being female. Although she was by nature an introvert, she had modelled herself on her father who was very active and extroverted. Developing the masculine side of her nature allowed her to survive but she felt hollow and empty. She did not know who she was. Driven to achieve by a tyrannical force she was, at first, dissociated and split. She had developed into a teenager who had wanted to emulate father (as he was alive for her) and developed her own masculine side and intellect. This brought intense conflict as father wanted her to be very feminine. (He seemed to want her to represent an aspect of his anima. He had definite ideas about how his daughter should look and he thought that a woman's place was in the home. At the same time he placed high value on her education.) For Annette, being female was equated with being nothing. As puberty arrived she wished she had been born male and tried to deny the physical changes occurring in her body. Her need for affection, exacerbated by her father turning away from her during adolescence, led her to become seductive and promiscuous – desperate for men, yet despising them for not seeing her despair. She wished to control men and seduce them. Having done so, she felt disempowered and in order to regain her power she would turn away from them and refuse any contact. This caused her great distress as she really wanted closeness, but was driven to having shallow, unsatisfactory, angry relationships.

As she regressed in analysis, more sense was made of her childhood. She had few memories of her early years except feelings of terror and acute anxiety and a sense of black all around her. Her analysis took her back to early birth experiences where, during a long and difficult birth, she and mother both nearly died. As a result, early defences of the self (Fordham, 1986) came into being which made it difficult for her to relate when a baby, especially as her attempts at relating were met by a poor response from her severely depressed mother. She retreated into a shell. We might express her development by noting how the archetypal image of the anima was not shaped by a good enough mother, so she remained at the mercy of the primordial 'bad mother', the devouring witch. This she projected outside herself, often hallucinating that she was a witch when she caught sight of herself in reflections in windows. The witch also appeared in her paintings. When, in the transference, the analyst became the witch, Annette was so terrified she lay petrified, unable to speak. It was fairy stories such as 'Hansel and Gretel', and 'Jack the Giant Killer', that spoke to her fears and offered some hope of resolution.

Her 'masculine' armour had been used rather in the way Winnicott describes a false self (1987: 145). Slowly she let this go and found her way of communicating these terrifying, destroyed internal parental figures through painting, drawing and sculpture. Annette found that the means of expression came through her hands. She began to connect with her archetypal rage and also with her creativity. Previously her rage had been vented as the rage against 'all men' and against an impersonal society which was unfair and did not favour women. Once the rage became related to and she found creative outlets, less was projected outside and she became less of an ardent, angry feminist or seducer of men. This did not stop her from putting energy into writing equal opportunity policies and petitioning for nursery care at her place of work, but it was achieved more diplomatically.

The internal male and female figures changed. They became less hollow and more lifelike and male figures in her dreams emerged who were benevolent and helpful. In conjunction with this, female figures filled out, also becoming more lifelike and ordinary. One day, through role play, outside the analysis, Annette contacted a wise woman within herself. The wise woman 'knew' things. At first she was dumb. This we took to mean that her knowledge was not intellectual, but intuitive. Through this externalised anima image, Annette began to connect to her feminine, instinctual nature in a more embodied way. Relationships in the outside world became more fulfilling as the relationship with her 'internal parents' changed through the experience of the analysis modifying the archetypal images of the anima and animus and humanising them.

Ben

My second example is included to show how similar concerns and forces may operate in men. Ben had been brought up in a predominantly female household. He had four older sisters and while he was an infant and small boy, his father was frequently absent for long periods of time. He had great difficulty with his gender identification, although he did not feel deep down, that he was homosexual. An emotional man, he identified strongly with women. Yet, when he felt misunderstood, he could swing suddenly to hating 'all women' with an intense, murderous rage of which he was very scared; especially as, at first, external and internal reality could merge. To be assertive was confused with being aggressive and abusive. To be male, to have a penis, was equated with abuse. In a dream he had early on in analysis, he had strung up women, then cut them down and and buried them. When, in the dream, he then dug them up, to his surprise they were not dead – but alive and stronger than before. Often women in his dreams were split into good and bad: a bad seductress, in black, tries to entice him to follow her, but a good woman, in white, stops him. Over the years in analysis these figures changed. In one dream a baby emerged from his thigh, and then in his drawings a hermaphroditic figure emerged. Eventually more lifelike male and female figures grew from a tree. This we took to be signs of his individuation – that the male and female aspects were becoming integrated into his personality and were in a better relationship internally. It is interesting to note here that in the *Rosarium Philosophorum* (Jung, 1946) Jung describes how holding the tension of the opposites while they unite and change leads to depression – the *nigredo*. At this point the hermaphrodite emerges and there can be a new beginning. The huge archetypal forces were slowly modified through the analysis, and as the archetypes became more humanised Ben had to hold on with all his strength to the intense forces inside him, which he frequently wanted to act out. He began to see that only by doing this, by holding on to his rage rather than beating someone up or smashing up his house, could the forces start to change and modify. He began to feel loving feelings as well as hate, and was able to allow them to exist together. Here the opposites were held. As change occurred internally so he, too, became able to form relationships which were based on mutuality rather than power relations where he was either victim or agressor. His relationship with his anima had changed and in the process he could begin to value himself as a male and not equate his penis with abuse. As his emotions, this huge energy, were related to and made sense of, so he started to be able to link and then to regain his mind and think. He had been possessed by his anima and needed to develop his animus – logical, thinking qualities. Then his masculine and feminine sides could exist internally in a more creative relationship.

The anima cannot be buried. As Jung found out, she has to be related to and is the essence of relatedness. For some, however, huge archetypal forces and the anthropoid psyche have to be faced in the process, requiring intense courage, as with this patient. In Annette's case the story of her psychic journey was written as a piece of active imagination when she felt compelled to write a fairy story. In it she had to confront a ring of wolves which enabled her to find her voice. For women the wolf may represent the animus. In her case it might also be seen as a representation of the defences of the self. Annette had to confront all her worst fears before she could get into relationship. She had to confront her animus, her over-masculine nature, which was threatening to engulf her and rip her to pieces. It is often seen in cases of bulimia and anorexia how a masculine persona destroys the feminine nature and destroys the soul. This is a theme Woodman writes graphically about in *The Owl was a Baker's Daughter* (1980) and *The Ravaged Bridegroom* (1990). She shows how the destructive energy of the masculine principle is fixed and rigid and can destroy. It has to be either overcome or let go of and this requires great courage; just as it requires great courage for the man to face his anima. However, when there can be a good internal masculine and feminine and a dialogue between them, then there can be a good creative intercourse both internally and externally.

Infant observation and early development

Clearly there is a need to understand the ways in which anima and animus are shaped by early experience. The way we are, is shaped by a mixture of what we bring into the world innately and by how this is met by the environment. Initially, this means by our parents, who are the first people to whom we relate. Michael Fordham took Jungian ideas and applied them to early psychological development. Briefly, he suggests that consciousness forms like islands from the unconscious. The child is born with an innate archetypal disposition to meet the world and the child *deintegrates* or opens out towards the world. At first this may be feeling a sense of hunger, which if met by a good enough feed is then taken inside (*integrated*) through sleep. This process of deintegration–reintegration may begin even before birth and the experiences will begin to shape the individual's relation to the world. If the experiences the child has are good enough then, the child will build up a good and sustaining internal sense of self, which will help over periods of frustration. If the experience is not good enough or the child has had to wait too long between feeds, there may be disintegration – a feeling of falling to pieces. If this is repeated too often the child may develop a sense of being persecuted internally and develop defences of the self. Mara Sidoli describes this process well in *Jungian Child Psychotherapy* (Sidoli and Davies, 1988). Through this repeated experience of deintegration–reintegration and, where the parenting has been good enough, archetypal forces slowly become modified and lose some of their power. Where it has not been good enough, or because of overt trauma (for example, due to prolonged separation from mother), archetypal forces can assume terrifying power and may cause difficulties in relationship.

An example of this can be seen in the case of a 15-year-old school-phobic boy, Tim. His parents, because of their own substantial difficulties in their relationship, were unable to provide an emotional holding for him. Tim lacked a sense of containment and had problems in his own gender identity as a boy. If any teacher spoke in a tone of voice which Tim perceived as critical, then he or she could suddenly assume huge and terrifying dimensions. The intense archetypal rage within Tim could be projected out, in an instant, on to the teacher who then became a huge raging monster coming to attack him and Tim would have to retreat and run from school. His internalised mother was hard and cold and uncaring and his internalised father was over-emotional and uncontaining for him. This caused a terrible internal conflict for Tim and left him confused and either at the mercy of overwhelming emotions or cut off from his emotions and obsessionally trying to contain himself with rituals. Where there has been damage to the psyche at this level then the analyst may have to work with projective identification as the means of communication, as a way of contacting that part of the self relegated to the shadow. In Annette's case it was her anima.

Infant observation studies have provided much information about the psychological growth of the infant. They would seem to indicate that gender is innate, although there is always contention about what is inherent and what is due to socialisation. Certainly gender socialisation starts early, some would say from the womb. Attitudes towards the different sexes can be seen in some of the old wives' tales. For example, if a woman's looks improve during pregnancy she is expecting a boy; if they worsen, a girl. If a woman is placid during pregnancy she will have a boy, but if she is bad-tempered or cries a lot, she will have a girl. Usually the assumption is that if the woman suffers in any way she will have a female child. Studies comparing how mothers may treat their girl and boy babies showed that mothers tended to be more active with boy babies and breast feed them longer than girl babies, and taught their girl babies to feed in more delicate ways (Belotti, 1975). The point is that being male or female may be innate, but learning to be a girl or boy is through subtle interactions in infancy which are later reinforced with toys and wider social attitudes. The stereo-types of what it is to be male and female in western society have changed slowly over the last thirty years. It would have been difficult to conceive, thirty years ago, that Britain would elect so many women Members of Parliament as they elected in May 1997. One young female Member of Parliament was heard to say 'women are the doers'! Does this mean that they have a good balance of their masculine and feminine sides or are they animus driven? We wait to see.

Transference

Bringing the two opposites together, in this case the masculine and femi-nine elements, occurs in analysis through the process of the transference. This is the alchemical process I talked of earlier, where both analysand and analyst experience change. The process of alchemy can be seen as a meta-phor for the working of the unconscious. It is a process which must be allowed to work through. The alchemical symbol for the union of unlike opposites is the *coniunctio*. Out of this union a new element is conceived – there is rebirth. This was experienced in Ben's case when he painted the hermaphroditic pictures, and the child was born from his thigh in the dream. This process involves the experience of death and loss as well as of rebirth. The *coniunctio* provides a dynamic model of the transference and one which operates at both the unconscious and conscious level (Jung,

1946: para. 422). This is also clearly explained in M. Fordham's book *Jungian Psychotherapy* (1986).

Mythology

I will return now to the wounded feeling function. It has been well described by Robert A. Johnson in *The Fisher King and the Handless Maiden* (1993). He suggests that many of the issues – both at a societal and a personal level – with which we contend today in western society, have been expressed in myths. He says 'men and women suffer quite differently from the wounding of their feeling functions and much of the tension and lack of communication between man and woman springs from this difference' (1993: 9). 'The Fisher King' is a story about a young prince who is out fulfilling his knightly duties when he comes upon a campfire in the woods. No one is around and he sees a salmon roasting on a spit above the fire. He is hungry so he reaches for some salmon but it is hot and burns his fingers. He drops it and sucks his burnt fingers but a little salmon gets into his mouth and wounds him so badly that he is in agony for most of the rest of his life. (Some versions say he was wounded in the thigh.) He is only free from pain when fishing in the castle moat, that is, when in contact with his unconscious, and the wound is only relieved when he meets Parcival the fool. This wound stands for man's generative capacities, which may express themselves in his sexual activity, or in difficulties in relationships or in his creativity. It seems therefore very significant that the emergence of the baby from his thigh, in Ben's dream, signified a beginning of a new relationship with his wounded self which had been so repressed. He too could only ease the pain and be more at ease with himself when he went fishing.

For women the wound is somewhat different. Her ability to *do* is damaged. In the myth of 'The Handless Maiden', the father, a miller, makes a pact with the devil, believing that his mill will prosper with less work. The miller believes the devil will help him in return for an old tree. Little does he realise that the price for the increased output in his mill is for his daughter to be given to the devil. The devil cuts off the miller's daughter's hands and *she does not object.* We see how she becomes incapacitated and cannot do anything. Although we can examine this myth at many levels and pick out many aspects (see Coline Covington's paper 'In search of the heroine', 1989), I wish to suggest that by passively acquiescing to having her hands cut off the daughter effectively colludes with the wound in society at the collective level. The difficulty is that when something is so unconscious at the collective level both men and women are affected by it, and so the daughter may have no awareness that her reality could be different and therefore no words or voice with which to express her feelings. Both she and her father are out of touch with them. Loss of feeling can lead to a sense of meaninglessness, depression and dark moods. It is interesting to note here how Annette would somatise her rage and then her hands would swell and erupt in raw eczema.

These myths speak to both men and women. The Handless Maiden can be considered to speak directly to women and to the feminine side of a man, whereas the Fisher King may speak directly to men and the male side of women. Myth is useful when trying to illustrate the importance of the feeling function as it provides an imaginal space in which to relate to the deep underlying, unconscious issues which are often hard to express in words.

The women's movement

Earlier I indicated that I wished to consider the interplay of inner and outer influences. The feminist experience is apposite to the theme since it encapsulates many of the polarities and dynamics being discussed and outlines the struggle to become conscious of societal attitudes which are taken for granted. The wave of feminism, which had achieved emancipation of women in the 1920s and political equality with men after the Great War, died to a ripple as, after working in the munitions factories, women returned to the home to follow their traditional roles as housewives. The swell of feminism increased again in the 1970s with a generation of women who had been brought up and educated to assume they would follow careers and expected that they would compete equally with men, only to find that they were discriminated against. Many felt dissatisfied in their relationships and experienced conflict as mothers, as they felt the role of motherhood was not valued by their partners or by society. Support groups and consciousness-raising groups arose in which women shared their frustrations and their experiences. It was necessary, for a while, for them to isolate themselves in order to disentangle which issues were individual and which cultural (the Handless Maiden might have benefited from such a group). Initially they often emulated men – the dungarees were the uniform – or they became superwomen, doing a 'man's job' in addition to caring for the home and children. This emulation of men was an attempt by women to develop their animus. Sometimes the shadow side was projected out so that men collectively (not any one man) became the target for their dissatisfaction and anger. Women's groups brought out individual pain and made them aware of the inherent partriarchal structures of society. Many women started to look deep into themselves to find answers to questions about what belonged to them as women and might call for political change, in contrast to what was taken for granted as inherent in society. Although it was generally women who felt the most conflict and were the ones to challenge the assumptions underlying relationships, men were inevitably affected as well. Women became involved in implementing changes in the wider society, for example by petitioning for better childcare facilities and creating equal opportunities policies. The Women's Therapy Centre (WTC) opened in London in 1976 (see Ernst and Maguire, 1987, for a short history). Luise Eichenbaum, who, with Susie Orbach, founded this centre, spoke recently of its development and their changing theoretical perspectives. She suggested that they incorporated various analytical theories as seemed appropriate to them at the time, so that they could conceptualise and respond to whatever they found themselves dealing with. At first they concentrated on the mother/baby relationship. More recently they have focused on what makes the therapeutic relationship work. Here, it seems to me, they are close to Jungian ideas of the psychology of the transference (as I described above) and the alchemical process in which both analyst and analysand change. This is one aspect of Jungian ideas which could be more acknowledged by feminist writers, as could the Jungian ideas of the anima and animus.

The changing division of labour

In the 1970s, Jungian analysis was viewed sceptically by feminists as women's issues were not at the forefront of the work. Indeed Jung was criticised for being sexist and we have only to refer earlier to the quotes on the anima to realise how derogatory he was about the effects of the anima in men and of the animus in women. Many feminists criticised writers such as Bowlby, Winnicott and Klein because they focused on the importance of the mother/baby pair. Some women argued they did not want to be tied to this relationship or feel that they were the only, or main figure of importance, in a child's life. Yet others, who had regressed in their inner work, found these developmental theories helpful, particularly in enabling them to value the feminine, themselves and childcare and to understand how the feeling aspects of relationships have a place in family life and education.

As jobs changed in nature and more women had work outside the home, so the socialisation of children, it was thought, had to reflect this. Sociological views, that the social environment is the main vehicle for establishing behaviour, prevailed.

Ideas in the field of education suggested that if we socialised our children differently then we could make the relationships more equal between the sexes. Young children were encouraged to play with non-sexist toys and read literature which was less stereotypical of the division of labour. However, this did not make them more equal – if anything it served to make the sex differences greater; girls did not necessarily want to be dressed in dungarees and play with trains any more than boys wanted to wear pink dresses and cuddle dolls. Although there seemed to be an assumption that we needed sameness, not difference, the underlying trend was to honour the need for both sexes to have respect for each other and to respect their differences. Parity between the sexes needs more than external change; it requires inner changes within the psyche.

Conclusion

In this paper I have described how gender is culturally defined, although sex is innate. Jung's concepts of anima and animus allow us to understand how these gender roles may develop through the individual's early experiences, which are set within a particular culture. Anima and animus are opposites, yet are complementary to one another. If one changes so does the other. They are the divine syzygy. They have many aspects which have to articulate with each other and which must be lived within our inner and outer worlds. The clinical examples illustrate this and show how issues which appeared as external manifestations – the hating of 'all men' or of 'all women' or of patriarchal society as the impersonal, uncaring parent – may lead back to early damage within the psyche.

With his concepts of anima and animus, and his understanding of the transference given in the *Rosarium*, Jung has contributed a dynamic model which accounts for a variety of conscious and unconscious exchanges at many levels and which provides, through the transference, the possibility of reaching the repressed shadow elements of the psyche and allowing them to transform. At the present time this means women connecting to the unconscious aspect of their masculine and men re-contacting their feminine, so that both have a more complete view of themselves. Current cultural 'healing' of the patriarchal society may be taken forward by the masculine–feminine healing within the individual's psyche and the healing of the feeling function within the society. This might mean that different values become dominant. Healing might include more co-operation in problem solving, not having an all-out pursuit of profit, more concern for the environmental impact of modern living and care of the earth. We can in fact see a ground swell of opinion beginning to form over these issues.

References

Belotti, E.G. (1975) *Little Girls.* London: Writers and Readers Publishing Cooperative.

Covington, C. (1989) 'In search of the heroine'. *Journal of Analytical Psychology,* 34 (3): 243-54.

Ernst, S. and Maguire, M. (eds) (1987) *Living with the Sphinx: Papers from the Women's Therapy Centre.* London: The Women's Press.

Fordham, M. (1986) *Jungian Psychotherapy: A Study in Analytical Psychology.* London: H. Karnac (Books) Ltd.

Hillman, J. (1985) *Anima: An Anatomy of a Personified Notion.* Dallas: Spring Publications.

Humbert, E. (1988) *C.G. Jung.* Wilmette, IL: Chiron Publications.

Johnson, R.A. (1993) *The Fisher King and the Handless Maiden: Understanding the Wounded Feeling Function in Masculine and Feminine Psychology.* New York: HarperCollins Publishers.

—— (1974) *He: Understanding Masculine Psychology.* Toronto: Religious Publishing Company.

Jung, C.G. (1938) 'Commentary on "The Secret of the Golden Flower"'. *CW* 13, para. 58.

—— (1946) 'The Psychology of the Transference'. *CW* 16, paras 353-537.

—— (1953) 'Two Essays in Analytical Psychology', *Collected Works* 7.

—— (1983) *Memories, Dreams, Reflections.* London: Fontana Paperbacks.

Oakley, A. (1972) *Sex, Gender and Society.* London: Maurice Temple Smith.

Sidoli, M. and Davies, M. (eds) (1988) *Jungian Child Psychotherapy: Individuation in Childhood.* London: H. Karnac (Books) Ltd.

Stoller, R.J. (1968) *Sex and Gender.* London: Hogarth Press.

Winnicott, D.W. (1987) *The Maturational Processes and the Facilitating Environment.* London: Hogarth Press.

Woodman, M. (1980) *The Owl was a Baker's Daughter.* Toronto: Inner City Books.

—— (1982) *Addiction to Perfection: The Still Unravished Bride.* Toronto: Inner City Books.

—— (1990) *The Ravaged Bridegroom: Masculinity in Women.* Toronto: Inner City Books.

Contrasexuality and the Unknown Soul

Warren Colman

Introduction

Jung had much less to say about the sexual object than Freud but much more to say about the gendered subject. Where Freud spoke about bisexuality in relation to sexual orientation and the choice of either a same-sex or opposite-sex object, Jung spoke about contrasexuality in relation to gender identity and the internal relationship to the gender characteristics of the opposite sex. He believed the contrasexual archetypes of anima and animus gave each sex access to the gender characteristics of the other and that the integration of these characteristics constituted an important aspect of the individuation process.

It is not surprising, then, that the most common understanding of anima and animus sees them as representing the feminine aspect of a man and the masculine aspect of a woman. While this does not exactly misrepresent Jung's thinking, I shall argue that it is a gross simplification that fails to capture the significance of anima and animus for the individuation process. Nevertheless, it is important to start with masculinity and femininity, not least since the ambiguities and confusions in Jung's thinking can lead some readers to reject the concepts of anima and animus altogether.

Masculinity and femininity: relative or absolute?

The modern post-feminist reader is likely to regard the ascription of masculine or feminine gender categories to specific personality traits as a highly controversial undertaking, if not inherently flawed. Jung certainly did use descriptions that now seem very old-fashioned and which have a decidedly culture-bound ring to them. Although he was ahead of his time in recognising that men could be 'feminine' in the sense of being concerned with relationships, softness, and the emotional life and that women could be 'masculine' in the sense of having an intellectual, spiritual and creative life, many people today would seriously question whether these capacities are necessarily gender-related or, even if they are, would suggest that they have only become so through cultural usage. Gender, they would argue, is a relative, not an absolute phenomenon. Jung has therefore been heavily criticised for his essentialism: the belief that there are certain innate archetypal qualities that constitute a masculine or feminine essence (Samuels, 1989; Young-Eisendrath, 1992).

The present-day challenge to Jung's view of masculinity and femininity suggests that he took the cultural norms and stereotypes of his time and elevated them into ahistorical, eternal verities. He asserted an archetypal basis for them that put them beyond question and beyond change, removing the possibility of any questioning and/or debate about what factors make or influence them. Masculinity and femininity confront us as abstract archetypal principles, fixed and defined for all time, to which we all have to conform.

Perhaps the most extreme version of this kind of absolutism in Jung is his assertion that the nature of actual men and women can be deduced from the archetypal pattern existing in the opposite sex, rather like Eve being created from Adam:

> Every man carries within him the eternal image of woman, not the image of this or that particular woman, but a definite feminine image. . . . Even if no women existed, it would still be possible, at any given time, to deduce from this unconscious image exactly how a woman would have to be constituted psychically. The same is true of the woman: she too has her inborn image of man. . . .
>
> (Jung, 1925: para. 338)

Here Jung makes virtually no distinction between real women and the archetypal *image* of woman carried by men. Yet in the same paragraph he acknowledges that, in practice, each sex tends to have a highly distorted view of the other:

> most of what men say about feminine eroticism, and particularly about the emotional life of women, is derived from their own anima projections and distorted accordingly. On the other hand, the astonishing assumptions and fantasies that women make about men come from the activity of the animus, who produces an inexhaustible supply of illogical arguments and false explanations.
>
> (ibid.)

This link to projection leads to a much more complex, flexible and sophisticated area of Jung's thought. Here he is not making categorical statements about what men and women *are* like but is providing a conceptual framework for an understanding of what each sex *thinks* the other is like – and why. If anima and animus were merely fancy names for the masculine and feminine principles, we might safely lay them to rest as outdated and outmoded. But there is actually a great deal more to them than that.

Soul-image and soul-guide

Empirically speaking, anima and animus are not 'principles' or even 'concepts' but refer to a kaleidoscopic variety of *images*. It is only through the manifest images that the archetypal forms behind them can be deduced. Some postmodern critics have therefore argued that the concept of the archetype-in-itself is redundant – an unnecessary and unjustified hypothesis (Carrette, 1994). In any event, we are certainly incapable of making any final statement about it. We may recognise the penumbra of fascination and numinosity that surrounds certain images and marks them out as archetypal but the archetype itself is, by definition, beyond conscious awareness. This constitutes a powerful argument against any absolute judgements of 'the masculine' and 'the feminine' for, even if there is an inborn image of the other sex, it must be inherently unknowable and any specific manifestation of it can only be an approximation shaped by specific psychological and social contexts. Some manifestations may seem to approach closer than others to the 'pure form', such as those appearing in the work of great artists or in myths which have survived through many different contexts, but they will all be more or less distorted by the partial vision of consciousness. One might make similar comments about any archetype or, indeed, about God himself who again, by definition, passes human understanding.

Like other archetypes, anima and animus are personified in myths and legends, in art and literature, in dreams and via projection onto other people. They may appear as positive or negative figures: witches, fairies, beautiful maidens, hags, sexual goddesses for the anima; magicians, heroes, Beasts, and tall dark handsome strangers for the animus. Since they are especially connected to sexual relationships, at least as far as heterosexuals are concerned, one of their most typical manifestations is in the figure of the beloved. They can also appear in just as intense a form in the transference especially, but not necessarily, if the transference is an erotic one. But, in order to recognise and understand these archetypes, we need to see not only their contrasexuality but also their function, meaning and purpose in our psychic life. Here we must distinguish, as John Beebe (1993) has pointed out, between an anima or animus figure and the anima or animus function.

The contingent vs. the absolutist view

When we consider the way the archetype functions in the psyche we find Jung giving a totally different account of anima and animus – one in which masculinity and femininity are almost coincidental. I will refer to this as the *contingent* view as opposed to the *absolutist* view. This is similar, though not identical, to the rather more well-known contrast between *essentialism* (which asserts that the contents of the psyche are composed of predetermined essences) and *constructivism* (which asserts that the contents of the psyche are constructed in the course of each individual life).

This alternative view of anima and animus goes back to Jung's early definition of his concepts in 'Psychological types' (1921). There Jung described the anima as equivalent to what he called the soul-image or the inner attitude, which he contrasted with the persona or outer attitude. Anima, of course, *means* soul. Thus the anima when she appears in personified form is an image of a man's soul. The same is more or less true of the animus as an image of a woman's soul, although Jung's absolutism got him in a tangle here: he suggested that since the soul is feminine, women must have something else – an animus, characterised by spirit rather than soul. However, I doubt if women will take very kindly to the suggestion that they have no soul: even if it is only a word it is one with extensive connotations and it makes no sense to deprive women of it. A happier resolution might be to admit that the anima (as 'soul') belongs to both sexes but in men it usually takes a female form and in women a male form. This might also allow for the possibility of the anima turning up in same-sex guise, especially perhaps for homosexuals. Whether or not the soul is characterised by spirit would then depend, not on gender, but on the nature of the conscious attitude and the way the soul is complementary to it.

Jung suggested that the soul-image was an image of the unconscious depths of the personality, all that which is felt to be 'other' and unknown to the conscious mind. This makes the unknown man or unknown woman one of the most frequent manifestations of anima/animus projections: in love relationships they are always the elusive man or woman who may be just around the corner and would be the answer to all one's dreams.

This notion of the unconscious as Other is vividly represented in Celtic mythology where the world of gods, spirits and supernatural happenings is called the Otherworld. This is similar in a way to the Greek 'underworld', which we might think of as 'below consciousness' although the Greeks of course also had an 'upper world', Mount Olympus, where most of their Gods resided. This dualism has been carried over into the Christian tradition with its division of the spirit world into Heaven and Hell. No such division existed for the Celts for whom all spirits and magic emanated from the Otherworld.

Quite unlike the absolutist view of anima and animus in which they represent predetermined gender characteristics, the description of anima and animus as soul-images emphasises the *contingent* nature of their character: it depends on that which is felt to be other to the conscious mind. It is also important to bear in mind that when Jung first defined anima and animus in 1921, he had not yet introduced the concept of the shadow, so that in some respects shadow and anima/animus are conflated in these definitions and only become separated later. The unknown soul contains everything that is repudiated by the conscious mind and relegated to the 'otherworld' (that is, shadow contents), as well as those aspects that have not yet been developed – for example, the contrasexual qualities and also the inferior type function. This is why the soul-image or anima of a rational ascetic man, for example, is likely to appear as an emotional, seductive and voluptuous woman – consider, for example, the relationship between Arthur Miller and Marilyn Monroe or, in darker form, the old professor who is led to his destruction by Marlene Dietrich's showgirl in *The Blue Angel* (Paramount Pictures, 1930).

As Jung says, 'the character of the soul can be deduced from that of the persona. Everything that should normally be in the outer attitude, but is conspicuously absent, will invariably be found in the inner attitude' (1921: para. 806). Jung then gives a contingent reason why the soul-image appears in contrasexual form: it is because the other gender epitomises the quality of 'otherness' which defines the inner attitude from the point of view of consciousness. The contingency of the relationship between otherness and contrasexuality is apparent in a number of qualifications such as 'the anima is *usually* personified . . . as a woman' (1921: para. 808); 'very masculine men have . . . a very soft emotional life, *often incorrectly* described as "feminine"' (1928: para. 297); and, most clearly, in this reference from 1934: 'What is not-I, not masculine, is *most probably* feminine, and because the not-I is felt as not belonging to me and therefore as outside me, the anima-image is *usually* projected upon women' (1934/54, para. 58, italics added). This suggests that the unconscious only represents itself as contrasexual because, and in so far as, the conscious outer attitude, the persona, is identified with the same-sex gender. In other words, contrasexuality is a function of the particular form taken by the persona.

The role of anima and animus as soul-images also explains their particularly intense fascination: they are suffused with enigmatic hints of hidden depths which are, in fact, intimations of the unknown continent of our own interior being. The longing and desire we feel for those who personify them, whether actual love objects, or imaginary figures of dream or artistic representation, is a reflection of the longing we feel to be united with our 'other half', it is the thirst for wholeness and for the union of opposites – the mystery of the *coniunctio*, the sacred marriage or *hieros gamos*.

Someone who is captured by a projection of their anima or animus knows that they are in the grip of no ordinary love affair. Suddenly the universe is flooded with meaning – trivial events take on cosmic significance, synchronistic happenings abound. No account which does not acknowledge the power and ferocity of these encounters can ever do justice to what anima and animus truly mean. Sexual they may be, but they always go beyond the sexual towards the spiritual and the divine.

Anima and animus are more than *images* of the soul: they also frequently appear in the role of soul-*guides*, or psychopomps, messengers and mediums of all kinds leading us inwards or outwards, upwards or downwards. Any figure who seems to partake both of this world and the Otherworld, the spirit world, is likely to represent anima or animus. Such figures frequently appear in dreams of which the following are typical examples (with obvious transference implications!). A woman dreams of being trapped in a tomb. The door opens and a man stands in the doorway beckoning her to follow. The patient who dreamt this associated the man with the figure of Hermes as she had seen him depicted on a tarot card, but he might equally have been Orpheus coming to reclaim Eurydice from the unconscious underworld. Just as Orpheus might represent the animus coming to release a woman from her mother-bound state of unconsciousness in the tomb/womb, so Eurydice might represent the anima whom the man seeks in his own unconscious depths where she is entrapped by the Hades-shadow.

A man dreamt of a fiery red-headed girl who opened a door in his analyst's small and rather cramped and crowded house into a great mansion with many rooms. Eventually, he found his way out into a garden where he ending up having sex with Princess Diana. Here the anima appears first as a guide leading from the cramped world of ego-consciousness into the great vastness of the unconscious and second as the anima-princess with whom he is eventually united in the *coniunctio*.

Integration and loss: *Blood on the Tracks*

Perhaps the most famous example of the anima as soul-guide is Beatrice who became Dante's guide to paradise. Bob Dylan makes an oblique reference to Dante to indicate his own encounter with the anima in the song 'Tangled up in blue', the opening track to *Blood on the Tracks* (1974). The song tells the story of a relationship, first made, then broken, then found again by chance. It is when the couple meet again that the anima-woman reveals her true nature as soul-guide – ironically, in the very act of revealing to the narrator the parallel between Dante and himself:

> She lit a burner on the stove and offered me a pipe
> I thought you'd never say hello, she said: you look like the silent type
> . . . Then she opened up a book of poems and handed it to me
> Written by an Italian poet from the thirteenth century
> And every one of them words rang true and glowed like burning coal
> Pouring off of every page like it was written in my soul
> From me to you –
> Tangled up in blue. . .

The implied reference to Beatrice suggests that this is a meeting with the divine image of the soul: a woman who offers not the mere satisfaction of physical love but a gateway to paradise. Dylan's imagery indicates both the timelessness and the intense heat of such an encounter. Subsequent songs on *Blood on the Tracks* are full of images of sparks, shooting stars, explosions, and, 'like a corkscrew to my heart', the sheer violent agony of love.

Dylan wrote and recorded *Blood on the Tracks* following the break up of his own marriage. The songs are primarily about pain and loss, sometimes, as in 'Idiot wind', with a harrowing sense of grief and fury. For him, as for Othello who loved 'not wisely, but too well', the loss of the anima was due to his failure to recognise her and he is left full of poignant and bitter regrets. Yet Dylan seems to find a way through the suffering to some sense of reconciliation and redemption. For the songs also contain the possibility of transformation: when she is integrated into the self, the anima acts as a bridge to the unconscious, bringing meaning and vitality into the everyday world of ordinary life. Sometimes it is only through the loss of an actual relationship that this becomes possible: in the absence of the physical reality of the beloved, the archetypal projections that animate the relationship become intensified and are revealed in all their 'raging glory'. *Blood on the Tracks* represents a personal experience that has been heated in the furnace of creative suffering until it has taken on archetypal form: no longer merely a record of a failed marriage, it has become an archetypal story about losing and finding the anima-soul.

In 'You're gonna make me lonesome when you go', the pain of loss is offset by the carefree, almost madcap style of the song. Dylan sings of finding his lost love 'in the sky above, in the tall grass, in the ones I love'. Ultimately, loss is transformed into spirituality, the loved one becomes like some immanent godhead who is felt in all things. The externally loved object, she who carried the projection of anima, is transformed into a feeling, into a relationship to the world that gives it meaning and joy.

Only when we can experience the world as being in harmony with the internal background of our own unconscious can we find our place in it. This is what I understand Jung to mean by the anima or animus being a bridge to the unconscious: a bridge implies a two-way traffic, a *coniunctio* even, so that the outer attitude (persona) and inner attitude (soul) work together, complementing each other. In this way, our ordinary, everyday lives are enriched by inner meaning, while our inner lives are enriched by outward relationships. There is a connection here with Jung's definition of individuation as both 'an internal and subjective process of integration and an equally indispensable process of objective relationship' (1946: para. 448). In projection, anima and animus embody the image of, and longing for, integration: when they are reclaimed as part of the self, they act as the function which links inner and outer together. Ultimately, they are the image of relationship itself.

The integration of anima and animus always involves a capacity to come to terms with loss and disappointment since we have to be able to tolerate the knowledge that they are intrinsically elusive and cannot be possessed. When they are projected in actual love relationships – whether in ordinary life or in the transference – we have to come to terms with the distinction between the fascinating, idealised projection and the ordinary reality of the lover or therapist.

Aspects of the shadow

Another factor which may seriously impede the integration of anima and animus is their contamination with shadow elements due to the overlapping connection with 'otherness' referred to earlier. This is perhaps why Jung argued that it is necessary to come to terms with the shadow before dealing with anima and animus. It is not possible to listen to what anima and animus are trying to tell us until we are prepared to recognise that they are more than our enemy. But anima and animus also have a critical role in forcing us to pay attention to the shadow. The link between them is a potent brew since that which is repudiated is always cast in the guise of that which is also glamorous, exciting, alluring and seductive:

> For an idealistic woman, a depraved man is often the bearer of the soul-image; hence the saviour fantasy so frequent in such cases. The same thing happens with men, when the prostitute is surrounded with the halo of a soul crying for succour.
>
> (Jung, 1921: para. 811)

Thus anima and animus do not allow us to escape our shadow contents but always bring them back to our attention. Whereas pure shadow contents are feared, avoided and wholly repudiated, anima/shadow contents always draw us into relationship with them – often against our conscious will and even when they seem to represent that which we most hate and despise.

This linkage provides one of the key motivators underlying couples' choice of each other. Each is attracted to an other who represents their own unknown soul in its most desirable aspect. But if the shadow projections informing such choices cannot be re-owned, couples end up coming to hate and fear in the other all that originally attracted them to each other: shadow projections unmediated by introjection become reinforced and intensified until the relationship degenerates into a marriage between Bluebeard and Medusa, each one trapped in the horrendous clutches of the other. The inability to separate that holds these couples together is eventually the only remaining feature of the original anima /animus attraction. Shadow aspects have otherwise completely driven out the anima /animus function of promoting integration by offering a 'bridge to the unconscious'.

In this situation the potential for psychic liberation is blocked: anima and animus appear only as dangerous, threatening figures which have to be avoided or destroyed. For example, a male patient who had been sexually abused as a child dreamt that he was being pursued by Myra Hindley with a knife. This dream occurred at a point when his growing trust and closeness with his female therapist had been threatened by oedipal jealousy, aroused by her having to attend to a visitor who arrived as the patient was leaving a session. The figure of the dangerous sexual abuser and murderess reflected not only his anxieties about abuse but represented an extremely primitive anima figure filled up with his own feared sexual violence. Like many people who have been abused, this man had become extremely confused about his own sexuality since it was horribly tangled up with something terrible that had been done to him. Thus, all these feelings and impulses had been relegated to the shadow. Consciously, he was preoccupied with an insipid and sexless anima figure represented by churchyard angels and porcelain madonnas. The dream indicated the savage split in him and could be seen as an attempt to heal it. The murderous anima with the phallic knife represents a power he must deal with before he can integrate his sentimental childlike love with the full-bloodedness of adult sexuality. In the dream he wanted to kill Myra Hindley: it will be painful for him to realise that when he does, as symbolically he must, he will also have killed off his angelic idealised therapist. Perhaps then he may be able to manage a real relationship with a real woman.

Conclusion

Jung maintained that unconscious contents always appear first in projection. By this he did not only mean projection onto other people: he included all the various forms in which archetypal imagery appears. It is as though all of culture is a great Rorschach test through which we may gain access to our own internal depths. These projections have a purpose – they enable us to see ourselves as in a glass darkly and, if we have eyes to see, to make contact with our own unconscious through them.

The anima /animus has a special place amongst archetypes in that it is the gateway to all the others. It therefore leads towards the self and is in some way akin to it, as I have attempted to show by emphasising the connection with soul. In one of his late works, *Aion* (1951), Jung referred to the anima as the projection-making factor itself and identified her with Maya, the Indian goddess of illusion. In this context, the link with gender becomes only a small part of the anima's equipment due to her association with otherness. Yet it remains an important link because through gender, anima and animus are also linked to sexuality – and through sexuality to desire.

Desire may express itself through sexuality but, certainly for Jung, it is much more than that – it is the unquenchable desire for wholeness and for union with the divine within us and without us. Anima and animus represent the image of that which is most desirable to us. This image may be experienced through sexual relationships but it is never satisfied by them. Only when sexual relationships let us down, as sooner or later they inevitably must, are we forced back on the unquenchable nature of desire which requires us to go beyond the physical to 'the sky above'. In this way, desire creates its own fulfilment through the creative and sustaining role of Imagination which, like soul, contains infinite, inexhaustible possibilities. These imaginative constructions, stimulated by desire, both enrich the soul and constitute its discovery. And so desire is linked to soul and the circle is complete.

References

Beebe, J. (1993) 'Towards an image of male partnership'. In R.H. Hopcke, K. Lofthus-Carrington and S. Wirth (eds), *Same Sex Love and the Path to Wholeness*, Boston and London: Shambhala.

Carrette, J. (1994) 'The language of archetypes: A conspiracy in psychological theory'. *Harvest*, 40: 168–92.

Dylan, B. (1974) *Blood on the Tracks*, CBS Records.

Jung, C.G. (1921) 'Psychological types'. In *Collected Works* 6, London: Routledge and Kegan Paul.

—— (1925) 'Marriage as a psychological relationship'. In *Collected Works* 17, paras 324–45, London: Routledge and Kegan Paul.

—— (1928) 'The relations between the ego and the unconscious'. In *Collected Works* 7, paras 202–406, London: Routledge and Kegan Paul.

—— (1934/54) 'Archetypes of the collective unconscious'. In *Collected Works* 9.i, paras 1–86, London: Routledge and Kegan Paul.

—— (1946) 'The psychology of the transference'. In *Collected Works* 16, London: Routledge and Kegan Paul.

—— (1951) 'The syzygy: anima and animus'. Ch. 3 in *Aion*, *Collected Works* 9.ii, London: Routledge and Kegan Paul.

Paramount Pictures (1930) *The Blue Angel*. Directed by Joseph von Sternberg, starring Marlene Dietrich and Emil Jannings.

Samuels, A. (1989) *The Plural Psyche: Personality, Morality and the Father*. London and New York: Routledge.

Young-Eisendrath, P. (1992) 'Gender, animus and related topics'. In N. Schwartz-Salant and M. Stein (eds), *Gender and Soul in Psychotherapy*, Wilmette, IL: Chiron Publications.

Chapter 9

Myth and Fairy Tales

Catherine Crowther, Jane Haynes and Kathleen Newton consider the innate archetypal motifs symbolised in fairy tales and the range of ways in which we respond to them. They expand on the interaction between the motifs and cultural, sociological and clinical orientations. The authors explore how the individual resonates to fairy tales in the course of different life stages; their lasting appeal to generations of children and adults; their adaptability to changing society. They examine the interplay between the ancient oral folk tale tradition and the familiar fairy tales of the European literary genre handed down to us by Perrault (1697) and the Brothers Grimm (1812–56). The paper refers to the difference in the focus of psychological understanding between Freud and Jung, and von Franz and Bettelheim. The developments in the application of fairy tales to clinical work is illustrated by Dieckmann, Jacoby and Kast. The authors give two clinical vignettes to illustrate the role of the personal equation in the spectrum of analytical approaches they have developed.

The Psychological Use of Fairy Tales

Catherine Crowther, Jane Haynes and Kathleen Newton

In Jung's understanding both myths and fairy tales reflect innate archetypal motifs arising from the collective unconscious. While both symbolise archetypal dynamics, there is a great difference between the two. In his book *Myth and Reality*, Mircea Eliade states:

> Myth narrates a sacred history: it relates an event that took place in primordial Time, the fabled Time of 'beginnings'. In other words myth tells how through the deeds of Supernatural Beings, a reality came into existence. . . . Myth tells only of that which really happened. . . . The actors in myth are Supernatural Beings. . . . In short, myths describe the various and sometimes dramatic breakthrough of the sacred (or supernatural) into the World. Furthermore it is as a result of the intervention of the Supernatural Beings that man is himself what he is today, a mortal, sexed, and cultural being.
>
> (Eliade, 1964)

Myths underline the mysteries of birth and death, the place of the divine in human life, the violent power of erotic love, the tragic pulls of divided loyalties, the compulsion to make war. Often the endings of myths leave one to ponder the endurance of human suffering.

By contrast, the personae of fairy tales are two-dimensional and typical figures: the simpleton younger son, the wicked witch, the beautiful princess. Fairy tales exist in a timeless and spaceless world, for example, 'Once upon a time', or 'Far beyond the end of the world, and even beyond the Seven Dog Mountains, there was once a king'. Mircea Eliade calls it 'the timeless eternity, now and forever'. At the same time as being fantastical the atmosphere is also recognisably domestic and familial, even in royal palaces. Royalty, talking animals and supernatural figures mingle with ordinary merchants and country folk. The stories often begin at a period of calamity or transition ('The old king is dying', 'A baby princess is born', 'The family are hungry') and they pose a perennial and problematic situation, which is then elaborated symbolically. It is more in the denouement of the action than in the character development of the protagonists that the ripening of conscious awareness and learning from experience is suggested.

The reading of fairy tales continues to attract large audiences and their appeal seems to be contagious. They have the power to reveal and simultaneously conceal their readers' underlying motives and desires which cannot always find a rational outlet for their expression. They allow the reader's instincts and feelings to be released into consciousness through their eternal archetypal forms. These are often projected on to talking animals and birds, kings and queens, and frequently conjure into consciousness their opposites. For example the spirit of the good dead mother is opposed by the wicked stepmother, the power of the wicked magician by the wise old man.

We will be discussing the many different ways of responding to fairy tales later in the chapter. Post-Jungians have responded to, developed and raised challenges in relation to some assumptions in the classical Jungian approach innovated by Marie Louise von Franz. Clinical vignettes illustrating our own practice will be presented.

It is beyond the scope of this chapter to go into detail about myth and international folk tale traditions. Our intention is to concentrate on the significance for clinical practice of the genre with which we, and our patients, are most familiar: that is, European fairy tales, with particular reference to the work of the Brothers Grimm. Three different approaches will be developed:

1   The relevance of the different theoretical, cultural and sociological theories to our understanding of the tales.
2   The ways in which we resonate to fairy tales at different times in our lives.
3   The clinical application of fairy tales:

    a   How do we relate to the symbolism in our analysands' material?
    b   The bridging of fairy tale images and motifs with metapsychological models.

The relevance of the different theoretical, cultural and sociological theories to our understanding of the tales

In the light of modern research by historians, linguists, folklorists and anthropologists, it is necessary to question some of the previously held assumptions about the psychological meaning of fairy tales. This section will trace an outline of some of the commentators on fairy tale interpretation and show their influence on our current understanding of fairy tales.

Both Freud and Jung recognised a similarity between dream symbolism and the symbolic motifs of myths, legends and fairy tales. In 'The phenomenology of the spirit in fairy tales' (1948) Jung writes that fairy tales express 'the anatomy of the psyche'. He enlarges on the spirit as the dynamic which can function both creatively and destructively. He talks in terms of the archetype of the spirit which is symbolised in the tales by personifications, for example the old wise man, magicians, animals or birds. These symbolic figures often add depth and paradox to the stories, as a counterpoint to the main protagonists who remain two-dimensional.

Von Franz has been the most influential commentator on fairy stories from a classical Jungian perspective, in particular through her thesis that fairy stories reveal the collective unconscious in a direct way. 'Fairy tales are the purest and simplest expression of the collective unconscious psychic processes. . . they represent the archetypes in their barest and most concise form' (von Franz, 1970).

Following Jung, who believed that the dream is its own best explanation, von Franz sees fairy tales as unadulterated unconscious utterances from the 'objective psyche', that is, those phylogenetic layers which are impersonal and not coloured by an individual's own history and experience. She is inclined to idealise the wisdom of the folk fairy tale, believing the Brothers Grimm and other collectors were tapping into the 'purity' of the archaic oral heritage of our ancestors. She contrasts myths – which are 'national', and are closer to consciousness because they carry ancient collective memory about known and historical material – with fairy tales which, she says, depict in the most simple form, the most general, most basic human structure:

> Because the fairy tale is beyond cultural and racial differences it can migrate so easily. Fairy tale language seems to be the international language of all mankind – of all ages and of all races and cultures.
>
> (von Franz, 1970)

For von Franz the best way to understand the tales was to circumscribe their events with comparative studies in motifs and images. She had a wealth of knowledge in this area, and thus aimed to 'bring into the light the whole network of associations in which archetypes are enmeshed' (ibid.). In this way she translated the motifs into Jungian metapsychology saying: 'It is the archetypes which function as the regulators of the psyche and fairy tale motifs are the best clues to unconscious processes.' She relates this understanding to universal human situations and challenges such as the shadow, evil, femininity, individuation and many other themes. In relation to clinical work she says that we interpret:

> For the same reason as that for which fairy tales and myths were told because it has a vivifying effect and gives a satisfactory reaction and

brings one into peace with one's unconscious and instinctive substratum, just as the telling of fairy stories always did.

(von Franz, 1970)

She takes up general themes such as femininity, individuation, the shadow and evil. 'It is the archetypes which function as the regulators of the psyche and fairy tale motifs are the best clues to unconscious processes'. Therefore her therapeutic method tends to amplify the archetypal qualities of the fairy story itself.

Dieckmann (1978), Jacoby, Kast and Riedel (1992) and Kast (1986 and 1990) extend von Franz's approach by placing more emphasis on the use of fairy tales in their work with patients. They see the therapeutic benefit of contact with the collective unconscious, and especially the unique ability of fairy tales to speak to us on the level of images and feelings. They also provide some indications of how they may be answered, thus carrying the 'archetypally encapsulated hope' (Bloch, 1986) that difficulties can be overcome and maturity realised. Kast sometimes prescribes a fairy tale to a patient in the belief that the overall theme symbolises the patient's particular complex or developmental needs at that time. Her recognition of a shared archetypal language between dreams and fairy tales steers her towards a dream analysis technique: to interpret the entire cast of characters in the tale as subpersonalities of the protagonist.

Like von Franz, Kast thinks amplification is helpful clinically but her focus is more on active imagination and on facilitating patients to evolve their own images. She also stresses the necessity of emotional involvement if symbolic images are to become meaningful. Both Kast and Jacoby agree on the many possible levels of interpretation of fairy tales whereby they can be related to both on a collective and individual level. Both authors give examples in which fairy tale motifs and images symbolise patterns in their patients' pathology and describe the ways these can be worked with in the transference and 'be of significant help to the therapist in formulating interpretations' (Jacoby, Kast and Riedel 1992).

Alongside the classical Jungian exploration of the pathological meaning of fairy tales should be mentioned the work of an influential Freudian, Bruno Bettelheim, whose *The Uses of Enchantment* (1975) has been widely read. His distinctive contribution was to try to understand fairy stories from the perspective of the child's inner world, and in this respect he was a pioneer of current psychological approaches to the genre. Both von Franz and Bettelheim believed there is such a thing as a *'true'* fairy story, which Bettelheim distinguishes from a cautionary tale or fable which merely scares a child into good behaviour. The true fairy story, he says, gains its effect in the child's imagination by virtue of its happy ending which relieves the child's anxiety and speaks of escape from danger, of recovery and consolation. What is significant here is that Bettelheim, on the one hand, regards fairy stories primarily as a didactic tool consciously used by adults to promote the moral education of children, while, on the other, he reveres the stories themselves as in some way 'naturally' expressing children's universal anxieties and preoccupations, using oblique and symbolic images. He refers to the power of fairy tales to provide the 'image language' of childhood.

The paradox in his approach reflects a common debate about the balance between cultural and archetypal influences on the creation of fairy tales. Embedded in his own era's devotion to Freud's exposition of the Oedipus complex Bettelheim saw predominantly oedipal material in the tales he studied, and clearly his interpretations were influenced by both cultural and personal factors. We should say here that von Franz recognised that the many different responses to fairy tales, including her own, were influenced by both personal and cultural factors and in that sense the tales could be regarded as a Rorschach test.

Jack Zipes' (1989) research gives us a historical and cultural perspective on the fairy tale tradition, in particular pointing to the transformation of the oral folk tales into a more consciously contrived literary genre, throughout the eighteenth and nineteenth centuries. The substantial rewriting of the tales reveals the changing cultural mores of the times and means we must be more sceptical about traditional attempts to attribute primordial psychological truths too directly to fairy story material known to us only through the anthologies of Perrault and the Brothers Grimm.

Although the principal anthologisers and architects of the classical fairy tale genre have been male, this has by no means always been the case. In mediaeval Europe fairy tales were often constructed by women who were gathered together day after day to spin cloth and who, in order to make the activity less monotonous, amused themselves by spinning a yarn. Zipes describes how:

> In a good part of Europe where spinning was prevalent, peasant women would work in the spinning rooms from morning until evening, and the men and young boys would join them in the evenings, where there might be some singing, games, dancing, eating and storytelling. It was the place where women could demonstrate their skills to win a husband. . . . There is a great deal of evidence that from the late middle ages up to the beginning of the nineteenth century the spinning rooms were types of cultural or social centres and that the tales were exchanged by women as well as men to pass the time of day.
>
> (Zipes, 1994)

The literary revisions of the peasant tales made by both Perrault (1697) and the Brothers Grimm (1812–56) show a distinctively male influence which reflects significant changes in cultural attitudes to the social order. Perrault was writing for the court in Versailles at the very end of the seventeenth century, to entertain aristocratic adults and their children, who were the only class able to afford to buy books at that time. He wrote in a cultural climate in which childhood was increasingly recognised as a distinct phase of growth which provided the base for the future development of individual character. His popular stories reinforced the male-dominated establishment of norms for an ordered society.

The Brothers Grimm were not merely collectors of tales. They were heavily influenced by Perrault's collection of stories, some of which they further adapted. Their major accomplishment in publishing two volumes of 156 tales was to create an ideal type for the literary fairy tale, one that sought to be as close to the oral tradition as possible. Recent research has challenged and discredited the notion that the Brothers Grimm were simply collectors and archivists of stories that had been handed down in rural communities, through the oral tradition. They wanted to preserve, contain and present to the German public what they believed to be profound truths about the origins of German culture and European civilisation. They saw the 'childhood of humankind' as embedded in customs that Germans had cultivated. What made for good economy in the house was selected by the Christian church and bourgeois class to legitimise particular interests. Originally the tales were not addressed to children, who nevertheless may well have been present when there were communal story-telling gatherings.

It is now known that the Brothers Grimm collected their tales from different sources, including versions recited by various aristocratic women who had collected the tales from their servants. After the publication of the first editions of *Children's and Household Tales* in 1812 and 1815, the Brothers Grimm were advised by literary scholars that if they wanted their tales to appeal to an audience other than scholars they should alter their style to appeal to children. To quote Jack Zipes:

> They eliminated erotic and sexual elements that might be too offensive to middle class morality, added numerous Christian expressions and references, emphasised specific role models for male and female protagonists according to the dominant patriarchal code of the time, and endowed many of the tales with a 'homey' flavour by using diminutives and quaint expressions. They regarded the tales as an educational manual.
>
> (Zipes, 1994)

Readers who are interested to see how the tales of the Brothers Grimm were edited can make a comparison between the first editions published in 1812 and 1815 and the final version of 1857 which is the basis of the contemporary anthologies with which we are now familiar. By the end of the nineteenth century the popularity of the tales was so great in Germany that, with the exception of the Bible, no other publication rivalled their sales.

Not only did the Brothers Grimm alter the style of these tales in order to cultivate their ideas of a bourgeois and hierarchical society, they also transferred on to them many of their own conscious and unconscious fears, betrayals and longings which related to the traumatic biographical details of their own lives. Their initial experience of childhood was almost Eden-like. Their father was a successful lawyer and the six children grew up in idyllic countryside and material well-being. Things changed dramatically when their father died suddenly and they were forced to move into cramped quarters in the centre of town. Jacob, the eldest, was only eleven when he had to take on the role of father. He was continually worried on his mother's behalf at the lack of provision for the family. Two years later when the brothers were about to attend the gymnasium their beloved grandfather died. After that, both Jacob and Wilhelm had to struggle to become educated without any sponsorship or funding. Late eighteenth-century German society was such that these circumstances frequently led to them being ostracised by their peers and teachers alike.

In various and subtle ways these experiences have crept into the tales where, through small editorial changes, the brothers could attempt to restore a sense of social justice and order. They were reluctant to attribute evil doings to parental figures, particularly the mother whom they frequently changed into a stepmother. Zipes suggests that the brothers' idealisation of their own mother may have been responsible for this sleight of hand. However we would point out that the stepmother and the witch are universal images of the negative aspect of the mother archetype, present in many fairy stories. Marina Warner in her study of fairy tales, *From the Beast to the Blonde* (1994), has an interesting discussion about the sociological presence and importance of stepmothers in pre-industrial society when so many women died in childbirth. There is also a large and illuminating collection of the brothers' correspondence. Jacob, in a letter to Wilhelm, is able to speak in private of his more primitive longings and disturbance.

The only time in which it might be possible for me to allow an idea of the past, and idea of the world of knights, if you will, to blossom anew within us and to break away from the norms that have restricted us until now and shall continue to do so, is generally transformed into the forest in which the wild animals roam about, for example wolves with whom one must howl if only to be able to live with them. I believe that I would have been naturally inclined to do this. A constant warning against this and my drive to be obedient have fortunately suppressed this inclination.

(Spence, 1981)

It is revealing to follow Zipes' careful tracking of the successive changes made to one of the best known fairy stories, 'Little Red Riding Hood' (Zipes, 1993). In our times, the Red Riding Hood story has inspired many contemporary images and adaptations – from witty advertisements, to moral and social satires, to erotic playful stories and musicals, to feminist revisions. This story's adaptability to so many levels of interpretation is testimony to the creative life intrinsic to fairy stories. It exemplifies the interplay between fairy stories' archetypal themes, and the social context which shapes them and reinvests them with symbolic meaning relevant to each generation and culture.

'Little Red Riding Hood' is almost certainly based on a mediaeval peasant story common in south-west France in the seventeenth century, which would have been familiar to Perrault. The oral tale is rooted in a hazardous and violent world where children had to be warned about the dangers of the forest, and where not only wolves were commonplace, but witches and werewolves – personifying society's collective projections of evil – were routinely convicted of killing children. In the surviving version of the oral tale, the little girl is not eaten by the werewolf, but tricks him into letting her get out of the bed by pretending to be suddenly 'caught short'. The werewolf allows her to go outside to defecate, and she makes 'a pile' and runs off. This ending surprises the modern reader, brought up with the later literary versions, which have sanitised the earthy denoue-ment. In the oral tale it is the little girl's own resourcefulness and shrewd use of her body that resolves the story.

A comparison of Perrault's familiar version with the oral tale is reveal-ing. The two most obvious changes are the striking addition of the red garment which gives the girl her famous name, and the abrupt ending of the story with the violent death of Little Red Riding Hood, who is devoured by the wolf. In Perrault's revision, a new moralising angle alters the tone and atmosphere of the original story. With the introduction of key elements – the seductive red garment (red is the colour of sin, passion, evil, sex), the renaming of the werewolf as 'old neighbour wolf', the motif of Red Riding Hood dallying pleasurably in the forest, gathering flowers and chasing butterflies instead of taking the straight path to her grandmother's house – the message of Perrault's story becomes a cautionary one of warning and punishment. The forthright and shrewd peasant girl who can look after herself has given way to a patriarchal and courtly view of the gullible young girl who must be admonished to conform to a strict and protective code of conduct.

A century after Perrault, the Brothers Grimm drew heavily on his story for their retelling of it as 'Little Red Cap'. They introduced two significant changes which underline the didactic direction of their revision, with the moral education of children primarily in mind. First, the replacement of Perrault's savage ending with a happy and restorative one, with the redeeming male hunter who cuts open the wolf's belly to release the Grandmother and Little Red Cap. Second, the much stronger emphasis now placed upon the girl's disobedience of her mother's prudent warning against straying off the 'straight' path of moral order. Her sexual initiation is therefore a punishing one. The last line of the Brothers Grimm's story shows Little Red Cap expressing remorse for her transgression. This is a long way from the humour and self-reliance of the heroine of the oral tale.

The versions of Perrault and the Brothers Grimm both carry different moral messages, according to the cultural climate of the times, which we question today. Indeed, modern adaptations of the tale usually have Red Riding Hood fighting back against the image of helplessness and sexual *naïveté*, thus coming closer to the original heroine. The universal conflicts of sexual initiation dramatised in the story have always had the power to provoke a strong reaction, both personal and societal, which speaks of their archetypal roots. Both the forest and the wolf are ancient and powerful symbols which still compel fear and fascination today, as representatives of the wild side of humanity and of wilderness. Layers nearer to the surface of consciousness retain their direct relevance to western culture: the young girl's psychological conflicts between inner and outer strivings, the ambivalent developmental stage of leaving mother, the mixed excitement and fear of the sexual encounter with the big, bad wolf, the violent doing-away with a maternal figure, and the entanglement of orality with genital sexuality in the devouring scene.

While it is important and informative to gain a historical perspective on the cultural influences which shaped the rewriting of the tales, and although it is no longer possible to regard fairy tales, as von Franz did, as pure archetypal form, we do still resonate, in all three versions of 'Little Red Riding Hood', to archetypal layers of meaning. The living tradition of fairy tales retains the capacity to pose us unresolved and universal questions.

The ways in which we resonate to fairy tales at different times in our lives

Fairy tales are a unique art form in the sense that they can accompany us throughout life: the fairy tale remains with us from infancy to old age. As infants we may listen to them, often just before sleep, later we may read them, play with them, imitate them, or have fantasies about controlling the world through their magic emblems, such as the wand and magic beans. An ancestor of the domestic wand must have been Asclepius' staff with the snakes coiled about it.

Fairy tale motifs are rooted in a priori archetypal dynamics clothed in the cultural values of the time in which they are told: they symbolise universal human problems played out in different cultural contexts. Therefore they can be understood as giving expression to unconscious fantasies relating to primitive impulses and anxieties, such as separation and loss, to which the tales also often provide resolutions. Children find that the 'image language', as conceived by Bettelheim, gives form to their fantasies which enables them to resonate to the unrealised creative potential of the psyche, prior to having any conscious understanding with which to verbalise the meaning of the tale as a whole.

Favourite stories have to be told over and over again and function as metaphors for the child's ongoing concerns which are often fraught with anxiety. On the whole, the most popular tales of the Brothers Grimm do supply happy endings which, as one grows older, may feel oversimplified but which, during infancy and childhood, offer hope for the possibility of resolution. Children respond to the tales in many different ways: they may experience joy, misery or reassurance that the tale relates, often in disguised form, feelings and emotions which they recognise to be true of their own experience.

The art critic John Berger writes of the psychic complexity of such an experience:

> If you remember listening to stories as a child, you will remember the pleasure of hearing a story repeated many times and you will remember that while you were listening you became three people. There is an incredible fusion: you become the story teller, the protagonist and you remember yourself listening to the story.
>
> (Berger, 1972)

With the passing of years the relatively innocent listener inevitably becomes the more experienced teller of the story, whose initial wonder may have changed to irony. Adult listeners may be put in touch with their internal child who may remain less sophisticated and more creative than the social persona they have constructed over the years. As we have indicated, at some time almost every child's unconscious fantasies are likely to be expressed in fairy tale motifs – for example the abandonment motif, which symbolises the child's separation anxieties, and their fears about survival. Another example would be the changeling motif which may function as a defence against the realities of the child's environmental and social experiences.

Often it is the men and women who have become disillusioned with the two-dimensional fairy tale stereotypes who enter our consulting rooms to wrestle with emotional conflicts in order to arrive at a more meaningful conscious/unconscious dialectic.Then it can become possible to construct a three-dimensional personal narrative with a coherent sense of self and responsibility. Post-Bowlby research in attachment theory (Holmes, 1993) has placed great importance on the way individuals use language, narrative and autobiographical coherence to organise, remember and ultimately understand their experiences of loss and separation.

Fairy tales are a principal source of the earliest development of our narrative and hermeneutic skills. They provide us with what may be the first example of the symbolic power of the image. They introduce infants, if they are fortunate enough to live in a good enough environment, where premature experiences of death, abandonment and abuse have not impinged, to crucial philosophical concepts of life and death, good and evil, that may not enter so immediately into the privileged and protected world of European twentieth-century childhood. From the moment that we are able to enjoy and follow a narrative, which usually occurs somewhere between the ages of 2 and 4, fairy tales demonstrate our need to relate to and make sense of our lives through symbolic patterns of thought. The tales stimulate our desires and longings, which are often omnipotent, to exert control over our environments. They provide us with imaginative opportunities for discovering there is a world outside the familiar one of our own limited domestic experience, for example the world of the forest. Today, when most children, if they have seen a wolf at all, will have seen one only in captivity, the forest is primarily meaningful as a threshold, or liminal terrain between conscious and unconscious processes. One contemporary equivalent is derelict urban wastelands where people are afraid to walk in the dark.

When we reach adolescence the tales may reverberate with new levels of meaning. How many daughters, as they have experimented, perhaps through the use of make-up and hair colour, with their reflections in the mirror, have not experienced their critical and perhaps envious mothers as cruel as the jealous queen in 'Snow White'? One of the authors found this motif helpful in her counselling work with sixth formers when she introduced an exercise where the pupils, in pairs, role played a similar situation in which both daughter and mother, in turn, expressed their envious feelings about the other's reflection.

Whenever a new baby is about to be born what parent has not wished to negotiate with those fairies who were so busy choosing the gifts for the Sleeping Beauty – even if it is only to ask for the gift of a perfect human form, replete with ten tiny fingers and toes? 'If only' is not only a recurring leitmotif of fairy tale idiom, it is also a recurring theme of the human condition. The forgotten fairy, the unwanted guests, the damaged or dumb ancestors, all have shadows who lurk in the nursery as the visitors from the unremembered parental past.

By contrast, there are some adults, including some of our patients, who do not share the same resonances from childhood. People who have had no fairy stories read to them as children often feel deprived of an auditory, shared experience with a caring adult, and may lack a sense of cultural mutuality with their peers. Dieckmann draws attention to the common impulse to discard fairy tales disparagingly after childhood, dismissing them as 'only fairy tales', until a situation arises – a severe emotional illness or a life crisis – which brings a fairy tale back to mind, perhaps through a dream. Thereby the power of the fairy tale imagery is revealed once again; now resonant with meanings both old and new.

As adults we encounter fairy tale motifs in our daily lives through the transmission of popular culture. Many of the experiences and symbolic images originating in the oral tradition of the tales and now committed to ink in the literary fairy tale genre, seem to play a vital role in our phylo-genetic and ontological development, and correspond to many of the archetypes of the collective unconscious. It is these patterns of archetypal emotional experiences which are symbolised and transmitted through the tales, that are eternal. Their contexts, or frames, have repeatedly been redesigned by different socio-cultural imaginations.

There is a tendency in today's culture of computer games, story books and Disney marketing to idealise the fairy tale as an achievement of a past age which was pastoral and innocent. Many of the Brothers Grimm tales, however, are about abandonment and survival in a harsh and antagonistic world where very little may turn out all right. Their fairy tales often contain narratives of child abuse and cruelty which they believed were too harsh for children to bear unless they were embellished with Christian ideals of salvation and a sense of utopian hope and justice. In order to make the tales more palatable to young egos they sometimes stitched on happy endings and distributed just punishment for evildoing. There are many tales, which are not included in most of the child anthologies, such as 'The juniper tree' and 'Fitcher's bird', and which contain all the ingredients for adult nightmares. Analysts need to wrestle with the terrible develop-mental difficulties that such tales portray and to unstitch the utopian endings of the more familiar tales, for the task of the adult reader is different from that of the child. One of the goals of individuation is to learn to endure 'the slings and arrows of outrageous fortune', to endure the intolerable and to speak the unspeakable. This is conveyed in Robert Hobson's perception that: 'Growing up is a matter of learning how to mourn. And of loving with loss' (Hobson, 1989).

The clinical application of fairy tales

Analysts need to understand the different levels of response to fairy tale symbolism in terms of both the patient's and their own personal equation, at any particular time, which will in turn be affected by the prevailing cultural values of the time. As we have said, von Franz refers to them as Rorschach tests and we can understand these different levels of response in terms of the individuation process which evolves throughout life. As already stated, fairy tale personae tend to be two-dimensional, and when change is present it tends to occur through events rather than character development. In 'Snow White' for example, the tale ends with Snow

White's marriage to the prince and the envious Queen dances herself to death in red hot shoes. So a new situation with a new potential has been achieved, but one gets no indication as to whether Snow White is now in a position to integrate her shadow. Such an ending raises the issue of the wide-ranging levels of integration which are symbolised in images of harmonious resolutions. This, in turn, raises the question of the relevance of fairy tales to our clinical work in which emotional integration and individuation are of central importance. The following vignettes illustrate the vital part which the analytic relationship plays in this respect.

We consider two metaphors for the analytical relationship to be relevant to the use of symbolism, including fairy tale imagery, in our therapeutic work.

1   Jung's metaphor of the alchemical *vas*, in which two chemical substances combine to create a third, in the process of which both are changed; here we can think of the patient's unconscious projections and the unconscious/conscious responses of the analyst.
2   Winnicott's hypothesis of transitional space, which can be established between analyst and patient, in which intrapsychic dynamics may come into play and be mediated by the analyst in an interpersonal context. Speaking from a clinical perspective it is this mediating function in the therapeutic relationship which introduces the potential for symbolic images to be translated into a three-dimensional personal experience.

In presenting the following clinical vignettes we will be referring to the analyst in the first person.

The patient, whom I will call Ann, is a woman in her thirties who was in despair as she felt that her life was passing her by. She came into analysis with desperate hopes. Soon she became disillusioned, extremely scornful and vindictive towards me and others in her life. Then she became silent in her sessions for weeks and eventually months on end. She lay rigid and still on the couch, either staring at the ceiling, or with her eyes closed, and making as little response as possible to any commentary I could make on our predicament. I discovered that interpretations, either in terms of Ann's fear and hopelessness, or in terms of her envy, revenge and destructiveness, had no effect. The alternative of remaining silent and waiting also had a despairing and deadening quality.

Ann's silences vividly communicated her annihilation anxiety and need to defend her sense of identity against any disruption. After a time I began to feel paralysed, as though turned to stone. I was literally petrified; scared of shifting in my chair, clearing my throat, or even breathing audibly. My voice emerged in squeaky stutters, and I felt quite dislocated from my usual self-awareness. Eventually I regained my balance in the silence and found I could begin to contemplate my own responses. Then the story of 'The Sleeping Beauty' began to occupy my mind. I broke the paralysing silence and told Ann that I felt that she was lying asleep for a hundred years, like the Sleeping Beauty, surrounded by an impenetrable thicket of thorns, which almost concealed her from all human contact. Unusually, Ann reacted: she jumped and grunted in what seemed like surprise. Then, more silence. After a while I said that I supposed that Ann might not dare to recognise, or even wish, that I could be the Prince who would try to fight his way through her prickly and protective brambles, to bring her back to life. Ann continued to meet my interactions with a silent response, but there was a difference: instead of lying like a statue, there were now signs of restlessness and I was aware that she continued to make very small body movements for the rest of the session.

It would not be true to say that Ann and I 'lived happily ever after', after that session, but there was a shift as Ann now started to speak. In the same way that some patients learn to play with dream material, the fairy story now became the vehicle through which we could communicate about some of the meaning and feeling behind her defensive thicket. She was already familiar with the fairy story and we discovered that only certain of its elements now became pertinent to her own narrative. Our task was to evolve our combined version of the story to suit Ann's context. I was struck by how much more ready Ann was to recognise parts of her personality, as represented by characters, or situations in the story, than had ever been possible before. It was as if the form of the fairy tale, like the prince's kiss, had released us to engage in an imaginative exchange.

Over the next months she could acknowledge her sense of having been trapped and numbed inside her defensive fortress. She came to identify the image of the entire court sleeping alongside the Princess as her dead, or dormant internal objects; inhabiting but not interacting in her inner world. She was readily able to relate the pricking of the Princess's finger, on the fateful spindle, to her own narcissistic wounding, which she feared had halted or even annihilated her life potential. Now she could identify with the thirteenth wise woman who had not been invited to the christening feast, and who turned her hurt into a deadly and envious attack. I was perceived both as this wise woman turned witch and as the Prince. The disturbance caused by the Prince's intrusion, albeit in the name of rescue, together with my own disturbing presence, now made her more aware of her terror of living. In addition she was able to begin to recognise all her fears and hopes for relationship which had been hitherto concealed by her prickly and defensive scorn about acknowledging her dependency and need of me.

This vignette gives an illustration of the way in which Ann's entrenched defences of her self-structure elicited a powerful response in her analyst, who was experiencing Ann's split-off projected pain and despair in a process of projective identification. It was only after the analyst was able to contain the sense of paralysis and dislocation that the image of the Sleeping Beauty occurred to her. In Jung's analogy it was only after the tensions between the two alien substances in the alchemical *vas* had been mutually experienced and contained in the transference/countertransference, that the third position could materialise, enabling both to change. This shift created a transitional space in which Ann and her analyst could interact in an imaginative personal exchange. The fairy tale images had created the possibility of access to deep and primitive anxieties which had hitherto been inaccessible.

The next vignette provides a condensed account of the work with a patient for whom the character of Rumpelstiltskin became a key image.

Joan was a single woman in her thirties, successful in her profession. She came into analysis because of a broken love affair. Joan's view of her parents' marriage was of an unequal partnership: her mother idealised her father who, in his turn, denigrated her mother, and in Joan's opinion showed signs of being disgusted by his wife's body. Joan experienced her mother as distant when she was a baby and she turned, as a substitute, to an idealised dependency relationship with her father, whose approval became a matter of life and death to her.

In the analytic relationship I started by being a stand-in for the father. Joan experienced me as an austere woman who was relatively disembodied, to whom she was a good daughter. The material Joan brought was controlled and controlling and she manifested entrenched defences of her sense of identity. In the countertransference I felt progressively more frustrated: stuck in a sense of unreality in our exchanges. Gradually Joan became more aware of her own frustration. One day she brought up the image of Rumpelstiltskin, from the Brothers Grimm fairy story. She associated him with a feeling of tension in her body which began to localise in the pubic area as a penis which gave her a sense of phallic control – or of being controlled. This body sensation, which she experienced as having its own autonomy, she both resented and clung to. What would happen if there was no control? Rumpelstiltskin symbolised a vital defence structure. Her evocation of the figure of Rumpelstiltskin led us to contemplate the need for perfection (straw into gold), and the life-and-death issues of this persecutory ideal which are played out in the fairy story: if the girl cannot spin straw into gold, fulfilling her father's boastful claim, she will die. If she can, the King will marry her.

A shift occurred in our work when she started to have outbursts of rage when I did not live up to her expectations of our having moments of blissful harmony together. These outbursts seemed to Joan to have their own autonomy, and in the next session she would become dissociated from them, and sink back into resigned good behaviour. However, we could now begin to link her rage to Rumpelstiltskin. We related her body tensions and penis sensations to her bottled-up rage. Rumpelstiltskin's narcissistic rage, when he could not have the Queen's baby, became a vivid parallel to Joan's narcissistic pain and rage when she could not have an all-good relationship with me.

Later in our work, Joan became much freer and able to give vent to her negative feelings in a more personal way. She expressed these feelings in terms of her disgust with my body, which then led on to shame and disgust with her own body, and body fantasies. This personal expression of the dislike and hate of the embodied mother/me felt an immense risk to her. Between sessions she began to experience panic states in which she felt that all her defensive structures, which she had relied on to enable her to sustain a coherent sense of identity, were crumbling. Could she survive? Would I survive? Or would I be too hurt and throw her out?

Her Rumpelstiltskin image has remained in constant interplay and we have amplified his dual function in her inner world. On the one hand, in relation to her father/King's demand that she should be an ideal daughter, Rumpelstiltskin, who symbolises her defensive self-structure, does save her life by enabling her to have the illusion of winning and keeping the approval of the father/King. On the other hand, paradoxically, this same structure robs her of her baby, in terms of her bodily and emotional spontaneity, thus perpetuating the split in her personality. We are still in a spiralling process in terms of defences, aggression and anxiety. However there are now times when Joan can trust that our relationship is good enough to survive her negative attacks, and thus establish an ego position with which to integrate her aggression. Joan has resonated to fairy tale imagery in terms of her inner world and we are still in an ongoing dialogue with the imagery. While Rumpelstiltskin has not torn himself in two, he has become much less dominating and Joan's defences have loosened.

Given that both fairy tale motifs and our metapsychological models express archetypal determinants in our psyche – the one symbolically, the other in conceptual abstract form – relating the two can lead to a fruitful exchange with which to enrich our analytic understanding and skills. In our clinical vignettes we have related the symbolism to the opposites, splitting processes and part-object relations which are so necessary while we are establishing an individuated ego position in our chaotic emotional experience. The hypotheses of annihilation anxiety, defensive self-structures and projective identification, also deepened our responses in the transference–countertransference interactions. As already stated, the resolutions to the tales mainly come about through evolving events in which the protagonist, with the help of benign figures, survives and defeats the malignant opposites. As a result of this a situation with new potential evolves, symbolised by the happy ending. However, as we have said, this does not mean a final answer. Von Franz affirms this when she notes that in the oral tales there may also be a dual ending.

> And they married and there was a big feast, and they had beer and wine and a marvellous piece of meat, and I went to the kitchen but when I wanted to take some the cook gave me a kick in the pants and I rushed here to tell you the story.
>
> (von Franz, 1970)

This illustrates the story-teller's differentiation between the happy ending of the inner world and the reality of the outer world.

Our clinical vignettes illustrate the way in which working with the imagery in the transference/countertransference made inroads into both Ann's and Joan's defences and enabled them to become aware of and express ambivalent affects and associated anxieties. This process led them towards a more integrated ego position with an increased potential for whole-object relationships and reconciliation of the opposites. There was continuing interplay between creative/destructive, love/hate impulses and affects in an interpersonal context, which facilitated the painful recognition that good and bad belong to the same object, as well as the equally painful recognition that they are also aspects of oneself. In that sense the work spiralled round the transitional space between the paranoid schizoid and depressive positions and illustrates the ways in which fairy tale motifs and imagery can release a new potential for 'self-realisation' through the establishment of a three-dimensional ego position in which integration of the shadow, and therefore individuation can be an ongoing process.

We have already referred to the many different ways in which we can relate to fairy tales. We have described von Franz's approach and touched on the ways in which Dieckmann, Kast and Jacoby enrich their clinical work with fairy tale motifs. Any summary of the ways in which post-Jungians apply different techniques to their clinical work must include:

1 The use of imagery to facilitate active imagination.
2 Consideration of the fairy tale imagery as a symbolic representation of complexes when patient and analyst can both:

   a amplify the archetypal images and
   b amplify the emotional roots of the image in the analytic relationship.

3 Linking the symbolism with a range of metapsychological models.

These approaches all contribute to and enrich each other. The work with Ann and Joan illustrates that we can amplify symbolic images by releasing their emotional roots in the transference/countertransference, as well as through active imagination, or by tracking parallel motifs in other tales. These methods are not mutually exclusive and as von Franz (1970) stated, 'There are no final answers.'

In conclusion, we look forward to further collaboration between the different perspectives of analysts, socio-historians, anthropologists, literary critics and story tellers to develop our understanding of the symbolic processes at the heart of human experience.

References

Berger, J. (1972) *Ways of Seeing*, London: Penguin.
Bettelheim, B. (1975) *The Uses of Enchantment: The Meaning and Importance of Fairy Tales*, London: Penguin.
Birkhauser-Oeri, S. (1977, trans. 1980) *The Mother: Archetypal Image in Fairy Tales*, Toronto: Inner City Books.
Bloch, E. (1986) *The Principle of Hope*, Cambridge, MA: MIT Press.
Davidson, D. (1966) 'Transference as a form of active imagination', *Journal of Analytical Psychology*, 11(2).
Dieckmann, H. (1978) *Twice-told Tales: The Psychological Use of Fairy Tales*, Wilmette, IL: Chiron.
Eliade, M. (1964) *Myth and Reality*, London: Allen and Unwin.
Franz, M.-L. von (1970) *An Introduction to the Interpretation of Fairy Tales*, Dallas, TX: Spring Publications.
—— (1974) *Shadow and Evil in Fairy Tales*, Dallas, TX: Spring Publications.
Grimm, J. and Grimm, W. (1992) *The Complete Fairy Tales of the Brothers Grimm*, trans. J. Zipes, New York: Bantam Books.
Hobson, R. (1989) *Forms of Feeling*, London: Routledge.
Holmes, J. (1993) *John Bowlby and Attachment Theory*, London: Routledge.
Jacoby, M., Kast, V. and Riedel, I. (1992) *Witches, Ogres and the Devil's Daughter: Encounters with Evil in Fairy Tales*, Boston: Shambhala.
Jung, C.G. (1948) 'The phenomenology of the spirit in fairy tales', in *Collected Works* 9.i, London: Routledge and Kegan Paul.
Kast, V. (1986, trans. 1995) *Folk Tales as Therapy*, New York: Fromm.
—— (1990, trans. 1992) *The Dynamics of Symbols*, New York: Fromm.
Perrault, C. (1697) *Contes*, ed. G. Rougier, Paris: Garnier.
Plaut, A. (1966) 'Reflections about not being able to imagine', *Journal of Analytical Psychology*, 11(2).
Spence, L. (1981) *British Fairy Origins*, Northants: Aquarian Press.
Warner, M. (1994) *From the Beast to the Blonde: on Fairy Tales and their Tellers*, London: Chatto and Windus.
Zipes, J. (1989) *The Brothers Grimm: From Enchanted Forests to Modern Worlds*, New York: Routledge, Chapman and Hall Inc.
—— (ed.) (1993) *The Trials and Tribulations of Little Red Riding Hood*, New York: Routledge.
—— (1994) *Fairy Tale as Myth, Myth as Fairy Tale*, Kentucky: University Press of Kentucky.

Chapter 10

The Creative Interface with Culture

Ian Alister sees popular culture as growing out of the structures of the personal and collective unconscious and as central to a Jungian view of the psyche's capacity for self-healing. He shows how, in an analytic setting, a highly organised cultural system such as team sport can provide the symbolic language for a therapeutic relationship hindered by problems in the transference. Alister considers the archetypal elements in the game of football and how the ball functions as a medium of co-operative activity. Aware of the symbolic significance of the game and the ball, he is able to use the patient's devotion to football as a meaningful metaphor which gives access to deeper unconscious levels.

Fiona Ross presents a very imaginative analysis of 'pattern', which she sees as the 'rawest form of archetypal expression, weaving a tapestry from opposing threads', giving examples of pattern in craftworks like textiles, patchwork and quilts. She explores 'pattern' as a mediator linking the internal patterning of mind and body to the expressive and receptive aspects of patterned artistic activity. She also relates the concept of pattern to the art of analysis and to the analytic relationship. Ross makes the point that the acknowledgement of 'pattern' provides a life-enhancing insight.

The Creative Interface with Culture

Popular Culture
Keeping ourselves together

Ian Alister

Patrick was 32 when he came into therapy. His internal world was silent –
no dreams that could be shared, no spontaneity, and a strikingly reluctant
manner. I took him to be in permanent fear of attack. A great deal of what
I later understood as his paranoia got into me, and I felt singularly unim-
aginative, angry and heavy in the body. My interpretations and speculations fell on barren ground. I sensed that I was a contemptible and hated
mother whose frightening power meant that nothing could be allowed to
happen. It created a painful situation. Patrick needed very much to be
reached. Part of me hated being with him and understood graphically how
assaulted he felt. The problem with interpretation was that it relieved me
but not him, or so it appeared.

One day he asked for a change of session so that he might play in an
important football match. This came as a bolt from the blue. The fact that
he was asking for something was as much a shock as the news that this
apparently lifeless man was appearing in the final of a respectable local
competition. I agreed.

As we sat again in silence I found myself having grim thoughts of the
national stadium in Chile after the overthrow of Salvador Allende. I
remembered seeing news pictures of football grounds which had been
converted into prison areas during the right-wing aftermath. Political
conditions were murderous. The pitch was occupied by reactive repression.
In the session he and I were in the grip of the same process.

My mind wandered to a scene of German and British soldiers playing
soccer with each other in no man's land at Christmas during the First
World War. Here the atmosphere was lighter though both sides were
entrenched. Could we play out in the middle somewhere or would that
be avoiding the pain of the conflict? My feeling was that although these
associations were mine, they were grounded in the work between the two of
us, and that play needed to happen.

We were able to survive a stuttering and inhibited beginning and share
conversations about football born of a genuine interest, and out of a need
shared by both of us to make contact (Hobson, 1985). Sometimes he

repressed the freedom this gave and sometimes he played ball. It depended on his mood.

By suspending fixed ideas of the transference, I was able to take my part in creating an in-between area where Patrick felt himself to be a person, no longer under siege. Football – with its players, teams, clubs, leagues and fixtures – was a family with which he felt at home. Its collective reflection of a psychological world – why some players, managers and teams did well and some badly – enabled us to find a context in which Patrick could begin to be understood, and to understand himself.

Until then, my attempts to interpret Patrick's need for continuity in our sessions, and the attacks he made on remembering our work in between them, had been met by silence. Interpretation of his need for reassurance that he continued to exist in relation to his football was, however, all right because it was set in a world that was consciously real to him. It was embodied and it was practical. He could test it out. Not long afterwards Patrick stepped down to a lower league in order to move from keeping goal to outfield, which offered an unbroken involvement in play (and a move from purely defensive responsibilities). In goal he had found himself detached and losing concentration. This shift had a meaning in our sessions. With the ball now arriving more often, both in the consulting room and on the pitch, the gaps that Patrick might fall into were not so big.

Because of our shared interest in football we now had 'common ground', and it was as if we remained in contact, through football, between the sessions. We belonged to a collectivity that bound us, even when we were apart. This seemed to attenuate Patrick's perception of me as all-powerful and devouring. I became a more boundaried, reliable and supportive parent in the unspoken transference, rather than someone intrusive who was always trying to get too close. Provided that I held in mind what wasn't being addressed, the process seemed to help us to a state of being together in the room that could be spoken about and enjoyed. Where there is stability and continuity, difference and negative transference can be negotiated. When defences are implacably rigid there can be little effective interpretation. Being 'together' at points in the week other than session times offered a form of flexible holding that could be interpreted as and when it was useful.

Patrick had sought therapy because of the break-up of his marriage. He felt violently towards a wife who he believed had abandoned him. The awfulness of the first period of our work was partly the result of his experiencing with me a hitherto unconscious disintegrative memory of his first 'marriage', which had been to his mother. This had gone disastrously wrong, and he had been caught up in her depression with little help from a father unable to form any bond with him. Traditionally football is a focus for father and son, but this was not the case in Patrick's family. His father had looked down on what he regarded as the proletarian excesses of soccer grounds, particularly the kissing and hugging, with its homoerotic undertones, after a goal was scored.

Although sport had always been very important to Patrick, there was something detached and do-it-yourself about it. He couldn't get stuck in, he couldn't tackle. He had never been coached, never had anyone to watch him and reflect back. In areas where his considerable natural ability was not enough to carry him through, he struggled. Technique was confused in his mind with restrictiveness and he tended to reject it.

He had been a small, shy child, with no siblings. He told me that one way he had managed to find company was by going out into the yard and playing with an elasticated net strung inside a rectangular metal frame. If you threw a ball at it, it would always come back with renewed speed and at a variety of angles. With his mother there had been little reciprocity, rhythm or knocking into. The frame in the yard gave a context to his energy, and anticipated the football pitch with its frames and nets. What he savoured most of all was to make catches at full stretch, so that he would have to dive to the grass and tumble over clinging on to the ball. He would finish grazed and bruised. This helped him carry a physical fearlessness into adult life, and gave him the feeling in his skin that he was alive, durable and engaged with the world. We were able to work increasingly well in the transference, though I continued to have a sense that an important part of my job was patiently to return what was thrown. This offered not only a sense of the containability of his life and aggression, but a realisation that showing it was essential to his growth and separation (Winnicott, 1971). His discovery on and off the pitch that he had a temper helped to break a static and controlling way of being which was passively aggressive, and to find workable limits with other people.

The repertory of sport was useful across a wide range of our work. Patrick had repeated fantasies of hitting a cricket ball, half of which stuck to the edge of his bat, while the other half flew to a fielder. It seemed to be a confirmation of a splitting defence that I felt with him in the room. If I delivered a comment, it was sometimes impossible for it to remain intact, and for the interplay to continue. He was then stuck; he couldn't be 'out', but he couldn't make any runs either.

He had a way also of enviously breaking up my states of mind by repeated shifts of direction or emphasis. It wasn't possible to get a hold of this until he related with great pleasure how he had defeated an especially good tennis player at his club by perfecting a wide variety of improvised groundstrokes – a lob, a drop-shot, a heavy slice followed by a wicked spin. In themselves they were not powerful. They could never have been: Patrick was too afraid of his own power to use it. In combination, his strokes were such an affront to rhythm and aesthetic sensibility that his opponent had become frustrated, angry and ineffective. I knew how he felt. Patrick could have given no better description of my countertransference at the start of sessions, and no better clue to something of the way he himself often felt. It was important for him to attack technique and stability in order to force the other person to feel what it was like to live in a world that was broken up by the unexpected and the erratic. He was delighted by John McEnroe. In his opinion McEnroe evacuated his self-destructive anxiety into umpires and opponents, which enabled him to recover his own equilibrium and to upset theirs.

Discussion

The process of playing is much more than establishing a rapport; it may at times constitute the very conditions of existence. Sport offers a mode of interaction that by-passes defences which continually frustrate a more 'meaningful' exchange. The meaning is in the feeling rather than in the thinking, and the feeling is generated in the reciprocity of the exchange. Establishing the to and fro is vital.

Jung wrote that 'dialectic was originally the art of conversation among the ancient philosophers, but very early became the term for creating new syntheses' (1954: para. 1). Conversation is an art, yet we can be tempted to take it for granted, forgetting that even in an apparently rudimentary form it can establish a vital link, or appear to be a magical achievement to someone with a badly damaged sense of self. I have been impressed by the emotional rewards of this kind of conversation, which can appear aimless to the cultivated areas of the mind. Louis Zinkin catches it very well when he writes on the human face of psychotherapy and the benefits for a baby of a wordless 'chat' (Zinkin, 1978).

I have been talking about the way in which the analytic relationship can be enhanced by opening out the context into a bigger grouping. The hope is that there may also be an opening out of the individual psyche into a wider group of characters, and an understanding of the internal drama in terms of its constituent parts, rather than compact exterior events which may not adequately represent the complications inside. The sporting parallel would be to look at the result rather than the game, which is what tends to happen in the modern, ultra-competitive environment.

When I began work with Patrick we could not be together as individuals with a wide range of emotions. His earliest experiences of love and hate had been locked away. Only when a great deal of negative transference had been survived by both of us, could his extreme emotions be experienced as safe and wanted. He began to remember dreams:

> I see myself as a prison guard sitting in a central observation point from which I can see along the length of four long corridors which radiate from where I'm sitting. There are other guards with swastikas on their arms, and perhaps I am wearing one myself.

Through associations he began to feel that the corridors were isolated parts of himself whose existence was known only to the ego centre. He saw them also as forming the arms of a swastika, and from his knowledge of architecture had the idea that the swastika shape might represent a support for a structure (usually a window) in the process of being built. This led us to speculate that a splitting (fascist) process had enabled him to support himself. He then felt he could see the swastika from above, revolving like a wheel, until the crooked arms seemed to form a circumference outside four spokes. This he saw as the prison buildings, but now the ends of each corridor were connected with each other to form a circumference. Patrick's feeling was straightforward. Contact had been established between the wings of the prison, and the beleaguered parts of his psyche now had the possibility of speaking to each other.

The dream and its telling produced a different sort of watching eye/ego whose aim seemed to be a connecting of the whole rather than an isolation of the parts. Following a news report on the radio about a murder, Patrick had heard a neighbour interviewed. She had remarked that if only there'd been more of a community where they lived, someone would have noticed the strangeness of the murderer's personality and reported him to the police. Patrick was shocked, having expected the neighbour to say that if there had been more of a community, no one would have got into this murderous state of mind.

This seemed to reflect a shift after the dream, between the splitting off and punishing of shadow elements and being able to envisage the possibility of integrating primitive impulses and coming to terms with a real rather than a fantasised destructiveness. Having one continuously safe area in which we could be together was the start. It enabled a slow unpacking of the intense feelings that had been criminalised, projected, and then experienced as a fear of external attack.

Team sport can provide a form of holding that helps build the sense of identity which is a prerequisite for the exploration of difference. Grounds, stadiums and patches of grass are the sacred places where ritual enactments can take place (Stein and Hollwitz, 1994). The rituals reflect in part an early human need – to be a member of a larger group in order to learn about individuality. They allow the risky business of a partial merging with others in the confidence that a sense of separateness can also be maintained and developed.

Ball-sports in particular rework the childhood experience of playing in an atmosphere of continuity and connectedness. The ball keeps everybody in a relationship, as well as being an 'in-between' object that is by and large constant and indestructible. It can be hit or it can be caressed, it can be retained, it can be let go. It is wayward and must be mastered if you are to enjoy its potency; it is of supreme importance, and too long without it causes anxiety (Stokes, 1956).

Of course all games involve an exchange – something passes between people to their mutual satisfaction. For a baby it is a gesture, an expression or a cry, expecting a response, hoping for a response. For a patient whose interaction with the world as an infant was seriously deficient, it may feel in the consulting room as though there is no viable medium of interaction, no ball, just a heavy sense of silence and deadness. Nothing is in play. In an encounter group you can warm up literally – throwing a cushion around generates the feeling of being physically alive and emotionally in connection.

In therapy we are trying to find a reliable way to allow sounds and feelings to pass back and forth. Past experience of a shared language can be very patchy; the language of interpretation and transference may evoke such painful memories of disconnection and aloneness that rage and paranoia appear as defences, and nothing useful happens.

The topic of sport can in itself be a useful 'ball' because it keys in to a conscious memory of being wholly and satisfactorily engaged with the world, and of being able to co-operate with others and manage emotional setbacks. An important aspect of football is its ritual encouragement of male identity, giving value to the combative and co-operative athletic skills no longer reserved for winning food and beating off intruders.

If we react to the primitivity of its strange obsessions and tribal displays, we lose touch with football's value as a space which can offer the male psyche a protection – which in Patrick's case was essential – against the power of the feminine. Masculine identity can be affirmed, and with that comes the possibility of relating to the feminine from a more secure position. This is particularly true during adolescence when boundaries are blurred and subject to continual re-negotiation.

Football's position as the most universal team ball-sport may be the reflection of a strong archetypal content. The pitch with its halves, lines, boxes, circles, and semi-circles has a mandala-like quality about it. It often figures in children's drawings. A match can be played on almost any surface with minimal equipment. There is a great deal of freedom and a lot of rules; and god is everywhere in the shape of the referee. Ultimately only his perceptions matter.

The game is not about any civilised principle of truth or justice. If it were, a goal not a penalty kick would be awarded when a player handles on the goal-line. The game is more basic, whether you're a fan or a player. It is about spectacle and teamwork, learning to be, and be seen to be, in a collective, assertive and committed state of mind. In spite of what everyone says, it doesn't really matter whether you win. What really matters is that you care, and that others care with you.

As a player, the worst thing that can happen to you is not losing your captain through injury, or going three-nil down, or having the goalkeeper sent off, but that you argue amongst yourselves, which is an offence against your collective pursuit. The pleasure is in the sharing (Ward & Alister

1981). Football is a game about holding frustration. As a team you are likely to score, with all the obvious connotations of the word, only once or twice in a match. Tolerating strict prohibition is important, particularly on the use of the hands, which are normally so potent (Richards, 1994). The concentration of sexual and aggressive energy is principally into the foot which, Jung notes, 'has a notorious phallic significance' (1953: para. 128).

Culture is always present in the analytic relationship as an intermediate layer between collective and personal unconscious. Jung understood the importance of the sharing of cultural experience; his ideas have been expanded by Joseph Henderson in his work on the archetypal contents of culture and on the cultural unconscious, which he calls 'an area of historical memory that lies between the collective unconscious and the manifest pattern of culture' (Henderson, 1990). James Hillman (1985) has followed this theme in terms of the *anima mundi*, a concept linked by Jung to the role of Mercurius in the alchemical process – 'the third part in the alliance' (Jung, 1954: para. 384).

As a third element in the analytic relationship, culture can occupy a position on the boundary between the consulting room and the world. It may connect the inner workings of the mind and the outer structures of society – facilitating the psyche's striving for integration into the social and political world which Andrew Samuels explored in relation to depth psychology (Samuels, 1989: 1993).

The culture for which Patrick had a need was fundamental – the culture of play, that activity of which we never tire, and which in the earliest months and years of life fosters a vital creative space between self and other. The enormous significance of this intermediate area in the establishing of identity and relationship was repeatedly elaborated by Donald Winnicott. He asserted, with characteristic acuity, that 'psychoanalysis has been developed as a highly specialised form of playing in the service of communication with oneself and others', and continually underlined the power contained within the 'tremendous intensity of these non-climactic experiences of relating to objects'. 'Cultural experience', he added, 'has not found its true place in the theory used by analysts in their work and in their thinking' (Winnicott, 1971).

Humour is a universal phenomenon seldom explored in analytic writing, except in its defensive and aggressive aspects. This absence is all the more striking in view of the forceful presence which joking enjoys in the experience and activities of children. That analysis might sometimes be fun is not a popular topic (Coltart, 1992; Bion, 1980), and I suspect that humour finds its way into analytic sessions far more easily than the trickster does into the literature.

Yet laughter is a bond that matters as much to an analytic relationship as to any other. We feel differently about people who make us smile and about those who find us funny. Laughing at what is scary – and more often than not it's our own vulnerability – is an important everyday way of keeping ourselves together. It is one aspect of finding a shared emotional language that offers us a collective identity as ordinary human beings, and a sigh of relief at not having to be special all the time.

Soap operas, game shows, news bulletins, are all daily rituals like the sunrise, including us in a larger group than our immediate circle. Without some sort of shared experience we live with a fractured sense of ourselves, which leads to restlessness and to a loss of belief in the possibility of stable, pleasurable relationships. This is as true inside the mind as out. It is limiting to be too focused on our differences, just as it is to have narrow ideas about the various characters within us that are jockeying for expression. If they are neglected or poorly integrated, we will tend to project them into groups which can easily be scapegoated, particularly under the label of mad or criminal (Colman, 1995).

We no longer give family, state and church their former primacy as embodiments of our collective identity. Popular culture has filled the spaces, making bridge after bridge between the individual and the group, particularly through radio, television and the newsstands. They're not called the media for nothing. The Olympic Games and the World Cup, 'Twin Peaks' and 'Friends', 'Oasis' and 'Madonna' are forces which bind us. We follow them with something akin to religious devotion – we honour them together and we talk about them together. They are both deities and familiars. Popular culture is part of the furniture for most of us, and it holds us even when we're not in its material presence.

Today counselling, psychotherapy and analysis are a part of the culture, features of everyday life and the objects both of worship and of superstition. The profession struggles to understand itself in terms of the popular and the sophisticated, and to establish whether the value judgements that are inevitably made about the relative merits of counselling and psychoanalysis are based on an adequate understanding of psychic need. In my view an effective approach requires a respect for the holding capacities of the collective, as well as a watchful eye on its lack of differentiation.

Popular culture expresses a need to be openly primitive together, to have emotion and immediacy, which are characteristics of early psychic functioning that are never far beneath the surface. Its importance is precisely that it is popular, of the people, and by extension it expresses all aspects of the psyche. If we are condescending about the apparent lack of sophistication in a popular form – the constant melodramatic crises of soap opera would be a good example – we run the risk of a definitive splitting between 'high' and 'low' cultures which ducks the fundamental Jungian question: 'what is it for?'

It is important that we, as analysts, are wary of our own resistance to interests that may not be to our own taste. Untrammelled enjoyment of the bodily and of the unsophisticated is something deep inside us, though it is also frightening. It draws us back into a sensual and emotional world where there is always the danger of becoming merged with something else, which may wholly or partially possess us. The rituals of popular culture reassure us that a lowering of the threshold of consciousness may be enjoyed as part of a process that has a beginning, a middle and an end.

To understand what this means clinically, we could speculate that the work we do falls between two extremes. At one, the psyches of analyst and patient are together in a sealed vessel, and both are transformed in the heat generated by the intense interaction. In its degree of differentiation this process has many of the classical characteristics of an art form; it tends towards the personal. But what if the heat generated in this alchemical relationship is too much for the integrity of the patient to stand, and leads to a re-experiencing of infantile anxiety with its splitting and projecting defences? It might be more appropriate to turn the flame down and recognise that the objects of transference may be experienced more fruitfully in a symbolic form other than that represented by the analyst (Peters, 1991). This idea leans towards the collective and is closer to the processes of popular culture.

Conclusion

Sport and humour are but two of the many cultural narratives that appear in analytic work. More often it is something from TV, radio, or current events. It is always helpful to consider whether the introduction of a big news drama by a patient is, amongst other things, the best means available to describe something that is going on internally. Conversely, some dialogue may enter my own mind during a session or in connection with a patient, with my conscious or unconscious knowledge of it acting as a symbolic contribution to what the patient is wanting to show me. We need to be adequately versed in contemporary myth, as well as in the classical.

Jung knew a lot about the limitations of relying too heavily on the personal (Jung, 1963). He enjoyed no satisfactory sense of identity in his parents and he had no analyst. Although he started an impassioned relationship with Freud, in the end the transferences between the two of them were too much to bear (McGuire, 1974). Freud's world view appeared to Jung to have too narrow a focus, and he was forced back upon internal material. Instead of narrowing the focus still further, this took him wider, to the collective, to the shared elements within the personal. The evolution of his belief in the collective unconscious gave him crucial intuitions which were grounded in anthropology rather than biology.

Jung opened up the possibility of a new psychology which sets value on the variety of creative forms that inhabit us as a result of millions of years of living together. He made a massive investment in the capacity of the psyche for self-healing through its own history, and encouraged therapists to be imaginative and individual by placing patients' concerns both in the transference, and in a wider context. He valued culture in terms of its function, not in terms of its origin.

Popular culture is in the ether; it cuts across social and economic divides and is in a curious way classless. We can tune in to it and make use of its rhythms, its structures and its spaces. The work Patrick and I have achieved could have been done with a different analyst in a different language, but a language is always needed. Popular culture touches everyone somewhere. It helps us keep ourselves together.

References

Bion, W.R. (1980) *Bion in New York and São Paulo*, Perthshire: Clunie Press.
Colman, A. (1995) *Up from Scapegoating*. Wilmette, IL: Chiron.
Coltart, N. (1992) *Slouching Towards Bethlehem*. London: Free Association Books.
Henderson, J. (1990) *Shadow and Self*. Wilmette, IL: Chiron.
Hillman, J. (1985) *Anima: An Anatomy of a Personified Notion*. Dallas, TX: Spring Publications.
Hobson, R. (1985) *Forms of Feeling*. London: Tavistock.
Jung, C.G. (1953) 'Two Essays in Analytical Psychology', *Collected Works* 7. London: Routledge.
—— (1954) 'The Practice of Psychotherapy', *Collected Works* 16. London: Routledge.
—— (1963) *Memories, Dreams, Reflections*. London: Collins and Routledge and Kegan Paul.
McGuire, W. (1974) *The Freud/Jung Letters*. London: Hogarth and Routledge.
Peters, R. (1991) 'The therapist's expectations of the transference'. *Journal of Analytical Psychology* 36 (1).
Richards, B. (1994) *Disciplines of Delight*. London: Free Association Books.
Samuels, A. (1989) *The Plural Psyche: Personality, Morality and the Father*. London: Routledge.
—— (1993) *The Political Psyche*. London: Routledge.
Stein, M. and Hollwitz, J. (1994) (eds) *Psyche and Sports*. Wilmette, IL: Chiron.
Stokes, A. (1956) 'Psychoanalytic reflections on the development of ball games, particularly cricket'. *International Journal of Psychoanalysis* 37.
Ward, A. and Alister, I. (1981) *Barnsley – A Study in Football 1953–59*. Barton, Staffs: Crowberry.
Winnicott, D.W. (1971) *Playing and Reality*. London: Tavistock Publications.
Zinkin, L. (1978) 'Face to face – the human dimension in psychotherapy'. *British Journal of Medical Psychology* 51: 25–34.

Pattern

Fiona Ross

Princess Kinga, daughter of the thirteenth century King Bela IV of Hungary, journeyed to Poland to be united with her betrothed, Boleslaus the Bashful, Duke of Cracow. The Poland she came to was a prosperous country but it had no salt. When Kinga's father realised this, he included in her dowry the salt mine at Maramures. Guided by intuition, Kinga went to the mine and cast her betrothal ring into the depths of the shaft. She then journeyed on towards the city of Cracow where she had a deep pit dug in the ground. A large lump of salt was discovered in the pit with the princess's ring wedged in its crust. Further down, more and more salt was extracted, so much indeed it was enough for the whole country even to the present day.

(Majka, 1994)

The reader may not be familiar with the content of this tale but may nevertheless recognise its shape or form. Embedded in the pattern of the story, like jewels within a necklace, lie the promise, the ring, the royal wedding, the search, the dark creative space and the treasure. None of these elements stands alone, but each derives meaning from its relationship to another – they live within a pattern.

Looking at the whole story, what meaning might we place on such an impressive act of creation, or re-creation, by the Princess? How do we understand the assurance with which she trusted in her intuition? And why is it so easy for the reader to enter her enchanted space?

Jung's model of the psyche was built on a powerful substratum, the collective unconscious, the archetypal core of personality. Perhaps we accept the conscious elaboration of the Princess's adventure because we are able to relate to this archetypal core. Stein (1980) described the 'architect' of mythological form as identical to the psychological factor which continues to design and erect the structures of the modern psyche. So we can see both the conscious face of the story and recognise the primordial imagery. Each of us can excavate, with the power of primary process thought, into the depths of our own life-sustaining mine.

Where is the mine? We could locate it in Winnicott's potential space, where fantasy and reality interact, the place for creative union between prince and princess, Poland and Hungary, the place which provides forever one of the necessities of life.

This thirteenth-century legend holds a recognisable pattern which resonates in our understanding. Our relationship with the pattern is complex. It is the mediator between author and reader but also between the conscious and unconscious minds of both. Does this pattern-sharing demonstrate a will to re-create and communicate the essential pattern of our being: a will to express our nature both consciously and unconsciously? The legend of the princess may tell us of a compelling metaphor which forcefully structures our imagination. This is what Otto Rank referred to as an 'urge to externalization of the personality' (Rank, 1989).

The Princess's activity is open to many interpretations. For some analysts she might be sublimating her desire to re-create the lost loved object of her infancy through sublimation and creativity – her depressive fantasies leading to a wish to repair and restore. But we could see the relationship between internally and externally created objects not as a sublimation, nor a symptom, but as a positive life-enhancer. Jung was able to value the unconscious in this way. For him it was not so much a pit of repression as a lively, deep and positive creative power feeding the milk of history to the workings of our conscious mind. He saw the profundity of the collective unconscious and its more conscious personalised imagery as affording us a depth of mutuality and understanding of others, as well as the private satisfaction of intrapersonal connectedness (Jung, 1960b). In mythical images and tales Stein (1980) saw the archetypal patterns of self-organisation, which form the unconscious background of the psyche, acting as psychological 'magnets', drawing fantasy, behaviour and perception toward specific forms. Within this framework, any one of us could be a princess, set in a pattern of fairy-tale endeavour, her personal state of mind in tune with the universal mind, symbolised by the ring in the unconscious space she created, the archetypal dimension of her personal story.

The thread

Let us now take an imaginative leap, transposing this journey of the princess to another, to the journey of the thread, in the needle, through the hook or round the shuttle, the thread which brings together and which creates the patchwork, which knits the structure of entwining stitches, which weaves a tapestry from opposing threads, which creates pattern. I would like to suggest that such structures and patterns are examples of the rawest form of archetypal expression, being not images themselves but structures which direct, order and hold. They are a way of gaining acquaintance with archetypal form through parallel structuring. The repetition of stitch after stitch, row after row, the back and forth movement of the weft, the recurring tatting or lace motif, the layering and patterning of quilting and the repetitious use of the patchwork template: these privilege the form above the image, the language above the word. Not that there is no representation at all, but here lies the pattern of the holding structure, not the finished, or held, content. It is perhaps relevant that in cultures where there has been a fear and prohibition of the representational, sometimes leading to iconophobic repression, there has been a complementary recognition of the numinosity of non-representational symbolic creation, a deeper understanding of the power of the sacred expressed through the immortality of geometry, of space, shape and colour in patterned relationship.

The emphasis here is on the externalisation of an internally existent form. This was acknowledged by the artist Clive Bell, who claimed that works of art achieve their status not because of their content but their form (Winner, 1982). He understood that the effect of 'significant form' was to arouse aesthetic emotions in the observer. The projection involved in this experience is of a form of the whole self; it does not have the one-sided negative connotation of shadow projection.

This recognition of the power of form, or No-Image, holds great prominence in eastern thought. Toshihiko Izutsu describes its presence in the I-Ching:

> The I Ching symbols, whether fully developed into Hexagrams or reduced to their most elementary forms, the Yin line and the Yang line, are purely abstract or vacant forms having in themselves nothing to do with concrete imagery.
>
> (Izutsu, 1981)

Back to the thread. The power of pattern is often not fully acknowledged when it arises from repetitive craft activity. This is particularly true in the field of textiles, not least because it has traditionally been associated with women and domesticity. The work may then be judged externally, by the value of the finished object in the world, and not for the creative expression of patterning.

The following are two illustrations of combining pattern with textiles. In the first, the formal properties of the pattern can be difficult to decipher without close scrutiny. It could be said that the power of the pattern is held in the creator but only partly in consciousness. The communication to the beholder is also largely unconscious and consequently has greater impact. It is a description of the complex patterning process underlying some of the designs on fabric (and skin) of the people of the African Kingdom of Kuba.

There are three processes of partitioning compartments and inscribing in them . . . exploratory, starting from a variable number of diagonals, with one compartment symmetrically reflecting the next in both axes; analytic, based on a diagonal running in a symmetrically opposite direction from one compartment to the next, with alternately contrasted parts, or synthetic starting from the simple diagonal unit repeated and symmetrically reflected in both axes. With the elaboration of the pattern the original compartments disappear but the sense of pattern remains.

(Meurant, 1986)

The second example clearly demonstrates the entwining of personal experience and formal properties of shape, line and colour in relationship. It is a description of the Log Cabin Patchwork of the American frontier commonly worked by women living at subsistence level using scraps of salvaged fabric cut into strips. These were traditionally arranged around a central square so as to give a dark and a light side to the square. The squares were then sewn together to form a quilt.

The Log Cabin Quilt is a symbol and a celebration of the determination of the settler to create a home out of the wilderness. The strips represent the logs and the resourcefulness of the pioneer in meeting his needs with what materials were available to him. The center square symbolized the heart of the home, a red center representing the chimney, the source of warmth and sustenance, a yellow center symbolizing a lantern placed in the window to guide the menfolk safely home or to welcome the weary traveler.

(Leman and Martin, 1980)

Reading this description we could view the finished patchwork as a pleasing expression of domestic life from one period of American history. Alternatively, we could be amazed that people who were often exhausted by their struggles to acquire the basic necessities of life should bother to spend hundreds of hours creating elaborately constructed squares for decorative quilts. Even more surprising might be the fact that more than a century later, people with no financial hardship buy lengths of fabric, tear them into strips or cut them into pieces in order to reconstruct them into a single piece. Are these people merely copying the American settlers, or have they discovered that the creation of pattern offers a rewarding opportunity for self-expression? Such work is often unfinished, the objects unwanted and unneeded. But what about the activity itself: where does the desire to break up and re-form, as we have seen in both examples, come from? It may not be difficult to appreciate destructiveness as an essential part of the creative process and then to understand the analogy between repetitive craft work and the internal processes of deintegration and reintegration in the creative development of the self.

Perhaps this brings us back to the Princess: this time it is the knitting/ sewing/crocheting/lace-making/tatting/weaving Princess. It is the Princess who not only has her feet on the ground but also knows how much there is below the surface, who squares the circle, who creates both by intuition and by conscious design.

The material

In looking for the material source of this creativity and understanding, we need search no further than our bodies for confirmation of an inherent understanding of pattern within ourselves: in our hearts, sensations and motor processes, in the reciprocal inhibition of our muscle groups, in the symmetry of our skeletal structure and in the cycles of menstruation and of waking and sleep. Through an understanding of our own bodies we can appreciate the body/mind isomorphism recognised by Klein in infantile fantasy and can contextualise the more recent work of Johnson who looked at the ways in which even the most abstract and rational explanations could be seen as 'embodied'. He described the outer linking through the body with the inner, the body as a microcosm of society and the pattern of the world (Johnson, 1987). This theme was explored more broadly by Osterman (1969) who became a psychiatrist and analyst from a background in biology and explored some of the many 'striking analogies' to be found in the patterning of the outer world of matter and the inner world of the psyche.

The philosophical difficulties of relating inner and outer reality are addressed in the work of Plotkin who points out that even if we do not take the rationalist Platonic view that all sensory knowledge is 'a shadow of the real thing', yet we have to admit that it is not 'real' in the sense that it is not 'the thing' (Plotkin, 1994). It what sense is pattern a 'real thing'? The movement in modern art away from the representational has been described as a regression backwards through the various phases of differentiation seen in the graphic accomplishments of the developing child. Seen from this perspective, the focus of interest shifts from the finished object to the artist's relationship with the process of creation, including the body and its movements. Desmond Morris (1962) looked at this creative process in painting by apes and was able to decipher six 'biological principles' in their picture-making activities. Two of these are particularly relevant here – the Principle of Self-Rewarding Activation and the Principle of Universal Imagery. Given that primates have the basic needs of life met so that they have time for other activities, they will show great interest in the process of painting regardless of the results. They will also be rewarded by watching others paint. In the compositions which they create and in those which they appreciate 'Certain characteristic arrangements crop up independently . . . giving ape pictures as a whole a recognisable character.' Morris points out the similarity of the ape pictures to those found in the developing art of human infants. Winner (1982) described similar features in the development of children's art, with characteristic configurations, such as the mandala configuration, coming before figurative representation. Morris found out that the structures which apes create are in part determined by the type of movements they naturally make. Perhaps kinaesthetic imagery is not greatly thought about, compared with visual and auditory imagery, on account of its essentially abstract nature; but because of this it may be particularly important in the creation and appreciation of pattern.

The laws of humanly created pattern are the laws of relationship, not only the relationship between the pattern and the pattern-maker or observer, but between the unconscious and conscious mind and between the given and the fantasised other. They imply movement, rhythm, repetition, condensation and reversal. These are the laws of the unconscious mind and of Matte Blanco's bi-logic in which the unconscious treats the asymmetrical as if it were symmetrical: this is also the schema of recurrent pattern described by Jung (1960a). He emphasised the way in which unconscious influences, including those from the collective unconscious, continuously and actively pattern our conscious experience. Archetypes, although form, are also dynamisms which direct our lives in deeply unconscious but purposive ways.

The nature of our language can cause us to lose a sense of pattern and of continuous flow as the art of words is limited by the emphasis on a subject–object structure. The same dependency is found in much psychological thought. This may restrict us, stunting our expression because we feel we have nothing to create within an over-restraining structure. How many people (particularly women) have, in their inner or outer worlds, drawerfuls of fabric or balls of wool – untapped reservoirs of hope and of symbolic potential?

Dropped stitches, tangles and tears

Do we need an appreciation of the development, elaboration and communication of pattern to ensure our psychic health and to understand psychopathology? We might think of the patterning of our own development as beginning in the depths of time and personalising for each of us within our own recent genealogy, particularly through our immediate biological parents. The pattern then develops through life, influenced by individual and group relationships and by culture. While immature, we are limited in our capacity for integration of experience into our own pattern and may easily be traumatised by forced imposition of frightening experiences with high emotional impact which our immature and unelaborated pattern cannot accommodate. The classic example of such incompatibility is child sexual abuse: the abused child is traumatised by the imposition of adult sexual experiences which s/he is unable to integrate. Adults also may lack a sufficiently well developed or elaborated psychic pattern to allow for traumatic experiences, causing the pattern which is in place to crack or even fragment. The less comprehensive, flexible and accommodating the structure, the greater the damage likely to be suffered.

When a patient reveals unusual patterns of experience or behaviour associated with anxiety, distress and psychological dysfunction we may look at these as pathology. When making an assessment, the pathology is usually seen in terms of a pattern which recurs with predisposing and triggering factors. As Jungians, we might also see such symptomatology as a creative expression of the patient's inner world and as a flagging of areas of need and of useful psychotherapeutic focus.

Some symptomatology can most usefully be seen in terms of pattern. Phobic conditions come particularly to mind. Rey (1994) describes how claustrophobic and agoraphobic patients suffer from a reorganisation of objects in space, including themselves. These patients could be seen as not contained within a pattern. In certain other conditions the pattern has been lost, such as post-traumatic stress disorder, in which the earlier and familiar pattern has been attacked or blasted and remains fragmented as intrusive thoughts and flashbacks usurp power within the psyche. This leads to hypersensitivity and avoidance of new challenges with a turning away from pattern-building.

In obsessive-compulsive disorders and in addictions the pattern distortion takes a different form, becoming tightly located in one area of the patient's functioning. Such people often feel unpatterned in other areas of life with consequent experiences of anxiety exposure and insecurity. I believe that sexual perversion is one field of pathology particularly open to understanding in terms of uneven patterning. Symptoms present themselves in a rigidly patterned form, employing the psychic mechanisms of splitting, part object relating, idealisation and denigration. When the patients are not involved in complicated and sometimes apparently bizarre or incomprehensible activities, the rest of their lives often appear very unstructured, with the principal patterning being the cycles of growing anxiety, leading to a trigger which throws them into the anxiety-reducing activity of a tightly patterned perversion.

Is there a connection between the expressive satisfaction of rhythmic or repetitious art and craft activities and this specifically patterned psychopathology? Perhaps a comparison could be made between the knitting of a largely plain sweater with small areas of elaborate pattern, such as cables or Fair Isle bands, that is, areas which are highly codified, challenging and exciting and hold particular meaning to anyone who can interpret a complicated (knitting) pattern. Stoller (1975) appreciated this connection, suggesting that perversion could be lifted into art, both involving 'a search for (controlled, managed) ambiguity'.

Knitting two together – patterning the transference

Morris demonstrated how the creation of artistic form takes place in primates who are cared for by others and do not spend all their energy on survival. Perhaps this is analogous to the situation of the analytic patient who is looking for something more from life. This patient is making time and space for creative relationship and for furthering self-understanding.

Metaphorically, pattern is the artistry of the transference manifested in the consulting room. The medium of the analytic relationship, the ball of wool or the reel of thread, is unwound and thrown, hidden, passed, knitted, dropped and tangled in feelings and thought. What is experienced as happening *is* the treatment. Here the pattern of the everyday routine is imbued with the pattern of the archetypal form – the fifty-minute encounter is both ordinary and visionary, it is the time when the petty repetition symbolises the immeasurable pattern, when last night's dream becomes prophetic of the developing art of both patient and analyst as they draw in new threads and twists, colour and texture to the elaborately patterned path towards individuation. In one session the creation in the consulting room could be part of a delicate piece of lace, another day it could be an elaborately knitted Fair Isle, another time there could be a boldly coloured rag rug with gaping patches of uncovered canvas, in another a ball of wool could remain in the space between analyst and patient, demanding but unused. We may well assume that there is always a wish to pattern, to place oneself in context and to understand the cycles, links and repetitions which map our experience of life. This is part of the patient's inner will to health and was also observed by Willeford (1967) in the process of group psychotherapy, where recurrent forms give rise to 'symbols expressive of the integrating process described by C.G. Jung'.

People come into analysis knowing parts of their own patterning are missing or distorted and that they need a different quality of experience to repattern their understanding of themselves. We hope that they come with some ability to break away from the entrapment of old patterns and will find the freedom to develop new ones; just as Freud's understanding broke from his acquired pattern of the medical model, and as Jung, in turn, moved away from Freud's pattern which could not fully accommodate the ideas and images of his own transconscious disposition or his understanding of the collective.

Kenneth Clark understood Coleridge's 'something within us that already and forever exists' as an expression of the power and numinosity of our inner patterning – 'we possess and are possessed' (Clark, 1981). Pattern has an all-pervasive, timeless quality about it – it is endless although there are many endings within it. The tale of the princess reaches a conclusion, but the salt continues to be produced.

Intarsia

(Intarsia – a knitting technique employed when a number of differently coloured yarns are used in close proximity. The yarns are worked together at the back so that each part of the pattern is bound to the adjacent parts but the connections are out of sight.)

It may be true that most patients nowadays are not looking for the 'why' of their predicament. Even if the patient's conscious model of self-understanding is initially reductive, this may soon become just the dull model of winter which allowed the first commitment to analysis. With the coming of spring the patient may begin to wriggle free of both dry logic and chrysalis persona and to spread colourful wings. Learning to fly in the consulting room may be difficult: it demands an understanding of oneself in relation to the analyst and to the possibilities of movement, shape and pattern within the analytic space.

Developing an understanding of possibilities involves a search for meaning which combines the discovery of existing patterns with the creation of new patterning. This work takes place within a constant flow of pattern and of recurring imagery. Common forms in dream and fantasy are the square and circle or their combination in the mandala, where the centre or self-representation is wrapped in pattern. The patient has endless internal patterns, as does the analyst. The process of analysis involves the sharing of those patterns which can incorporate enough meaning for both patient and analyst to feel part of something developing between them, without a sense of either feeling incapacitated or misdirected by the patterns of the other (although such feelings might arise profitably for short periods). Zabriskie (1997), who sees the archetypal dimension of the psyche in terms of fields, suggests that we might conceptualise transference and countertransference as nodal points through which the symptoms and complexes of the personal psyche and the forms of the collective unconscious come into consciousness. Within this process, both analyst and patient must be able to retain the individuality of their own texture, colour and stitchery but also appreciate it as it relates to the other. Such patterning allows for pluralism in that it is constantly being created, modified, remade and elaborated. It changes as the patient changes, the analyst changes and the work changes. It is always in movement, its future is unkown. This quality of uncertainty is described by Perera (1990) who looks at form and design in dreams, comparing them with those of Celtic art, where the pattern is 'unpredictable, unknown in advance. It is found only during and after the experiential process itself'. In the art of analysis there is no end product, the creation is the ongoing work with the development of patterning. I believe that the first experiences of creative patterning form the beginnings of the therapeutic alliance, and later the developing pattern holds the patient because it is experienced as nourishing. Such strong emphasis on pattern may appear to make external objects, and likewise internal objects, relatively unimportant. But it might be helpful to regard an internal object as a process, not only part of a pattern but a pattern in motion with the ability to relate to other patterns and a desire to map itself. Analysis could then be thought of as the continuous transformation of one pattern into another: if progressive, the second would be more elaborate, more comprehensive and more colourful than the first but retain an imprint or memory of its predecessor. The safety to achieve this development would lie in the structure of the analysis, itself a pattern of sessions, times, place etc.

Modern science is no longer static. Quantum physics conceptualises a world in motion with fluxes of energy governed by archetypal principles, and Neo-Darwinism is based on an understanding of the patterning of genetic materials rather than on individual characteristics. Enlivening the use of pattern as an organic concept within the analytic relationship may help us to appreciate the artistry of analytic work in both discovery and creation, and to view the acknowledgement of pattern as a life-enhancing insight.

References

Clark, K. (1981) *Moments of Vision*. London: John Murray.

Izutsu, T. (1981) *Eranos Lectures 7*. Ascona, Switzerland: The Eranos Foundation.

Johnson, M. (1987) *The Body in the Mind*. Chicago and London: University of Chicago Press.

Jung, C.G. (1960a) 'The Psychogenesis of Mental Disease'. *Collected Works* 3, para. 565. London: Routledge.

—— (1960b) 'The Structure and Dynamics of the Psyche'. *Collected Works* 8, para. 339. London: Routledge.

Leman, B. and Martin, J. (1980) *Log Cabin Quilts*. Wheatbridge, CO: Moon Over the Mountain.

Majka, J. (1994) *Wieliczka Salt Mine and Subterranean Museum of Salt Mining*. Guide Book, Wieliczka.

Matte Blanco, I. (1975) *The Unconscious as Infinite Sets. An Essay in Bi-logic*. London: Duckworth.

Meurant, G. (1986) *Shoowa Design. African Textiles from the Kingdom of Kuba*. London: Thames and Hudson.

Morris, D. (1962) *The Biology of Art*. London: Methuen.

Osterman, E.K. (1969) 'The tendency toward patterning and order in matter and in the psyche'. In J. Wheelwright (ed.), *The Reality of the Psyche*. London: Barrie and Rockcliff.

Perera, S.B. (1990) 'Dream design: Some operations underlying clinical dream appreciation'. In N. Schwartz-Salant and M. Stein (eds), *Dreams in Analysis*. Wilmette, IL: Chiron Publications.

Plotkin, H. (1994) *Darwin Machines and the Nature of Knowledge*. London: Allen Lane, The Penguin Press.

Rank, O. (1989) *Art and Artist. Creative Urge and Personality Development*. London: W.W. Norton & Co. Ltd.

Rey, H. (1994) 'The schizoid mode of being and the space-time continuum'. In J. Magagna (ed.), *Universals of Psychoanalysis in the Treatment of Psychotic and Borderline States*. London: Free Association Books.

Stein, M. (1980) 'Hephaistos: a pattern of introversion'. In *Facing the Gods*. Dallas, TX: Spring Publications, Inc.

Stoller, R.J. (1975) *Perversion. The Erotic Form of Hatred*. New York: Pantheon Books.

Willeford, W. (1967) 'Group psychotherapy and symbol formation'. *Journal of Analytical Psychology*, 12(2).

Winner, E. (1982) *Invented Worlds. The Psychology of the Arts*. Cambridge, MA, and London: Harvard University Press.

Zabriskie, B. (1997) 'Thawing the 'frozen accidents': the archetypal view in countertransference'. *Journal of Analytical Psychology*, 42(1).

Chapter 11

Social Issues

These two papers place Jungian depth psychology in a social and political context. They explore ways in which this context has affected, and is affecting, the individual and the process of individuation through the interplay of an activated personal and collective unconscious with contemporary socio-cultural expectations and ideals. Jean Thomson demonstrates how the impact of monetarism – with its advocacy of efficiency as a priority and the consequent demands to 'slim down' the work force – was first generated through the media. She sees the more profound effect of these economic ideas as stemming from the activation of the archetypes of the collective unconscious, where our deepest human fears about dependency and the failure to survive in a hostile environment reside. Bion's Basic Assumption Theory is discussed and compared with Jung's notion of the collective unconscious. Rosemary Gordon reflects on the process of individuation in an ever-changing world. Advances in the sciences and in technology have triggered enormous social and ideological changes, giving rise not only to extended personal freedom of choice, but also to great uncertainty, insecurity and even depersonalisation. Gordon demonstrates that the process of individuation – a concept of central importance to Jung's metapsychology – is an absolute necessity for the survival of the planet and ourselves. She suggests that we are already witnessing actual, and potential, psychological consequences of not attending to these processes.

Slimming Down
A discussion suggesting archetypal roots for a contemporary metaphor

Jean Thomson

All memory has to be re-imagined. (Bachelard, 1969)

Introduction

In the 1980s the term 'slimming down' began to be used to refer to cost-cutting drives in industry where staff were made redundant or given early retirement. Although some of the 'deals' made to achieve voluntary loss of staff were lucrative and welcome for the staff concerned, the shift from expectations of job security was generally a severe shock, the equivalent of bereavement, particularly as jobs became scarcer and less easy to find. At the same time, official emphasis was on how such procedures were leading to more opportunity for individual aspirations and thus creating a much more efficient and affluent country. It became obvious that, in order to be part of such a trend, it was necessary to be as young and as fit as possible. A health industry evolved to offer to achieve slimness and trimness, particularly for women. Eating disorders became more publicised, if not more prevalent. Even royalty apparently suffered from anorexia and bulimia, terms hardly known a few years ago and now familiar. Under the umbrella terms of competitiveness, monetarism and consumerism, a number of metaphors connected with taking in and expelling came to form constellations in which personal and archetypal coincided with social issues.

The term, 'slimming down', had become a metaphor for reducing not only overweight bodies but the social economy, as if to acknowledge that individual and social systems are enmeshed. Health and fitness were implied on the one hand; on the other, pathological obsession with resources – either there was too much or too little. Paradoxically, in either case the remedy was to get rid of as much as possible.

As a metaphor the term 'slimming down' had entered the public imagination and I intend to suggest that this was because not only does it reach down into every individual's earliest apprehensions and conflicts about having the food on which to survive, but it manifests such fears at the collective species level in every human being, the archetypal unconscious, available to be brought out by nurture and culture. As such, 'slimming down' became as meaningful an analogy in the political economy as in the psycho-physical system, although later it came to be called 'down-sizing'.

In the consulting room

I hope to give my version, by discussion of individual and group theory and by illustration from work in my consulting room, of how social issues permeate perceptions of what is going on and affect transference manifestations. In the one-to-one relationship in the consulting room, therapist and patient both engage in the task of realising singularity. My theme is that wherever they are practising, they are affected by involvement in a culture with whose mores and organisation they form interlocking systems of projective identifications. From a Jungian point of view, individuation is about becoming as differentiated as possible in a contextual relationship to the collectivities of cultural life. Through individual integration, wholeness can be relatively experienced.

Sometimes this goal may seem to disappear in the beliefs which have arisen in contemporary culture, where emphases on individualism as an aim have gradually become *opposed* to collaboration as a social goal, thus obscuring the understanding organisation as a manifestation of collective interaction (Hutton, 1996). Therefore, I am suggesting, the 'slimming down' of organisations, as illustrated above, represents societally, as it does in individuals, an avoidance of facing depressive realities in the economy. The cost of carrying too many people has come to represent the disaster of a constipated bulk preventing healthy movement and change.

In contrast, the collaborative demands of the analytic relationship cannot ignore the contradictions of dealing with the apparent opposites in individuation where the achievement of balanced functioning requires a recognition of collective organisation within every system and part-system. In the therapist's consulting room, where the task is formulated and focused on the patient's psyche-soma, the individual's involvement in wholeness, the enterprise can only work, if it is to work, as a collaborative (transferential) relationship. Yet this also carries its shadow, the negative opposite, the tendency to formulate the task of individuation as if it were unrelated to any system other than the inner world of the patient. 'Transference' implies the formation of a microcosm in the therapy of the patient's perceptions of his or her life. The dialogue depends on what the patient (and indeed the therapist) can stand of the possibilities of this 'remembered present' (Edelman, 1992) of individual experience stored in the patient's memory system. The memory is part of the psyche-soma, not necessarily available to verbalisation and consciousness.

As work with the concept of transference has shown by now, the minimum therapy system is the therapist/patient duo. All relationships are imaginally mirrored through self and its relation to 'other' in the form of the therapist couple. This system cannot be slimmed down any further. Therefore, many Jungian analysts have become concerned with how much of the external, changing, social world is reflected in this here-and-now task and how it is to be included. Indeed, Andrew Samuels (1993) has devoted a research project to the subject. Is what is actually going on, or thought to be going on, in the everyday socio-political worlds of home, work, the 'news', the information networks, relevant when the patient's self is the focus for scrutiny? The answer, I suggest, is 'Yes', if it is the 'material' by which the patient can understand what is happening to him- or herself.

George

As an example of how the 'slimming down' metaphor has emerged in analytic work and been relevant in understanding the patient's dilemmas, I want to describe some aspects of work with George who was seriously affected by the recession which caused changes in employment and contracts. His established professional persona was undermined traumatically and our analytic work was shaken by an upsurge of defences against psychic change in the face of what he felt to be catastrophic environmental change.

Up to this time, his working life had sustained George's image of himself and concealed his difficulties in achieving a separate identity from that of his father and brother, while his relationship with his mother was with someone whom he felt to be wild and unreliable because his main memories were of her threatening to leave them, although she never actually did so. His individuation process as a child had been mangled by an image of himself which he described early in the analysis. He sat in a cot, smiling, while his brother, the 'real boy', was being naughty. He had been admired ever since for being placid, good and slow-moving. This image of himself formed a frozen frame in his re-imaginings and he had wordless struggles with conflicts about the risks of adult life – were risks necessary or not? He kept himself in order with, if necessary, punishing self-discipline. His persona was rather inflexible with an apparently passive compliance which hid a compulsion not to be dominated by the members of his family or by any person or any thing. Obviously, analysis was slow and difficult.

About a year after we had begun, the economic recession started and George's firm, a fairly large conglomerate of architects, engineers and draftsmen, began to lay off staff, eventually removing contracts altogether. George worked from week to week, paid as a part-timer. As his idea of working life, upon which his persona depended, was to remain in a firm on a long-term basis, and he was used to being on a permanent contract and salary, George was filled with fear. That he was a little over 30 only convinced him that he was 'finished', and he remembered his father's admonitions to be reliable and undemanding at work. The employment situation became described in the press as 'slimming down', and in line with the imagery – 'long, lean' – of the phrase, his firm said they intended to remain 'on the fast track'. There might always be redundancies. George felt driven to excesses of showing how hard-working and reliable he was. He took to carrying a bag of files to and from work. He wanted to be indispensable. By being good and no trouble, he could show that he could save the business as if it were, as he felt it to be, his family at risk of break-up. His sexual and personal life were put into abeyance.

His existential terror was difficult to be with and it was hard to find imagery which fostered dialogue. This came mostly from links with his earlier family experiences and memories that his father, who had been in the army in the Second World War, had survived horrifying experiences which had left him determined to live a post-war life of family harmony and uneventfulness. George, born into this, believed it was how life ought to be, and could have been had his father not developed an illness. Much of his effort as a young adult had gone into pleasing and supporting his father, while fearing that his own ambitions, the desire for a life and family of his own, were destructive to his parents, who, he believed, needed him to prevent his mother from leaving them.

He had, however, been able to combine conscientious work with some professional achievements and in the analysis was beginning to be less ritualised. But in response to the threats of redundancy, he was drawn into the collective panic where the processes ordering and giving bound-aries to the work system had been abandoned.

In keeping up with the contemporary mythology of monetarism as saviour, rapidly invading the collective psyche as a messianic belief, the firm held on through the deepest recession by dispensing with the 'old values', ironically soon to be vaunted as representing past morality. George's conflicts with his own inner parents, one over-protective, the other veering ambivalently between risk and commitment, were exacerbated by the new *coniunctio* of social life, a rejecting, greedy Father/Mother, relying on technology rather than humanity. He observed that the people who survived the mills of the slimmed-down economy, which spewed them on to the uncaring streets, were saying that only money could be productive, other needs were a burden. George was sucked into such fantasies and only his determination neither to be devoured nor spewed out enabled him to hold on to a continuing hope that analysis suggested a different philo-sophy, where he had less fear of losing everything if he had to separate from his job. The analytic relationship seemed to enable the growth of a less terrifying image of his predicament. He could differentiate his individual fears from the collective psychosis. In losing his contract, it was as if

George felt devoured in his sense of autonomous worker by the boss–father, as the unconsciously perceived shadow of his personal father. He had felt eaten up from within by his 'remembered present', the fantasy of desperately saving a disintegrating family by denying his own needs. They had apparently to be protected from his need to break away and live his own life. The image of bland passivity, which paralysed his energy, caught him and arrested change until, little by little, he discovered that he could move more safely than he felt while staying still.

Some theory of conscious and unconscious

Working with transference in psychotherapy brings a realisation of mystery. The mind is revealed to be part of the human psyche-soma and not something separate from the physical self. Jung's notions about 'the unconscious' show how little of human thinking can ever be conscious because, despite the facts of the discoveries of conscious cognition, thought processes consist not only of repressed life experience, but also of our collectively shared roots, as the tendency to produce similar behaviours demonstrates. There is a substructure carried in the genes by all humans as part of the body–mind system and without which consciousness and its repressions could not exist. The inner life of the individual is as much a series of interlocking systems as the external environment. So, it can be deduced that each person is as much influenced by unrealised thought as by cognitive mental processes.

At a conscious level, understanding of everyday life is subject to the influence of increasingly numerous networks of communication which form our news, views and analogies in daily repetition of words and pictures. News informs, but how do we understand what exactly it informs us of and to what extent? The two layers of unconscious processes differentiated by Jungians, personal and collective, influence groups and organisations as well as individuals. First, the 'personal' unconscious, through being held and protected by numerous individuals in systems of projective identifications, widens into the psychoanalytic concept of a shared social unconscious, acted out in family life and in the culture's group life (as described by Bion (1961) in his early work with groups – Basic Assumption Theory). Second, the Jungian notion of a collective unconscious influencing groups refers to our underlying human sameness, where a search for food and health depends on the capacity to share out scarce resources. Some order is implied, but also impending chaos and destruction. To perhaps labour the point, 'slimming down' has entered the public consciousness through media repetition of a felicitous conflation which has resonated with socially acquired views about body-shape, which are in turn linked to the deepest layer of unconscious thinking about resources, energy and survival in a dangerous environment.

Jung distinguished between 'collective man' and 'individuated man', always emphasising that there is a relationship between opposites. In our analytic fascination with the latter – how the baby grows to be an autonomous individual and how, as adults, we continue to individuate – much of Jung's writing on the continuing interplay of environments, inner and outer, by implication widening his interest in culture and its groups, has been ignored. He did emphasise that people tend to be sucked into and driven by mob reactions and expressed horror about this tendency, but his emphasis on individuation always contained the recognition that the individual is behaving in relationship to collective processes, the socio-political group and the archetypal unconscious where individuals and, indeed, whole groups can become dissociated from processes leading to integration and thus to differentiation. Sometimes it seems that the aim of individual development is the self, or at most the capacity to relate to one other, but as Samuels (1993) has recently pointed out, as the individual matures, s/he develops a pluralistic capacity to comprehend the links between a plethora of relationships. Group life demands such a capacity. Hutton (1996) discusses the problems of the present economy and its financial measures as stemming from a failure to recognise industrial life as systemic. From a psychotherapy point of view, through such failures, the equivalent of dissociations, pathologies such as addiction, narcissism, schizoid states, can ensue. Socio-political alienation is played out in the individual and his or her groups. A metaphor, such as 'slimming down', with its possibilities of demonstrating the verbal and non-verbal implications of complex interactions, may have an integrative effect or become 'split off' from conscious use, ultimately pathologically. This can be an individual or a cultural phenomenon.

George's obsessional personality rendered him vulnerable to addictive behaviours. Faced with the idea of the firm's slimming down and evacuating him, he was forced to prove himself worthy to be a retained part of the system and not part of its redundant material. He responded with obsessional defences.

The modern persona

Jung did discuss alienation in societal terms, as did later writers such as Laing (1967) or Kovel (1984), and puts individuation theory into context. As far back as 1912, in *New Paths in Pathology*, he suggested that the clinical situation was a cultural problem of our time in which 'modern man was separated and alienated from his roots in the past'. People coming for analysis, he found, were looking for meaning and spiritual paths in a world fraught with war and threat of war, and he conceptualised this as the need for dissolution of the rigid persona demanded by adaptation to the demands of mass culture. Such a persona, he considered, was anti-thought and subsumed in the societal manifestations of the collective unconscious. By 1957, he suggests: 'Modern man's consciousness was caught up in a conflict between natural, archaic and instinctual endowments . . . and his contemporary need to adapt to rationalistic and collectivistic norms' (Jung, 1977). Homans (1979) discusses this and suggests that 'analytical psychology is a diagnostic tool for problems of modernity'.

Through the experiences of his own life, as we can read in his autobiography (1963), Jung thought that there was a developmental drive which brought about a greater capacity in mid-life, amongst other developments, to take a more objective view of behaviour in relation to life's groups and organisations. The adapted persona of earlier years could change, although often with great pain and difficulty. He wrote about individuation as a mid-life phenomenon. Subsequently, Fordham and the child analytic group, extending the SAP into the wider psychoanalytic context, have enlarged the concept to apply to the earliest development of the baby and as a process continuing throughout life. Crisis theory (Parad, 1965) shows that the facing of life crises, normative or unexpected, is related to how the individual's development has prepared him or her to deal with problems. The crisis of the end of youth, as Jung describes it, or mid-life crisis as it has become (Jaques, 1970) depends, therefore, on many factors.

If the individual persona is rigid it is necessary to work in analysis on this as an individual complex, but this must take into account the extent to which the individual's perceptions are bound by societal convictions. At the present time, it seems that the 'modern persona of mass culture' described by Jung has taken a plunge into a different modern set of convictions. It is as if society itself has shifted into a state analogous to the Kleinian paranoid–schizoid position, fragmenting from a previously predictable form of organisation in which family and work life functioned according to rules which have come to seem archaic in their use of human labour. Whether this might suggest progress or regression, I shall not attempt to argue. The influence of mass communication remains but its messages are more turbulent. George, as an example of this, of a man who knew at least what the workplace expected of him, was beset by a complete change in the structure he had been entitled to expect. He could be said to have a rigid work persona, in the sense that Jung describes it, at home in the workplace but unintegrated within himSelf. He was internally prone to splits and, although young for the 'mid-life crisis', had come into analysis because he realised that 'youth' was coming to an end. This had been expressed in terms of his personal relationships, and we could see that he had not separated from the 'inner' parents, because, as already indicated, he was possessed by the fear that his development would split those parents. As far as work went, he had hoped to gain more qualifications but had come to the same internal barrier, how to remain in the firm in a more individual role. Through analysis, he wanted to achieve a more integrative functioning, which would allow him to progress in his career as well as be able to have a more fulfilling home life. This he hoped would come about by personal change and, in the end, it is personal change which will be required to enable him to deal with a work environment whose rules have to be relearnt. The imagery of slimming down, of down-sizing, smote him at the most primitive level of his inner self, where dependency of one organism on another happens but is not conceptualised. The 'remembered present' cannot be re-imagined, it can only be borne with extreme anxiety. However, the problem remains – is it enough to think of tackling alienation at an individual level?

Group relations theory

Derived from Bion's pre-Kleinian work (Bion 1961), group relations theory describes social organisation as a complex interweaving of group-systems, of inner and outer worlds, including that of the individual as system. Groups are swayed from their tasks by shared unconscious and irrational beliefs derived from cultural understandings (basic assumptions). Such unconscious assumptions are basic because developmentally acquired in the course of the individual's life in family and other groups. Cultural assumptions can evolve over centuries and become perpetuated and embedded in the psychological organisation of systems. They are not, of course, genetic blueprints.

An application of the group relations model was Isabel Menzies Lyth's (1988) description of how nursing structures grew to enable workers to cope with unbearable experiences by producing shared beliefs about admissible and inadmissible behaviour upon which the system depended. Powerful emotions about injury, disease and death were made tolerable through the work role and its uniforms. An ex-nurse colleague told me recently that when she put on her uniform she could deal with medical situations which otherwise disturbed her. She could 'manage' her feelings and fantasies. As with the metaphoric use of slimming down, the wider symbolic implications of 'management' have become reduced to the idea that 'efficient' use of resources applies to the inanimate only, so that when applied to people it contains the hope that people can be moved and manipulated like technological items. For example, the change from 'patients' to 'units' in the allocation of hospital beds is one indication of the avoidance of the fact that management of people means management of emotions as much as of behaviours. By such metaphors, it becomes possible to 'down-size' the work force as a logical response to lack of funding.

Group relations theory demonstrates how groups can be taken over by technological terminologies which become beliefs within the system and cease to be a matter for doubt or discussion. New metaphors are produced to describe how an organisation, in this case the NHS, will work better if it gives up the idea of inter-dependency of people in health care and takes on a more technologically related perception of how a system fits together and how its redundancies are arrived at.

While a recognition of how a shared cultural unconscious functions in systems of projective identifications which can be determined and analysed, archetype theory shows how such changes in assumptions reverberate with the most archaic needs. The unconscious is informed by instinctual manifestations and not simply arrived at in the course of personal experience. The work of the neuroscientist Gerald Edelman (1992) and of Anthony Stevens (1993) and Joe Redfearn (1992), who take Jung's work into contemporary medico-scientific areas, develops this theme. The patterns which form complexes in the human psyche are analogues of those which form in the body and brain. This is why repetition is so much of a hazard in the path of change. Repetition is required to set up a complex system and keep it going. Yet repetition reinforces the working of the human psyche and interferes with the need to find the new, to adapt, to change. This is the repetition compulsion described by Freud. The rigid persona, eliminating imagination and flexibility, is reinforced by an inability to contemplate change, even when it is happening. Family groups can be seen to play their part in the internalisation of cultural beliefs, developing an unconscious through their histories, as much of the psychoanalytical approach to family therapy shows (Byng-Hall, 1973).

These various ideas are intended to demonstrate an archetypally collective basis for processes in a system, necessarily mostly unconsciously held, which makes certain pictures and patterns so familiar and resonant with satisfaction when they *are* recognised and felt to be understood. Often, as in Bion's Basic Assumptions formula, there is a sense of mathematical symmetry and truth, where the conscious calculation and the unconscious apperceptions exist at the same time in the same space. Symmetrical thinking in which the opposites coincide is satisfied, while the asymmetries which bring meaning to conscious thought fall into their rightful configuration.

Summary

I hope I have demonstrated that there are reverberations from news items to archetypal depths which make analytic communications meaningful. In the transference, metaphors signify both individual development and collective processes and show the infinite overlapping of systems of human life. Complexes may be installed in the infant's earliest experiences, but their imagery comes to be 're-imagined' as life goes on. Trauma and crisis provide spurs to understanding inner societal functioning as necessary and inevitable.

I am also suggesting, through the discussion of group process, that the term 'slimming down' is itself a conglomerate of transferential projections (in systems of projective identifications). I am aware of writing at a time when we have been passing through a post-industrial revolution and are entering an era in which governments and nations will have little power over global systems of organisation or of information, beamed by satellite and controlled by a few people in an apparently unrealised delegation of power and authority. This implies the evolution of myths and metaphors which can hardly be imagined as an influence on behaviour. Slimming down has allowed 'industries' to adapt to immediate economic demands by a metaphoric persuasion that less money spent on human labour means a healthier state. Whereas a well-trained athlete has attended to his or her whole system, mental and emotional as well as physical, the industrial organisation is expected to work without its human feelings and brains. No wonder 'slimming down' rouses chilling anxieties if it does, as I suggest, reverberate with childlike familiarity into each individual's historic understanding and 'seeds of the future' implications. Its implications of pathology, anorexic dissociations preventing whole-system functioning, seem at present to be lost in an admiration of 'fast-track' competition rather than collaboration within systems such as that which underpins the National Health Service. Analysis undertaken in this era of swift-moving changes bears greater and greater responsibility for awareness of its involvement in social processes.

REFERENCES

Bachelard, Gaston (1969) *The Poetics of Space.* London: Beacon Press.

Bion, W.R. (1961) *Experiences in Groups.* London: Tavistock.

Byng-Hall, John (1973) 'Family myths used as a defence in conjoint family therapy'. *British Journal of Medical Psychology,* 46: 239–50.

Edelman, Gerald (1992) *Bright Air, Brilliant Fire: On the Matter of the Mind.* Harmondsworth: Penguin Books.

Fordham, Michael (1978) *Jungian Psychotherapy.* Chichester: Wiley.

Freud, Sigmund (1949) *Three Essays in Sexuality.* London: Hogarth.

Homans, Peter (1979) *Jung in Context.* London and Chicago: University of Chicago Press.

Hutton, Will (1996) *The State We're In.* London: Vintage.

Jaques, Elliott (1970) 'Death and the mid-life crisis'. Ch. 3 in *Work, Creativity and Social Justice.* London: Heinemann.

Jung, C.G. (1946) 'The Psychology of the Transference'. *Collected Works* 16.

—— (1963) *Memories, Dreams, Reflections.* London: Collins and Routledge and Kegan Paul.

—— (1977) 'The Structure of the Unconscious', in *Two Essays. Collected Works* 7. Trans. Hull, 5th edn, London and Henley: Routledge and Kegan Paul.

Kovel, Joel (1984) 'Rationalisation and the family', in *Capitalism and Infancy,* ed. Barry Richards. London: Free Association Books.

Laing, R.D. (1967) *The Politics of Experience.* Harmondsworth: Penguin.

Matte Blanco, I. (1975) *The Unconscious as Infinite Sets: An Essay in Bi-logic.* London: Duckworth.
Menzies Lyth, Isabel (1988) *Containing Anxiety in Institutions.* London: Free Association Books.
Padel, Ruth (1992) *In and Out of the Mind: Greek Images of the Tragic Self.* Princeton, NJ: Princeton University Press.
Parad, Howard (ed.) (1965) *Crisis Intervention: Selected Readings.* Family Service Association of America.
Reanney, Darryl (1991) *The Death of Forever: A New Future for Human Consciousness.* London: Souvenir Press.
Redfearn, Joseph (1992) *The Exploding Self: The Creative and Destructive Nucleus of the Personality.* Wilmette, IL: Chiron Publications.
Samuels, Andrew (1993) *The Political Psyche.* London: Routledge.
Searles, Harold (1965) *The Contribution of Family Therapy to the Psychotherapy of Schizophrenia.* New York: Harper and Row.
Stevens, Anthony (1993) *The Two-million-year-old Self.* Texas A&M University Press.
Zinkin, Louis 'The hologram as a model for analytical psychotherapy'. JAP 32 (1).

Individuation in the Age of Uncertainty

Rosemary Gordon

Jung's concept of individuation is a deeply ethical one. But the enormous and rapid changes in our century create situations which lead us to recognise that individuation is not just a sophisticated luxury, but indeed an indispensable necessity if we are to survive. It is the nature of these changes and the way in which they impinge on us that is my concern in this chapter.

In order to explore this thesis I will try to describe how I view the process of individuation and which of the many social issues I think of as particularly important, relevant and influential in relation to human development. The sort of social issues I have in mind are of course the family, but also changing attitudes to class, religion, sex and gender and the experience of time – both past and future. Then there is the awesome explosion of scientific knowledge which impinges on personal and social expectations, bringing with it either hope or despair.

In our twentieth-century world people – and that included Jung – are faced with changes happening at a pace hitherto unknown and the trend is likely to accelerate without foreseeable stop. Inevitably this creates a sense of uncertainty. Strangely enough this psycho-social experience of uncertainty has come about at almost the same time as, in the field of the 'hard' sciences, the concepts of uncertainty have exploded out of the enclave of the quantum physics laboratory. One need only to mention names such as Bohr, Heisenberg, Pauli. Jung, of course, knew and was a friend of Wolfgang Pauli and rapidly absorbed the basic tenets of the new quantum mechanics. With his concept of synchronicity he was able to make the connections between quantum physics and the workings of the psyche. As early as 1930 in his memorial address on the death of Richard Wilhelm he first used the term 'synchronicity'; he himself described this (see footnote in Jung, 1955: 452 § 866). David Peat in his remarkable and well-researched book *Synchronicity; The Bridge Between Matter and Mind* (1987: 25) explained that Pauli believed that synchronicity made it possible to begin a dialogue between physics and psychology in such a way that the subjective be introduced into physics and the objective into psychology. The concept of uncertainty is of course deeply embedded in quantum mechanics because Heisenberg's uncertainty principle indicated the extent to which an observer intervenes in the system he observes. Hence, as John Wheeler wrote, what we previously thought of as 'observers' are in fact 'participators' (ibid.: 4).

Individuation is a process, not a state. It is a continuing process that involves the search not for perfection, but for as much wholeness as possible. In other words there are no 'individuated' persons, only individuating persons. Individuation involves the development of ever-growing awareness of one's personal identity, with both its 'good' and desirable qualities and ego ideals as well as its bad, reprehensible and 'shadow' qualities. It encompasses an ever-growing consciousness of one's separateness, the development of oneself as a whole and unique person, relatively detached from personal and social origins and concerned to discover personal values. One becomes conscious of existence as an organic unit, separate from the collective, separate but not detached and impervious to the community's needs. While no longer identifying with others, one respects another person's rights, values and authenticity; and assumes personal responsibilities. In 'Aims of Psychotherapy' (1933) Jung wrote that he sought to bring about a psychic state in which his patients began to experiment with their own nature, that is, they were in a state of fluidity, change and growth, a state in which there was no longer anything eternally fixed and hopelessly petrified.

Naturally the process of individuation also facilitates an expanding capacity for comprehension, compassion and the construction of an ever enlarging system of bridges that link up the diverse and often opposing thoughts, feelings, moods and attitudes both inside oneself and also (and that is important, but not always sufficiently emphasised) between oneself and other persons and creatures.

Individuation encompasses processes that drive people to search for the meaning of their own lives, of life in general and of death and of the universe. It also allows them to forge links to their own creative centre and to their inner, real and secret self. It thus moves them towards the search for values, for meaning and for self-transcendence. One might almost say that an individuating person aims to achieve an optimum synthesis of the conscious and unconscious processes and fantasies, and so it may lead them to value their own individual uniqueness and yet remain aware that there are forces both within and without that transcend conscious understanding. This then opens the person up to experience processes that could be thought of or are felt to be mysterious. In turn, these processes may put the recipient in touch with and open to a sense and an experience of the spiritual, the holy as Otto (1926) has defined and described it.

My image of a person on the path towards individuation is of someone who battles against the seduction of remaining an undifferentiated item in a collective, be it either an external collective like a mob or a crowd and their pressures to conform to collective norms, or be it the internal collective, that is, the collective unconscious with its components – archetypal personages, themes and values.

As an example I think of a patient of mine. She was a young anorexic woman, still living at home, who had been referred to me. She started analysis in spite of her parents' attempt to dissuade her. One of the basic and deep conflicts was on the one hand a desire to be and to feel safe, sheltered and looked after, and on the other an almost compulsive wish to develop herself, to risk, to search and to become more and more conscious. After four years she ended analysis but came back several times for another period of two to three years. Each time she worked on this, her basic conflict. I was often surprised and impressed by the relentlessness of her quest for psychic development. Indeed my work with this patient made it very clear to me how much individuation and ego integration are linked and interdependent and how such relentless striving for individuation can drive a person towards the hard, grinding and gruelling work of integration.

Of course awareness of one's separateness can and does bring more freedom; and more freedom involves more choice and more choice brings with it more and increased responsibilities. Now the concept of identity is closely related not only to ego integration but also to the process of individuation. By identity, be it personal or that of a group, I imply that the person or the group has certain particular characteristic qualities and also a certain cohesion and continuity over time. Furthermore, consciousness of one's selfhood is of course one of the goals of individuation, as is the existence of boundaries that mark off the individual – person or group – from others. Jung was very concerned with an individual's ability to distinguish his own selfhood from:

1   The cultural and social norms and stereotypes.
2   The unconscious, archetypal and hence collective personages or images. Identification with them could indeed be very tempting and seductive, counteracting a personal fear of the experience of impotence and possibly depression.
3   One's social mask or persona. The concept of the persona is probably similar and has affinities with Winnicott's 'false self'.
4   The danger of losing oneself in who and what is indeed separate and distinct, that is the various emotionally significant persons around one, either now or in the past, such as mother, father, brother, sister, teacher, priest – or even analyst – or any impressive or even envied friend or colleague.

But if personal identity has been submerged in a social identity through identification with one's race, nation, religion, class, gender or with particular social or ethical norms, then one must suspect that an individual's experience of personal identity is weak, fractured, vulnerable or unreliable. For identification with a social group may have been sought in order to reassure, confirm and buttress one's sense of control, potency, or even omnipotence.

Obviously the path towards individuation bestows – or indeed burdens – an individual with much freedom. But freedom involves an extended range of choices. And, as Erich Fromm has argued in his classic book *The Fear of Freedom* (1942), freedom itself creates responsibilities and with this comes a potential experience of anxiety and a potential sense of guilt.

The problem of the interdependence of freedom and anxiety seems to be, in part at least, related to our most basic conflict: to exist, to be separate and unique or to be absorbed and to take part in a fusion or a union, that is to belong. Until recently most people have lived in societies in which only the special, the rare would – or could – choose to be separate, to find their own way and have their own unique identity and system of values. But in the modern western – or westernised – world this freedom to choose and to make oneself is laid upon the many, whether or not they want it or are up to it. Thus, while the drive towards separateness, identity and uniqueness is nowadays more readily satisfied, it leaves less satisfied the other, the opposite, the complementary need: the need to belong or to identify with some other person or group or community of persons.

Now the ethical value system of depth psychologists, and certainly the value system of Jung, is decisively on the side of the individual and on the development of the self, the individual. But one must remain aware of and accept that there can be different, and even opposing, ethical value judgements; for instance, some may consider that service to a group is really more important; and indeed those who are on the side of political and social involvement and commitment may condemn the former as being self-centred and narcissistic.

Clearly, concentrating exclusively on either the individual or the social is neither ideal, desirable nor practical. Instead there needs to be a certain interdependence and interaction of these different and opposing value systems. Such dialectical understanding corroborates the aim of individuation which, as I suggested at the beginning of this chapter, is not perfection but wholeness and integration, and union or communion of the opposites such as, for instance, light and dark, masculine and feminine, conscious and unconscious, sacred and profane, or even the private, personal and unique, and the social, the collective, and the otherness of others. One might even claim that individuation can involve an actual enjoyment and delight in diversity.

But it is important to be aware that besides the influence on the individual of the biological, the psychological and the historical forces, there are also the cultural factors that affect a person and imprint themselves on his or her images, dreams and fantasies. This has been recognised and discussed by Joseph Henderson who has argued that there also exists a 'cultural unconscious' which is intermediate between the personal and the collective unconscious (1990: 117).

I now want to move on to the exploration of the various contemporary, social, political, cultural, spiritual and religious conditions which, so I believe, affect the behaviour and the experience of modern man and affects also his self-image, goals and sense of place in the world.

The fact that psychotherapy and analysis have emerged, developed and become so prominent and so generally known – or at least known of – in this, the twentieth century, seems to be related to a number of social conditions and events. One of the most significant is, I believe, the fragmentation and disintegration of those social structures that had served to make people feel contained and secure, structures that made them feel they were special, known and noticed and that they belonged somewhere. Their goals and values were safely displayed and laid out before them. Now the institutions that are particularly important both in rooting a person and in transmitting the culture's ethos are of course first and foremost the family, but also the neighbourhood, the school, the workplace, class structures and political parties, as well as local and national boundaries, and the religions with their rituals, their faiths, their sanctions, their icons and artifacts, their buildings, pictures, statues, and music.

What has happened or is happening to dissolve these structures, these buttresses of our confidence and orientation in time and in space. There are, I think, several very powerful and influential forces which I will now describe briefly. My order of naming them will not be in terms of their importance, but simply as they present themselves to me.

Perhaps one of the conditions that people complain of most frequently is the speed of change. For all of us it means that one can no longer rely on anything or predict anything, neither partner, nor work, nor income, nor praise, nor blame, nor the pronouncements or guidelines of leaders of political parties or of governments, or even of nations. No wonder that there is an absence of what has been described as the 'feel-good' factor.

At the bottom of much of what is happening are the phenomenal advances of modern science and technology. The demands and consequences of modern technology have led to the geographical dispersal of the industrial centres. This has created enormous mobility of men and women and of the general workforce. It has broken up the idea and the experience of neighbourhood and communities. It is also the consequence of technology that the production of goods no longer relies on brute force; hence men and women are now seen as equally effective workers. Even in the armed forces women can aspire to pilot combat aircraft. Again as a result of science and technology, the accompanying sophistication of medicine has led to the reduction of infant mortality and the extension of the general life-span; so we are now faced with the scourge of population explosion. And with this comes ever-growing mobility and more and more inter-ethnic, inter-national and inter-religious meeting and mixing.

Of course, part of what we experience as the speed of change is the result of the fantastic growth of information and communication, through radio and television, which we can receive by cable, by satellite and even electronically by Internet and E-Mail and in the newly created 'Cyberspace'. Potentially, the whole world can now hear, read, see and know, almost instantaneously, what is happening practically anywhere on the planet and in near space. This new world-audience increasingly discovers how others – both neighbours and cosmonauts – look, experience, behave and believe.

This general meeting and mixing is wonderfully shown when one looks at people in the street. I have always been intrigued by what people wear, their clothes, hairstyles and the general trend of fashion. My attention to this was aroused and sharpened by Professor Flugel's book – written many decades ago – called *The Psycho-analysis of Clothes*. Certainly what strikes me nowadays is how fashions cease to distinguish men from women, old from young, and how even ethnic clothes become more and more a question of choice rather than a signal which announces one's cultural origins. Instead we are now free to find in what we wear an expression of our personality, our interests, aims and goals, and also how we want to be seen by others. So again much is left to us to choose, which of course depends once more on our idea of who we are, that is, on the sense of our identity.

But even our gender and sexual orientation have become a matter of choice and personal responsibility. Modern medicine and surgery can help us change from our original gender towards the opposite gender. Furthermore, the growth of tolerance and of psychological sophistication allows us now to love and to create a partnership with a person belonging to the same or to the opposite sex. In other words, we can now be guided not just by our biological make-up but also by our conscious or not-so-conscious knowledge of the character, temperament and the qualities of the 'other' and how well the two of us will form a compatible and emotionally enriching relationship.

But consciousness of personal identity can also bring in its wake the experience of anxiety or of isolation. It is thus not surprising that some may seek out defences like identification with a social group, or the excitement of extremisms, be they nationalistic, religious or sexual; for this releases an individual from doubt and from the discomfort of not knowing. It can even provide him or her with an enemy or enemies, for there is indeed much evidence that men and women need enemies – to reinforce their sense of identity, to be the target of their aggression and the 'host' of their shadow. Or else they may defend themselves by rushing into isolation and the avoidance of relationships, or into a belligerent fundamentalism.

Or they may cling to the past, be it viewed and idealised as a sweet domestic haven, or seen as the origin of the damage done to them, damage that leaves them angry and dissatisfied with others and also with themselves. They tend to long for perfection and demand of people, of events, and of themselves, absolute faithfulness to archetypal fantasies and personalities. Thus discrepancies between real persons and their archetypal prototypes is totally unacceptable to them. Jung has suggested that 'when a particular view of the world is collapsing, sweeping away all the formulae that purport to offer final answers to the great problems of life' then archetypal images, archetypal forms, fantasies and feelings will 'crop up autochthonously in anybody's head at any time and place' (1929: 8). Thus Jung's hypothesis confirms and explains the fact that in our clinical practice we do increasingly meet patients frustrated in their 'Don Quixote' hunt to find, catch and own pure archetypal objects. Certainly in our consulting rooms we encounter persons who feel lost, strangers to themselves, strangers in the world. Often they do not find it in themselves to love or at least to respect or to value or to care for themselves, nor do they feel that there is somebody somewhere who loves and cares, values and respects them. Indeed, they may claim that there is nothing and nobody inside them; it just feels empty and hollow and grey. Or they may feel themselves, as described by Sartre and some of the French Existentialists, cast upon an uncertain stormy sea without anchor or compass. And many more patients or friends are worried, wondering where they come from, where they belong, where they should go.

Is this uncertainty the reason why in our era, in which there ought not to be any longer real hunger, real poverty or real illiteracy, there stalks so much violence, hatred, murder, war, conflict, racism, ethnic cleansing, serial killing, genocide, torture, hostage taking?

What is it all about? What does it mean? Is it greed? Envy? Fear of boredom? Or is it freedom that drives people to ever greater, but ever more primitive exploits, experiments and exultations? Is it the lack of trust that one is loved or that one can be loved; or is it low self-esteem and despair that tempts some to grasp at power and control and so try to force others to notice them, to pay attention, to submit? Is it the need for excitement, for escape from the ordinary, the everyday, from consciousness and from the dominance of the ego-functions that is expressed in the search for drugs? Do we find ourselves in the drug culture because there is a search for out-of-the-body experiences, a search for otherness, for the unexpected, the unthinkable? Or is it a search for the 'big self' that Jung describes, or a search for spirit, the spiritual? Jung had already seen a link between alcoholism and the addiction to 'spirit' – when orally ingestible spirit has been confused with the spiritual spirit that one needs to 'breathe in' like Kwoth, the god-spirit of the Nuer; they think of it as 'intangible air' and as 'invisible and ubiquitous like wind or air' (Gordon,

1993: 90). Using drugs to reach 'Kwoth' or 'Spirit' or 'the big self' is, I believe, a kind of rape, an impatient bulldozing by a speed-obsessed technocratic society, using means that risk perverting and damaging the goal they seek.

I summarise here the changes in some of the social conditions and institutions that must have affected the psyche of the modern person:

1   The break-up or break-down of various social institutions – family, neighbourhood, community – which serve persons as containers for or as a dispenser of or as a substitute for a personal identity.
2   Accelerated social mobility – which deprives people of the security of neighbourhood and community and leads them into constant attempts to make new friends in relation to whom they have to cut a figure, and whom they must impress as being somebody worth knowing.
3   The presence and the proselytising of different faiths, beliefs and spiritual disciplines which require or tempt individuals not just to remain members of the religion into which they were born and brought up, but to recognise that here too they have to choose, are free to choose.
4   The much accelerated pace of change all around – in the external, the social world, in the sciences, in the arts, and in terms of what is known or can be known.

All this creates a world, and an experience of the world in which one cannot rely on or expect certainty. But this psychological disillusionment that certainty is neither dependable nor easily accessible, a psychological dis-illusionment that is mostly unconscious, has emerged and developed some seventy years after Heisenberg. Even the lay person now knows that the observer always intervenes and affects the system that he or she observes, and that therefore the product of observation is never totally certain. David Peat quotes John Wheeler in order to clarify the thinking that led to and underpins the uncertainty principle.

We had this old idea, that there was a universe out there, and here is a man, the observer, safely protected from the universe by a six-inch slab of plate glass. Now we learn from the quantum world that even to observe so minuscule an object as an electron, we have to shatter that plate glass, we have to reach in there . . . . so the word 'observer' simply has to be crossed off the books, and we must put instead the new word 'participator'. In this way we've come to realise that the universe is a participatory universe.

(1987: 4)

Thus both in physics, in the study of social structures and social issues and in the psychic experience of ourselves and of the world we have been driven to acknowledge that we have entered the era dominated by the 'death of certainty'. We have reached the age of uncertainty which then brings with it the experience of doubt. Yet, though uncomfortable, we must also remember and feel comforted by Jung's comment in his 'In Memory of Sigmund Freud' that 'Doubt alone is the mother of scientific truth' (1939: 47).

Finding ourselves in the age of uncertainty, the development of the process of individuation has ceased to be just cosmetic, a mere luxury. For individuation, as described, developed and understood by Jung and the later post-Jungian analysts, has come to be recognised as a vital necessity. To shirk it may bring real disaster, real dangers and possibly death. The dramatic bursting out of so much violence, conflict and destruction in our own time is surely a warning that unless we embark seriously on our psychological growth, the acceleration of the technological and sociological changes will surely lead us, like lemmings, towards the edge of the precipice.

References

Fromm, Erich (1942) *The Fear of Freedom*, London: Kegan Paul.
Gordon, R. (1993) *Bridges: Metaphor for Psychic Processes*, London: Karnac Books.
Henderson, Joseph (1990) *Shadow and Self*, Wilmette, IL: Chiron Publications.
Jung, C.G. (1929) 'Paracelsus: The Physician', *Collected Works* 5.
—— (1933) 'The Aims of Psychotherapy', *Collected Works* 16.
—— (1939) 'In Memory of Sigmund Freud', *Collected Works* 5.
—— (1955) 'Synchronicity: Principle', *Collected Works* 8.
Otto, R. (1926) *The Idea of the Holy*, Oxford: Oxford University Press.
Peat, David (1987) *Synchronicity: The Bridge between Matter and Mind*, New York: Bantam Books.

Chapter 12

Contemporary Overview of Jungian Perspectives

Fred Plaut gives a personal account of forty years as an analyst in England and in Germany. He observes how economic factors have forced changes in working practices for analysts, and caused conflicts of loyalties for new practitioners. A comparison is made between the quarrels of analytical 'families' in the past (which led to splits within and between training institutes) and current professional differences and anxieties about economic and political survival which need to be met by unity rather than further fragmentation. For Plaut, identification rather then 'identity' is seen as a useful container of these conflicts. However, there is a danger it may also destroy the development of individual originality as well as the organic growth of analytic institutions.

Christopher Hauke identifies Jung as a radical thinker whose ideas make a significant contribution to the contemporary critique of modern consciousness and culture. He contextualises Jungian concepts by comparison with Freudian theory and aspects of postmodern thought. Hauke surveys major themes in analytical psychology and relates these to the need for both individual and cultural healing. He places Jungian psychology at the centre of current discussion on society and the individual.

What Do I Mean by Identity?

Fred Plaut

> Misery acquaints a man with strange bedfellows.
>
> Shakespeare, *The Tempest*

Are we analysts to be judged by tests of cost/efficiency, by statistical comparisons between different methods of psychotherapy and by medical and social criteria? Or, alternatively, are we going to maintain that ours is a method which has no aim other than to embark on a long journey designed, for example, to link the past with the present, in order to assist the unfolding and realisation of the individual's psychic potential? It is a journey, moreover, that involves frustrations and will be costly. While the analyst's personal experience justifies a hopeful attitude, it must remain an open question whether, or to what extent, any particular journey with its hardships will also relieve suffering, particularly the suffering that led the patient to come to analysis.

These are considerations and dilemmas which become urgent under conditions of financial stringency, and I shall not go further into the situation than to point out that the question of our identity as analysts living in the post-Jungian era is not being raised in a social and political vacuum or as a theoretical subject of no great consequence to the art and craft of private analytical practice. It should be said that I am viewing the situation from Berlin, where I have been practising for the last ten years after having practised in London for thirty-five. In a previous paper I compared the conditions of practice and training in the two countries and showed that the administration and socio-cultural frame exert a marked influence on the practice of analysis. To modify the administrative influence, the British Confederation of Psychotherapists has recently drawn up a Register which includes 'Analysts (Jungian)' and 'Child Analysts (Jungian)'. This should be reassuring to the public and practitioners alike and leaves analysts free to get on with the essential task of defining their post-Jungian identity. A big job, to which this paper is meant as a small contribution.

Before setting out, we should note that Jung's definition of identity was much closer to what we now mean by identification, and restricted by him almost exclusively to descriptions of the ego's identification with aspects of the collective unconscious, or primal self. Thus his definitions of identity were preceded by adjectives such as original or unconscious and the term 'identity' was used by him as a synonym for Levy Bruhl's 'participation mystique', meaning the animistic fusion of an individual's experience, in a participatory way, with that of collective nature, setting up an emotional continuum between the self and its objects. Of course, in contemporary psychoanalytic (and, now, common) usage, 'identity' has come to mean almost exactly the opposite: we now use it to mean a step in the formation of a distinctive individual consciousness, based on the autonomy and self-affirmed authority of the person's own independent psychological style. 'Identification' today is applied solely to human objects, and implies less a participation in another's reality than the loss of one's own ego to the other person – as in 'projective identification'.

We can think of identity in structural terms, for example that a person has an identity when ego and self are in a state of balance, or, alternatively, it can be thought of as a state between integration and deintegration of the self. The balance would describe a state of mind in which the person might not be troubled by doubts as to who or what he is, yet is still curious to make new discoveries about himself in relation to his surroundings. But no intrapsychic definition will do when we want to say something about a person's relationship to another person or their professional group. I am therefore going to assume that on an interpersonal level it is possible to distinguish phases of identification followed by disidentification and the possible finding of identity which can, however, be lost again and be followed by another identification. I will say more about that later.

If we turn to different institutes of analytical training, we see that practitioners have responded in their different ways to the challenge of being Jung's heirs and are called, variously, 'analytical psychologists', or 'psychoanalysts (Jung)' or just 'Jungians'. The term 'post-Jungians' was introduced by Andrew Samuels (1985) in his first book and comes close enough to what we are. Anyhow, the way we live, practise and train the next generation depends on how we feel about our identity. An important psychological aspect of analytical work is that it depends on the angle from which it is viewed. The viewer's orientation includes both the special standpoint, or 'vertex', and the geographical–political location to which I drew attention in my paper 'The presence of the third' (Plaut, 1990). There I pointed out the ways in which analysts in different parts of the world compromise between what they would regard as the ideal conditions of practice and the external realities of the patient, in short what is financially feasible, not forgetting the socio-cultural environment in which both live.

Germany presented me with a shattering example of the influence that external reality can have on analytical practice. It had been a sinecure for analysts, who were very well paid by the insurance companies, and there were long waiting lists of patients for analysts and trainees to choose from. Within the space of a few months, the outlook drastically changed. There were budgetary cuts and the piper, in the form of the Government Department of Health and the insurance companies, began to call a different tune. The payment of all analysts and psychotherapists as well as of doctors generally was reduced while the contributions for health insurance went up. This coincided with there being fewer patients on the waiting lists for analysis. The length of analysis, determined by the number of hours for which insurance companies would pay, had been limited before. But now another interference with free practice was added: an analysis could not take place more than three times a week. This constituted a direct interference with analytic technique. Furthermore, the areas in which a certain number of analysts as well as other specialists could practise were defined and closed. In addition, the therapeutic cost efficiency of analysis as compared with other shorter forms of psychotherapy was questioned. These are the circumstances in which analysts cannot escape proving the efficacy of their method statistically. And that in turn makes us question whether we are employed as medical auxiliaries or whether we, as a professional group of psychotherapists, practise according to a concept of mental health that is grounded in western culture and civilisation. This concept includes such issues as job-satisfaction and a regard for the individual as being more than a cog in a wheel. In short, what is it we stand for or what is our professional identity in the community?

I shall make a distinction between the first person singular 'I'- or ego-identity with which we are familiar, and the first person plural identity, the 'we-identity'. The latter term is borrowed from a sociologist, Norbert Elias, who maintained that it is neglected in our society and emphasised the meritocratic hypertrophy of the ego, hence the exclusive 'I-identity'. At the other extreme, we find the historically and prehistorically older 'we-identity' that, if unbalanced by a humanistic view, leads to destructive and self-destructive wars, as well as rabid sectarianism and religious fundamentalism, as we see in daily news bulletins. In any case, the we-identity remains hard to distinguish from the identification with a cause, sailing under the respectable flag called 'the faith' or 'loyalty'. It becomes comparable to an oath of allegiance. An outstanding example of it was Freud's secret committee, the seven members of which he presented with a ring. In this context, we also remember the ideological as well as personality-centred differences and polarisations in our professional societies. These examples could be extended but I must limit myself to observing that identification has gained a negative connotation: nobody wants to be told that they are identified with anything or anyone. It is the 'others' who are identified; 'we' are individuals.

Now I can hear somebody say: 'When are you going to tell us what you actually mean by identity?' By way of an answer, I shall introduce a model of phasic variations between identification and identity, which applies both to the I- as well as the we-identity. This model will also serve as a metaphor in lieu of a generally agreed psychodynamic definition of 'identity'. It is taken from daily life and refers to the states and transitions between 'being in love' and 'loving' (or, conversely, hating. We do not say 'being in hate' presumably because it is such a hateful condition to be in.) We all know about being in love as a state that alters our perception of reality. It does not change matters to know about projective identification, 'participation mystique', fascination (for example by a projected male/female image, such as Jung's animus/anima) or narcissistic mirroring, sex hormones and the like. We also know that 'All mankind loves a lover', in other words *we* tend to identify with the 'afflicted individual' who is like *ourselves* no matter how 'individuated' we may be. This leads me to draw attention to the transitions and oscillations that are in practice between identification and identity and between the I- (ego-) and the we-identity, as indeed between being in love and loving. The we-identity would have been anathema to Jung whose ideas about human groups were close to Le Bon's *The Crowd* (1896), where a human is characterised as a mindless mob. The we-identity in the form of solidarity appears to have been necessary for the survival of prehistoric human groups. It remains essential when common interests are threatened, in, for instance, peacetime when the survival of a professional group is at stake or, as in times of war, the survival of the nation. It looks as if there were a psychodynamic relationship between the two kinds of identity, both of which are required to a varying degree and for different purposes.

Is there such a thing as a Jungian identity?

Jung himself has often been quoted to the effect that he wanted no 'Jungians' and that people should become themselves. I took this to mean that they should do so, but that his teaching would be a help. Nevertheless, he had pupils who followed his teaching rather closely. Among them is Giegerich whose paper (1987) was entitled, in translation, 'The bottomlessness of Jungian psychology: concerning the question of our identity as Jungians'. Here Giegerich argues at length against colleagues who try to acquire an identity by illegitimate means, and castigates in particular those who do so. He categorises in detail and refers to these colleagues as follows: the good son, the heretic, the missionary (who delegates his identity to a group of initiates for the sake of his own comfort) and those who adopt an apologetic style in order to gain the approval of other analytical schools. Those analysts who try to define their identity by emphasising their differences from other analytic directions are equally on the wrong track. The sixth classification really rouses Giegerich's ire. I would briefly refer to it as the eclectic. I believe most of us would belong to this category. However, Giegerich's true Jungian identity cannot be found 'without the personal confession and personal bond with the founder of the school as the originator of a spiritual tradition'. Giegerich writes that, without it, the (analytical) psychologist becomes like a *croupier* 'who collects the tokens according to win or loss without risking together with theoretical work his own fate'. I respect Giegerich not only because he is so openly passionate in his convictions but also because he makes use of the word love when it comes to his positive criteria. He writes: 'like all transference phenomena, our Jungian identity is unthinkable without . . . the element of love.' This comes close to my metaphorical description of identity as an oscillation between being in love and loving, except that Giegerich omits any reference to hate, which I include in my feelings about Jung. As for the 'spiritual tradition', a free translation into English would probably call it 'cultural tradition'. I mention it here because the identity that is attributed to us depends not only on our own choice. The moment we carry a label with Jung's name on it, a cultural-spiritual aura will surround it. Whether we like it or not, Jung is known not only as an analyst but as a psychologist, therapist and a man of culture and vision.

As for the six categories of futile attempts to escape the question of identity as Giegerich sees it, I gladly confess that I committed all of these sins and remain unrepentant. Nevertheless, it is good to have a fundamentalist like Giegerich among us who will see to it that the master's words are not watered down by critics like myself.

Disidentification

There used to be a fairly large photograph behind the desk of my consulting room. It had not been autographed by Jung as the photographs in the consulting rooms of senior colleagues I knew had been. I had also seen photographs of Freud in the consulting rooms of psychoanalysts. The point is that my photo of Jung is no longer there and I am not sure where it has got to, though I am sure that I have not thrown it away. What has happened?

We saw that Giegerich goes out of his way to describe wrong and wrongful tracks which cannot lead to a Jungian identity. Yandell (1977), who had also written on the subject, expresses himself in a milder vein about schools one can attend, books one can read, teachers from whom one can learn but he says that there is only one self that one can become and for which there is no substitute. He closely follows Jung in this respect and adds that Jung's opus must have significance for Jungians. If I now turn to the details of Jung's ideas as applied to analytical psychotherapy and say what appeals to my thoughts and feelings and where I am critical and even rejecting, I am conscious that I am one of Giegerich's heretics and that, according to Guggenbühl-Craig (1988), who has also written on the subject, I must be counted as a traitor.

My first positive feeling for Jung is that I am grateful for having his approval when I criticise him. At least, in principle. Whether this would have been so in practice, I very much doubt. The second positive feeling for Jung is my admiration for his having survived the conflict with Freud and his subsequent breakdown. My admiration is tempered by Jung's evident weaknesses as a human being, about which Guggenbühl makes no bones. I also feel critical of Jung's leaning towards parapsychology, telepathy, astrology and synchronicity and other mantic procedures. These were very much in the fore in the 1950s and there are still Jungians about who throw the I-Ging several times a day. I make use of the oracle perhaps once or twice a year but I don't deny that it is due to a superstitious tendency of which Freud and most of us are by no means free. What I disapprove of is the use of these methods as part and parcel of the analysis, because as a procedure, they seem to divert from the analytic rigour.

So much for my feelings. Now to those of Jung's characteristics which I have incorporated into my analytical work. I can only summarise these here in the hope that they will strike chords without my having to go into detail. They are:

- The unalterable innate aspects of the personality.
- The relative autonomy of inner images, which are often more impressive than interpretations.
- Jung's concept of the Self, which is rooted in the body.
- Jung's appreciation of different cultures and historic happenings.

But it is my criticism of Jung that has helped me to disidentify and which is presumably responsible for the disappearance of the photograph from my desk. Here are some details.

Finding fault with Jung

The major disidentification from the Jungian vertex that was dominant in London about the time I became a member of the SAP forty years ago could be called 'from enthusiastic generalisations and the idealisation of Jung, the sage, to detailed observations and sobriety'. In more detail, the identification consisted of (a) being uncritical about the use of analogy between the alchemical model of the transference and personal projections and (b) the belief that the appearance of symbols of transformation would be accompanied or followed by a comparable evolution in the patient's

psyche.[1] It was assumed that the transformation would lead progressively
towards psychic wholeness and health. I could not find sufficient evidence
for this hypothesis, although the optimism that accompanied it was at first
infectious. However, it does do something for isolated patients to know
that their psyche is connected by means of symbolic images with others;
and further, that their analysts value them and their dreams and archetypal
images as living evidence of Jung's vision and intuitive discoveries. Clinical
evidence (i.e. improvement) supported these observations.

But as a method of analysis, and a discipline that could to some extent be
taught and handed on, I found that Jung's way was wide open to misuse.
The worst seems to me when the analyst cannot bear the patient's criticism,
thereby ignoring the value and necessity of the negative emotions in the
analytical relationship. Next: too many people know 'what he really meant'
and their credentials are that he had told them himself. This leads to Jung
becoming a cult figure.

I also found the misuse of mantic methods objectionable. Later 'synchronicity' was added when the mantic methods were supplanted by an a-
causal principle based on 'meaning' rather than causation. If one knew
'what the unconscious meant', why should one bother over-much with the
effect that events in the patient's past had had on their development and
psychopathology? I want to summarise my major criticism of Jung by
putting my question another way. Could one apply the principle of synchronicity to the analytic therapy of a child? It is easy to imagine that
children would love it at first and later become frightened. If, for example, I
were to interpret that father's angry outburst yesterday had coincided with
the thunderstorm we had or that mother was in a good mood because the
sun was shining, children would cotton on at once. But soon they would
realise that I was talking the language of correspondences (analogies) that
appeals to them like the magic of fairy tales. They would be too scared to
ask why I was doing that. I should not be surprised if they came to the
conclusion that I was trying to curry favour by talking like a child, perhaps
in order to gain their confidence and thereby get them into my power, like a
magician or a witch might do. Perhaps they would even get better quickly
rather than fall into my clutches. The situation seems to me quite different
when one is dealing with an adult, who has been to school and lived in a
world of cause and effect that one has to know about for the sake of sanity.

1 The reader who is not familiar with Jung's writings ahould know that (1), in Volume 16 of
the *Collected Works*, Jung draws a parellel between the illustrated account of the interplay
between the alchemical opposites and the transference problem in analysis – although
entitled 'Psychology of the Transference', it is not a clinical account of transference – and
(2) that 'Symbols of Transformation', published in a revised edition of 1952, was first
published in 1912, and counts as the first major publication that heralded the breakaway
from Freud.

The trouble was that one could not disagree with the unconscious and its wisdom, which nevertheless depended on its interpretation by fallible analysts. Too much emphasis on the person of the analyst – important though that is – meant that there was no room for a disciplined advancement of knowledge. It was as if analysis would become a pop-art in which everybody could dabble and practise as they wished, but the disciplined craft and method or technique would be neglected.

At this point I have to be autobiographical. My disidentification from what we in London called the Zürich interpretation would have taken very much longer without Fordham, who had begun to counterbalance Zürich by his more psychoanalytically orientated causal-genetic view of the transference and using it also in the analysis of children. On the technical side, this meant the analysis of transference projections on the analyst. This required a higher frequency of sessions. Twice a week had been standard for patients and trainees. Now three times began to be regarded as the minimum requirement for a proper analysis. At SAP, London, this has risen to four.

I noticed a tendency for a term to lose its orientating value and be treated no longer as an invention like a compass point but as if it were a lighthouse. The reification of 'anim-a-us' is a case in point. This occurs in other schools as well. Winnicott's 'transitional object' is a blatant example of a term that had a precise meaning within a genetic theory of object relations. The actual outer object that stood for the concept 'object' of a 'not-me-possession' was often a rag that a small child took about and used as a comfort before falling asleep. The paradox was that 'not-me' meant it was both outside his body, almost having a life of its own, and yet in relationship with the discoverer. But the term has been broadened out to comprise all mental phenomena between illusion and reality. If the genetic significance is ignored, all that remains of transitional phenomena and objects is an 'as if' capacity (closely related to Jung's transcendent function). However, all kinds of analysis require the ability to trust imagination and even to permit illusions; later on, strength is needed to bear disillusionment, disidentification and the frustrations of reality, and then to become disillusioned and disidentified depends on this capacity. Yet only if both, a person's genetic endowment as well as the developmental history, are borne in mind can we begin to understand how easily the requirements for analysis can get lost – and, how, with luck they might be restored.

Jung's preference for the method of amplification (including mythology) is in keeping with a purpose – rather than genetic- or cause-determined psycho(patho)logy. The method, so it seems to me, works and is effective as a restorative. However, it is lacking in boundaries between having hunches (intuitions) and discriminatory thoughts. The former (intuition) is essential for analysing, the latter for formulating consciously. Without being able to formulate what we stand for (our professional identity), unanalysed people cannot be expected to get to know and support us, nor can we be self-critical in a constructive way.

So what do post-Jungians stand for?

The first thing that needs to be repeated is that post-Jungians are neither homogeneous nor unanimous. In fact, they are polarised as the extreme variations in method indicate. For example, Toni Frey in Zürich prefers seeing patients once a week, while Fordham in London preferred to see them five times a week. The second thing is that no institute or school can stand alone in a tempest of administrative and political pressures. To quote from *The Tempest*: 'Misery acquaints a man with strange bed fellows.' In practical terms, this is expressed by organisations, such as that mentioned earlier, that have sprung up in places like the UK and Germany for the protection of the interests of all analysts, however different their line.

What else is there that post-Jungians and post-Freudians have in common? I have already said that in terms of optimistic analytical aims the end could, in both cases, be called to work or facilitate 'transformations', however different the methods may be. But I personally have reservations and think of this aim as utopian. Positively and all too briefly put, I would like to make a distinction that is meant purely for practical purposes.

Let one branch of the analytic tree be called therapeutic. Here I think the effect that all analytic endeavour can hope for as the result of a successful analysis, is that a central point of reference is created in the psyche of patients to which they can turn in times of need. In this respect analysis would fulfil the function that religions have fulfilled or still do; the difference being in the origin and route by which some major religions get to this centre. Let the other branch be called research. Here I would distinguish between three different approaches with a common aim. One is Jung's 'Symbols of Transformation'. In 1912, the subtitle of 'Transformations and Symbols of the Libido' was 'Contributions to the History of the Development of Thinking.' The second refers to Bion's work and revolves around the developmental aspects of how one becomes able to think by means of moderate frustrations, and with the help of a 'containing mother' who, when day-dreaming, talks to her infant and thereby gives words to his unspeakable affects. Bion was primarily concerned with clinical research; the same applied to Freud and Jung. If anything therapeutic would happen in the course of an analysis, that, however desirable, would be incidental. The two very different lines of investigation were concerned with the evolution of mankind, both as a species and as individuals. I think it is here that analysis still has a contribution to make. A third branch might be seen in the kind of statistical evidence that I mentioned at the beginning.

However, our *raison d'être* and our identity seem to me still determined by these two major branches, therapy *and* research. We are therefore in a minority *vis à vis* an establishment that looks for speedy medically and socially demonstrable results. The question is how to withstand these pressures. Our professional identity and survival depends on the answer.

There may well be an undeclared division of interests among analysts along the lines indicated that is more significant than the 'school' to which they subscribe. For instance, analysts of the therapeutic branch are subdivided into those who want to see the patient get well by criteria that insurance companies lay down, and others whose concern is with research into the development of the personality in different cultural and social settings.

Therefore I suggest that, on the whole and with the incidental help of economic pressures, our identity would best be served by a confederation of analytical schools with a measure of autonomy granted to each. I think of something like a common market with a free exchange between the different schools, yet all having their internal autonomy. It could well happen first that, in their state of anxiety and insecurity, the sectarians within each school will react with a 'fundamentalist backlash' that seeks to batten down the hatches against anything alien, each claiming to have found, if not the whole, then at least the most important part of the truth. I believe that neither the Society of Analytical Psychology, London, nor the Institut für Psychotherapie, Berlin, will take this course.

Note: Translations from works in German are by the author.

References

Elias, N. (1987) *Die Gesellschaft der Individuen*. Frankfurt/Main: Suhrkamp Verlag.

Fordham, M. (1992) Personal communication.

Frey, C.T. (1993) Personal communication.

Giegerich, W. (1987) 'Die Bodenlosigkeit der Jungschen Psychologie: Zur Frage unserer Identität als Jungianer'. In *Gorgo 12*.

Guggenbühl-Craig, A. (1988) 'How I do it'. In J. Marvin Spiegelman (ed.) *Jungian Analysts: Their Visions and Vulnerabilities*. Arizona: Falcon Press.

Jung, C. G. (1911–12) *Wandlungen und Symbole der Libido: Beiträge zur Entwicklungsgeschichte des Denkens*. Leipzig and Vienna: Franz Deuticke.

Le Bon, G. (1896) *The Crowd: A Study of the Popular Mind*. London: T. F. Unwin.

Plaut, F. (1990) 'The presence of the third: Intrusive factors in analysis'. *Journal of Analytical Psychology*, 35 (3).

Samuels, A. (1985) *Jung and the Post-Jungians*. London and Boston: Routledge and Kegan Paul.

Winnicott, D.W. (1971) *Playing and Reality*. London: Tavistock Publications, p. 89.

Yandell, J. (1977) *The Imitation of Jung*. Nashua, NH: Centrepoint Foundation, Inc.

Jung, Modernity and Postmodern Psychology

Christopher Hauke

We are in and of the moment we are attempting to analyse, in and of the structures we employ to analyse it. One might also say that this terminal self-consciousness . . . is what characterises our contemporary or 'postmodern' moment.

(Connor, 1989: 5)

Psychology and consciousness

Comparative discussions of psychoanalysis tend to place Freud centrally, so that other contributors or theories become fixed as either derived from Freud's thought, or deviating from it – or both. I find this misleading as it imposes a false evolutionary development upon psychoanalytic theorising, while simultaneously preserving Freud as the source *sui generis*. Jung falls victim to this tendency to the extent that the Jungian contribution to psychoanalytic thought has gone largely unacknowledged by the Freudian establishment, despite the opposite tendency among Jungians to acknowledge Freudian developments within a pluralistic frame that accepts the multiplicity of the psyche (Samuels, 1985; 1989; 1993).

The distinctive value of Jungian psychology becomes evident once the *difference* between Jung and Freud is acknowledged, rather than being hierarchised by viewing Jung as a deviant from the 'true path' of psychoanalysis. I agree with Malcolm Pines when he writes, 'both Adler and Jung were not so much deviationists but persons who for some years joined with Freud . . . bringing their own originality and creativity but who eventually found it necessary to follow their own paths' (Pines, 1995: 21).

In an effort to achieve scientific recognition for his new psychoanalytic theories, Freud formulated his ideas in the materialistic, mechanistic terms of the prevailing physical and biological models of his day. Jung himself was not free of these prevailing models, but being younger, with a different personality and background from Freud's, Jung was freer to formulate his psychology more along the lines of the radical thinking of his day. From the outset, Jung emphasised the fundamental *immateriality* of the psyche, so, for him, a psychology resting on materialistic biological theory alone would not do. That this is no 'deviation' is clear if we examine Jung's thought which, prior to meeting Freud, already reveals a critical attitude to the materialism of his day. In 'The Zofingia Lectures' which he delivered as a brilliant young student in 1896–7, Jung despairs of the uselessness of science with its modern, commercial and economic emphasis, 'the infinitely practical and . . . realistic trend of our age' (Jung, 1897: para. 166). Jung was sensitive to the growing realisation in society that the 'success' of scientific materialism had not made human beings any happier or more existentially at ease. In these lectures Jung reveals a radical attitude that influenced his conceptualising of the psyche and the treatment of psychological suffering in the individual, but, most importantly, did this within an analysis of the modern condition.

By the nineteenth century, the world view established by Enlightment rationalists such as Locke, Newton and Descartes, and expressed in social theory, the physical sciences and philosophy, had long prevailed – not simply as a paradigm, as we have now come to realise (Kuhn, 1962) but, illusorily, as *reality itself*. At the end of the century, there was an upheaval in European thought that undermined the 'common-sense' view of individual and social reality which had been based on the mechanics of Enlightenment science, and a revolution in consciousness began that has taken a hundred years to become established. It is now, in the late *nineteen*-nineties, that these radical challenges within the prevailing consciousness are becoming highly relevant. In the course of this chapter I hope to make clear the contribution of Jungian thought to this critique of consciousness, and to show how Jung's psychology has, from the start, been offering a radical critique of the human condition – one that now supersedes psychoanalytic attempts to claim the high ground of postmodern concerns in this field.

Pause: postmodern?

I realise it is unusual to be regarding Jungian psychology as somehow qualifying for postmodern status and, as importantly, to be regarding such postmodern thought optimistically as a positive, revaluing discourse. Let me take the second point first. There are those who regard postmodernism as roughly equivalent to nihilism. By selecting certain components – fragmentation, loss of essential beliefs or truths, surface without substance, deconstruction, loss of selfhood – and presenting these pessimistically, postmodernism is seen as an essentially negative turn in modern culture and expressive of a general malaise and decline. The psychoanalytic cultural commentator Stephen Frosh, for example, is inspired by Marshall Berman's splendid text on modernism *All That Is Solid Melts into Air* (1982), to compare the postmodern spirit unfavourably with modernism.

For Frosh there is in modernism a 'promise: not a certainty, but a chance that something more cohesive and supportive can be created' (Frosh, 1991: 31), and this he links to the hope carried within Freudian humanism that 'Psychoanalytically, there is an ego which can become infused with loving values and with an ability to form constructive and reparative object relationships, in even the most dismal of circumstances' (ibid.: 19). The promise of modernity, based largely on contemporary relations of production and consumption, has been that it will always deliver more than it will take away – in trusting this promise Frosh reveals himself, like Freud, to be linking the material world – in other words, modernity – directly to the psychological. Frosh finds a negativity in the postmodern, because

> Postmodernism emphasises the fragmented nature of contemporary experience – fragments which are exciting but also meaningless in their interchangeability and lack of significant relationships. From this perspective it is the *image* which is the most vibrant metaphor for modern reality . . . anarchistic because it offers no roots and no sources of value.
>
> (ibid.: 31)

I disagree with this view in a rather Jungian way. I believe it is Frosh's emphasis on the *ego* and its needs that keeps him and Freud in the realm of the material, and then, going along with all the material 'promises' of modernity, helps him with his optimism. In contrast, Jung's psychology has an additional, alternative focus for the individual – and also for the collective – the concept of the *self*, which is individual like ego, and yet also *other*, supra-individual and *in dialogue* with the ego. The essentialism of ego's needs immediately gets relativised in Jungian psychology. Moreover, the importance of the flow of *images*, which stem from the self and help shape ego's perception is taken in Jung's psychology not as negative and shallow but as the real expression of the psyche: 'there are things in the psyche which I do not produce, but which produce themselves and have their own life' (Jung, 1961).

I am having to sketch a view of a positive postmodernism and Jungian psychology's place in it in far too brief a fashion but it seems that the shift of focus between Freud–ego–modernism and Jung–self–postmodernism is central to the debate. I have already begun, now, on the first question which was how can Jungian psychology qualify as postmodern and what does this imply? For a start, there may well be objections to Jung's psychology on grounds of its apparent 'essentialism' and its constituting a 'meta-narrative'; in Lyotard's view it is the loss of meta-narratives and essentialisms that indicate the postmodern and especially postmodern scientific discourses (Lyotard, 1979). Lyotard is only one postmodern voice in a polyvocal movement (Connor, 1989), but let us look briefly at the 'essential' or 'meta-narrative' in Jung's psychology because in doing so I believe it is possible to see how this actually conceals and reveals postmodern qualities. Anti-essentialism in science indicates the movement from a position of claiming something to be *true* to one of emphasising *what works*; this is the attitude to psychological phenomena which Jung himself repeats time and again through his writing, and one with which post-Jungian therapists today would find no problem. Furthermore, if we examine a Jungian model of the psyche and its processes for the 'essentials' it is not the much promoted 'wholeness' and 'unity' that we find but multiplicity and plurality – of images, archetypes, complexes and subpersonalities – all in all a less hegemonic depiction of the psyche and one more sensitive to individual difference and expression than other modernist psychologies such as Watson's behaviourism, Freudian psychoanalysis, or object relations.

There are other comparisons such as the Jungian focus on the individual against the mass and mass behaviour which I would compare to Foucault's concept of heterotopia; or how the postmodern revision of power relationships placing the 'writer' and the 'reader' on more egalitarian ground compares with the Jungian emphasis on a parity between patient and analyst who are regarded as both 'in the work' of the psyche and subject to mutual, two-way influence and change. Even Jung's emphasis on religion can be viewed as comparatively postmodern and far from regressive when we find in David Harvey's analysis, 'the postmodern theological project is to reaffirm God's truth without abandoning the powers of reason' (Harvey, 1990: 41) – a point I will come back to later. But I need to leave this all too brief survey of linkages to pick up on the background to Jung's radicalism on which are based the shared roots of postmodernism and Jungian psychology.

Return: psychology and consciousness

Darwin and Freud have been viewed as seminal in overturning the rational certainties of the Enlightenment. But, upon examination, all they usurped was the artificial assumption which had been so useful in the development of modern scientific thought: that human consciousness itself could be regarded as somehow exempt and detached from the observed world. Freud's unconscious and Darwin's evolutionary theory deposed human consciousness from its privileged position – leaving a gap between consciousness and nature which could only be repaired through a new and completely different paradigm.

The healing began in a variety of fields – philosophy, physics, anthropology, psychiatry and, above all, in the new 'science' of psychology. Nietzsche's philosophy, which derived from *and* deconstructed contemporary European thought and values, formed one expression of a generally profound dissatisfaction with late nineteenth-century materialism. In doing so, it did not follow the form of its philosphical precursors, but was energetically subjective, polemical, full of emotion and desirous of *change*. We should remember that *Twilight of the Idols* was subtitled *Or How to Philosophise with a Hammer*.

German philosophy also underpinned another radical critique of the human condition which sought to destroy the old to make way for the new. In the field of political economy, Marx and Engels' deconstruction of the myth of *Kapital* exposed the 'false consciousness' which lay behind the unquestioned dominance of an exploitative style of socio-economic organisation. In the early twentieth century, it was to Marx that Freudian thinkers turned in an effort to wed a radical theory of mind to a radical theory of society within a critique which emphasised how false belief and fantasy underpinned common-sense 'reality', legitimised the *status quo* and undermined individual freedom. This project, initiated by what came to be known as the Frankfurt School, fell victim to the 'social amnesia' of conformist psychology (R. Jacoby, 1985). Since then, Freudian thought has seen its radical cultural dimension disappear beneath an overwhelming emphasis on clinical theory and the pathology of the individual. Jung's thought, however, while still keeping psychotherapy as its fulcrum, has always located psychology within its cultural manifestations.

From its beginnings in the last century, psychology has invariably taken its models from those of the physical sciences where Newtonian mechanics has prevailed. Jung's view, however, also had its roots in a subversive attitude to materialist and mechanistic thought. Apart from the paradigm shifts already mentioned, this was also being reflected in a radical new image of 'reality' arising from the theoretical physics of Einstein, Heisenberg and Bohr. The implication of the new physics, as Jung realised, was, above all, that the 'objective observer' – the lynch-pin of mechanistic classical science – could no longer be excluded from the frame of investigation. On the contrary, these discoveries confirmed how the consciousness of the human subject contributed to, and was indivisible from, all 'reality'. It is worth pointing out here how emphasis on the intersubjectivity of analyst and patient in Jungian psychotherapy contrasts with the Freudian analyst-as-observer – a position which is derived from classical science. However, it is important to note that, over the years, psychoanalysis has been developing a more intersubjective approach to analytic treatment as Jung emphasised from the outset.

The idea that psychology – a *logos* of the *psyche* (Hillman, 1995: 94) – is necessary for human consciousness arises, then, as much from a need to replace religion as a source of meaning and orientation in the world, as is often held, as from a need to replace the human subject back within the *field* of scientific investigation – and, consequently, back within the relationship between consciousness and the phenomenal world. Psychology, and for Jung, psychotherapy as a *method*, was to be *the* place where the most challenging response to modernity was forged. The importance of Jung's thought in this subversive sense is often masked by criticism of his so-called 'mysticism' and his exploration and valuing of ancient Greek and mediaeval expressions of the psyche. It is a mistake to think Jung's exploration of myth and alchemy is a Romantic regression rather than an indication of a postmodern revisioning of the human spirit in line with parallel developments in science, the arts and society. 'Mystics' tend to be those who, in every field, subvert conformity, challenge orthodoxies and herald fresh views. Such revisions in human consciousness can produce unexpected results, and throughout contemporary scientific thinking comparisons with ancient thought are becoming more and more evident and compelling (for example Capra, 1976; Peat, 1995).

Psychiatry and psychotherapy

In 'The Zofingia Lectures' Jung provides a critique of the overwhelming causal emphasis of mechanistic science, often in reference to Nietzsche's views (Jung, 1897: paras 187–8). We might speculate to what extent Nietzsche's ultimate expression of the suffering of his age through his own psychological torment may have influenced Jung choosing to investigate such universal discontent through psychiatry and psychotherapy. However, psychiatry would not have been as likely a choice for Jung had it not been for developments in the field in the late nineteenth century. Hypnotising and talking with patients diagnosed as 'hysterics' was being tried by Charcot and Breuer in Paris – with particular results that were to catch Freud's attention. In Zurich, Bleuler was one of the first to talk and listen to patients suffering from schizophrenic illness because, until the late nineteenth century, these individuals had been written off as less than human and as suffering from irreparable 'organic damage'. Bleuler, who was to be an important influence on Jung, had great success with his patient, humanistic approach which relied on an emotionally empathic attempt to understand the *meaning* in his patients' utterances.

Jung's own empathic approach to these patients not only increased his understanding, but also led to him developing a means for communicating with individuals who had been hitherto unreachable. Jung's *method* of psychotherapy, which places emphasis on the unconscious exchange between analyst and patient, not only values the particular form of empathic intuition that analysts call the countertransference, but also confirms the *non-material* nature of the psyche – operating outside classical mechanisms of cause and effect. This has led to much speculation around the 'quantum nature' of mind (Field, 1991; Zohar and Marshall, 1993), while, more practically, it is only relatively recently that Freudian psychoanalysis has valued empathy as a viable, if not a royal, road to the unconscious. This area of threorising as developed by Kohut (1971; 1977) still remains marginal to the psychoanalytic mainstream, while Jungians have made links and seen the value in Kohut's self psychology (see M. Jacoby, 1990; Hauke, 1995; Homans, 1979).

Analogies between the condition of modernity and of schizophrenic illness and its treatment were being made long before the critical formulations of Foucault and R.D. Laing. In *The Discovery of the Unconscious* Ellenberger notes how Bleuler's views on schizophrenia are comparable to Schlegel's philosophical theory where he states that, 'man is severed from communication with God, Nature and the universe because he is split within himself between reason, will, and fantasy, and that it is the task of philosophy to reestablish harmony within man' (Ellenberger, 1970: 288). This, of course, was the problem with modernity that Jung sought to heal through analytical psychology both as a theory and as a method. Jung's early experiences in psychiatry were to become the ground for his theory of the collective unconscious. The 'insane' were expressing themselves, rather like dreams do, outside the narrow restriction imposed by a consciousness dominated by instrumental rationality. In seeking to understand and give meaning to his patients' utterances, Jung began to discover images and symbols that did not seem to emanate from the personal unconscious as conceived within psychoanalysis. The psyche seemed to deliver up symbols and images that indicated a universal substratum to the unconscious: an aspect of psyche shared by all – the common ground of our psychologically shared humanity. In this insight lies the clue as to why psychotherapy and the attitude of analytical psychology may be so vital for the crisis of meaning in modern mankind. In former times, religion and ritual had served to carry the symbolic life which the psyche needs – not only for the individual to experience his or her existence as meaningful, but also to provide a sense of connectedness to the world: 'The applause of the heart before the approbation of reason' as Battye quotes (1995). Instrumental rationality and the mechanistic perspective, while advancing human progress in control and exploitation of the natural world, had robbed mankind and cut off that sense of connection through an artifice – the creation of consciousness as the detached observer. This has provoked a crisis for modernity that is psychological and cultural as much as it is spiritual. As Jung intuited, 'Mankind is hanging by a thread – and that thread is the psyche of man' (1961) – a warning that has been especially heeded by post-Jungian writers.

For Jung and many post-Jungians nowadays, psychological illness is viewed, in a broad sense, as arising as much from this modern crisis of the soul, that we all share, as from individual circumstances. But while Freud felt the best psychoanalysis could offer was to restore to the neurotic individual 'common unhappiness' in place of 'neurotic misery', Jungian psychology has the goal of healing through promoting the individuation of each sufferer and thereby contributing to the healing of the culture. For

Jung, the common unhappiness is not of *the* human condition but of the *specific* condition of modernity. Because of this focus on a crisis of meaning in those he treated, it is not surprising to find that much of Jung's practice involved the treatment of those suffering a 'mid-life crisis' – the moment when, after much has been accomplished through the consolidated efforts of the ego, the hollowness of life may be experienced for the first time. However, I think it is true to say that, in recent decades, this hollowness and dissatisfaction has been experienced by many not only at mid-life, but at an increasingly younger age. It is as if consciousness itself is experiencing a mid-life crisis, forcing us collectively to take stock of where we are heading.

The synthesis of Jungian and post-Freudian theory in recent years has provided many Jungians with the flexibility to offer a more comprehensive treatment according to the varied needs of their patients. But along with this has been a tendency to produce a model which prioritises the early environment and the mother–infant relationship, so that Jung's distinctively non-material and symbolic emphasis within psychology gets blurred. From this arises the risk of losing what, I believe, are the creative possibilities in Jung's approach for a radical critique of modernity. So far, psychoanalysis has failed in its attempt to provide a critique of modern culture as the essentialist and ahistorical assumptions within object relations theory demonstrate (see Samuels, 1993: 267–86; Gordon, 1993).

Psychology and culture

Although it takes only a minimal amount of reflection to realise that a theory of the conscious and unconscious mind must necessarily coincide with a theory of human culture, there has been considerable resistance to an awareness of this in mainstream psychoanalysis since the demise of the Frankfurt School's project. An exception to this is how the development of structural linguistics in France – away from the logical positivism of Britain and Germany – led a French psychoanalyst, Jacques Lacan, to begin to restore a cultural dimension to psychoanalytic theory. For example, for Lacan, the Oedipus complex becomes not simply the exclusion of the child from the mother–infant dyad and parental couple which is thought by Freudians to be crucial for developing individuality, but more a depiction of the beginnings of the *enculturated individual* – that is, the entry into, and the reproduction of, *culture itself* repeated in the development of each human being. Moreover, as it is the Father and the Law of the Father that typifies this moment, feminist theorists and psychoanalysts have found in it a theory of patriarchy (see Mitchell, 1975). We owe much to feminist theory and to Lacan for restoring this cultural dimension to psychoanalysis which other theoretical spin-offs ignore.

Jung's model of the mind has emphasised a cultural dimension from the outset and is distinctive in the way it can account for both individual and collective phenomena within the one psyche. In addition to a personal unconscious, Jung proposes the archetypes of the collective unconscious as structuring elements in the psyche which serve to render our experience of, and expression in, the world as distinctively and universally human. Specifically, archetypes function in the form of image, emotion, behaviour, ritual and belief – in other words the symbolic universe in which human consciousness lives and expresses its individual and collective being. Ultimately it is a theory of how the potentiality of all perceivable phenomena is registered within us as the contents of the particular human consciousness we all share despite our great differences; this is a theory which acknowledges and celebrates plurality, the individual and cultural *diversity* across peoples and history, in a positive postmodern fashion.

Jung's archetypal theory of mind goes further, however, than simply healing the artificial split between the 'individual' and the 'collective'. Within the theory of archetypes Jung goes for the geological ground of the fundamental fault on which modernity bases its achievements – the split between Matter and Mind, as formulated within the philosophy of the Enlightenment. Much like the 'form-giving cause' of mediaeval thought and Plato before this, the archetype is a structuring principle that at one end of its continuum manifests as matter, and at the other end, as mind. This aspect of archetypal theory, which Jung began to explore in his theory of synchronicity, brings us back to the links between Jungian thought and quantum physics mentioned earlier (cf. Card, 1991).

Although the concept of archetypes has a long history, Jung's intuitive grasp of this principle of consciousness and reality seems to be more and more in line with current ideas in biology, genetics, neuroscience and linguistics (Stevens, 1995). At the socio-political level of psyche, Andrew Samuels finds in the use of the transference/countertransference in Jungian analysis the tools with which we may also humanise our political lives within the context of a 'resacralisation of culture' (Samuels, 1993).

The postmodern spirit of not only valuing subjectivity but also deconstructing beliefs previously held as fundamentals, becomes most relevant once the extent of social construction and the 'givenness' of the commonsense view is fully realised. Previously, for Marx and Freud, *illusion*, or *fantasy*, were key concepts in understanding the profound unsatisfactoriness of modern life. But with Jung comes the insight that it is *modern consciousness that is the dis-ease* and not simply 'civilisation' and its discontents such as repressed sexuality or exploitative economic behaviour. And just as it has taken relativity theory and quantum science to shake us out of our Newtonian 'common-sense' assumptions about reality, so too does Jung's analytical psychology offer a theory and method to treat the subjective reality of the modern soul.

To a certain degree, all psychotherapies deconstruct consciousness to allow scope for choice and change in the individual's relationship with their inner and outer worlds. In the absence of traditional forms, beliefs and ritual, it is to the inner dialogue of the psyche that the individual has to turn for meaning. In Jungian analysis and psychotherapy, modern consciousness is healed by being nourished at the breast of the symbolic life-source which is contained in the unconscious and rediscovered in dreams, fantasies and symptoms – 'the pandaemonium of images – Jung's contribution to *Know Thyself*' (Hillman, 1983).

This image of nourishment and healing has a symbolic meaning that goes deeper than might at first be noticed. On first impressions, much of contemporary psychotherapy and psychoanalytic practice, with its emphasis on the treatment of individual pathology within a personal, causal and reductive frame, appears to be removed from broader cultural relevance. But if we view the phenomena of modern psychotherapy through Jungian lenses, the emphasis on the child, the infant and feeding metaphors may turn out to be informative about the crisis of psyche in late modernity, and about the hidden significance of psychotherapy as a cultural theory and a cultural healing. For example, the rise in empathy for the infant and the child since the end of World War Two may, in fact, be another way of expressing empathy for the suffering of modern humanity in general. This may also indicate a sense of the dependency and vulnerability – qualities which tend to be attributed to the 'child' – felt by many in these times. As each technological advance brings a new crisis – global warming, for example – we confront a universe found to be increasingly perplexing and uncontrollable in a way the Enlightenment rationality, with something of the certainty of adolescence, believed it had overcome for ever. The focus on *attachment* and *loss* may be reminding us how human consciousness, despite its achievements, can never be outside, or separated from Nature – the Great Mother herself. 'Feeding' and 'breast' then become symbolic of the modern ego needing to replenish itself not from the personal mother but from the self – psyche's source and the nourishment for consciousness. As Jung describes in 'The Psychology of the Child Archetype', the attention given to the historical child, both in contemporary psychotherapy and modern culture as a whole, is best understood as our deep concern for the historical roots of consciousness itself (Jung, 1951).

By addressing the crisis of culture and modern consciousness on several levels – the nature of matter and mind, the relationship between external 'reality' and psychological 'reality', or the problem of the individual and the mass – Jungian psychology provides a postmodern critique which is not only capable of healing the individual psyche through its therapeutic method, but, of equal importance, is also capable of contributing to the transformation of consciousness so urgently called for throughout modern culture.

References

Battye, N. (1995) *The Sublime*, Proceedings of the 13th Jung Studies Day. Centre for Psychoanalytic Studies, University of Kent.
Berman, M. (1982) *All That Is Solid Melts into Air*, London: Verso.
Bohm, D. (1980) *Wholeness and the Implicate Order*, London: Ark.
Capra, F. (1976) *The Tao of Physics*, London: Fontana.
Card, C.R. (1991) 'The archetypal view of Jung and Pauli', in *Psychological Perspectives*, 24 (Spring–Summer).
Connor, Steven (1989) *Postmodernist Culture*, Oxford: Blackwell.
Ellenberger, H.F. (1970) *The Discovery of the Unconscious*, London: Fontana.
Field, N. (1991) 'Projective identification: Mechanism or mystery?' *Journal of Analytical Psychology*, 36 (1).
Frosh, S. (1991) *Identity Crisis: Modernity, Psychoanalysis and the Self*, London: Macmillan.
Gordon, P. (1993) 'Souls in armour: Thoughts on psychoanalysis and racism', *British Journal of Psychotherapy*, 10 (1) (Autumn).
Harvey, David (1990) *The Condition of Postmodernity*, Oxford: Blackwell.
Hauke, C.C. (1995) 'Fragmentation and narcissism: A revaluation', in *Journal of Analytical Psychology*, 40 (4) (October).
Hillman, J. (1983/1995) *Healing Fiction*, Woodstock, CT: Spring.
Homans, P. (1979) *Jung in Context: Modernity and the Making of a Psychology*, London and Chicago: University of Chicago Press.
Jacoby, Mario (1990) *Individuation and Narcissism: The Psychology of Self in Jung and Kohut*, London: Routledge.
Jacoby, Russell (1985) 'Remembering Social Amnesia', Pilot Issue, *Radical Science* 15.
Jung, C.G. (1897) 'The Zofingia Lectures', *Collected Works*, supplementary vol. A.
—— (1951) 'The Psychology of the Child Archetype', *Collected Works* 9. i.
—— (1961) 'Face to Face', BBC filmed interview.
Kohut, H. (1971) *The Analysis of the Self*, New York: International Universities Press.
—— (1977) *The Restoration of the Self*, New York: International Universities Press.
Kuhn, T. (1962/1970) *The Structure of Scientific Revolutions*, Chicago: Chicago University Press.
Lyotard, Jean-François (1979) *The Postmodern Condition: A Report on Knowledge*, trans. (1984) G. Bennington and B. Massumi, Manchester: Manchester University Press.
Mitchell, J. (1975) *Psychoanalyis and Feminism*, Harmondsworth: Penguin.
Peat, F. David (1995) *Blackfoot Physics*, London: Fourth Estate.
Pines, M. (1995) 'Dissent in context: Schisms in the Psychoanalytic Movement', in *Bulletin of the Centre for Psychoanalytic Studies*, University of Kent.

Samuels, A. (1985) *Jung and the Post-Jungians*, London: Routledge.
—— (1989) *The Plural Psyche: Personality, Morality and the Father*, London: Routledge.
—— (1993) *The Political Psyche*, London: Routledge.
Stevens, A. (1995) 'Jungian psychology: the body and the future', in *Journal of Analytic Psychology*, 40 (3) (July).
Zohar, D. & Marshall, I. (1993) *The Quantum Society*, London: Bloomsbury.

Subject index

mass communication 261; *see also*
collective
materialism, critique of 287–94
maternal *see* mother
maturity, level of *see* development *and*
individuation
meaning: dreams 138–40, 143; fairy tale
212–19, 222; interpersonal 66; loss of
272, 289; search for 29, 30, 66, 121,
136, 160, 168, 186, 193, 204, 234,
249, 267, 292, 293, 294; *see also*
understanding
mechanistic perspective 287–94
memory: false 119; historical 237;
unconscious 256
mental illness *see* specific illness e.g.
depression; *see also* pathology
merging *see* fusion
metaphor 183, 192, 220, 229, 242, 263,
289; feeding 296; slimming down
255–65
mid-life crisis 261, 294
mind-body: integration 32; separation
32
mind-matter relationship 29–30, 44–54,
177, 295, 296
mirroring, narcissistic 280
misery, neurotic 293
mobility, and security 270, 271
modernism 288, 289
modernity 287–98, crisis of 253, 266,
267, 270, 271, 273, 274, 293, 295,
296; critique of 294
monetarism 253, 255; *see also* economy
mood 185, 186, 193, 232; *see also*
emotion
Mortificatio 166
mother archetype 133, 137, 146, 149,
150, 183, 188, 217, 226, 231
mother: good enough 77, 188, 191; role
194, 258; *see also* relationship,
mother-baby
mountain archetypal image 140
mourning 144, 222
mysterium tremendum 168
mystery: awareness of 259, 267; of birth/
death 211; pagan 137; of religion 168,
171; of transformation 136
mysticism, Jungian 292
myths 14, 76, 93, 161–2, 183, 193–4,
200, 203, 205, 209, 211–13, 241–2,
284, 292; archetypes 209, 211, 219;

Celtic 201; contemporary 239; in
dream amplification 139; evolution
of 264; Gnostic 163; of Janus 105,
111–12, 115–16; monetarist 258

narcissism 67, 120, 123, 260, 269, 280
narrative skills *see* storytelling
nature, links with 296
needs: analysand 224; developmental
214; ego 289; infantile 154
neighbourhood *see* community
neurosis 125, 293; transference 122; *see
also* anxiety *and* depression
nigredo 59, 190
norms, social 268
'not-me' possessions 77, 284; *see also* I/
not-I

object: analytic 70; combined 15; part
14–15, 76, 226, 247; reality 13; self
13–14, 37, 39, 40, 64, 77, 121;
transitional 284; whole 14–15, 76,
227; *see also* wholeness
object relations theory 57–8, 63, 64,
121–2, 237, 284, 290, 294
objectivity, valuing 184
observation, and participation 267,
273, 278, 291
obsessional rituals 191, 192
obsessive-compulsive disorders 247,
260
oedipal complex 186, 206, 215, 294
oneness, need for 27, 36, 37, 38; *see also*
individuality *and* wholeness
opposites 226, 256, 260; conflict of 69,
165, 171, 173; creative potential of 3;
dreams 175; fragmentation of 174;
meeting of 125, 151, 212; power of
183; reconciliation of 227; theory of
157; tolerance of 2; transcendence of
11, 27, 109; union of 45, 53, 58, 149,
174, 190, 202, 269; working with 143;
see also transcendent function
opus, alchemic 159, 161, 165, 166, 178
otherness 33, 201, 202, 205; denial of
67; reaction to 69; recognition of 67
otherworld, unconscious 181, 201–3
out-of-body experiences 31
outer: attitude *see* persona; world 296

pagan mysteries 137
pain, inner 143, 150, 151, 152, 194, 225

Name index

Addenbrooke, M. 85, 98–103
Adler, G. 1, 2, 287
Alister, I. 229, 231–40
Andrew, case study 172
Ann, case study 223–5, 227
Anna, case study 173, 174
Annette, case study 186, 187–9, 190, 192, 194
Anzieu, D. 37, 39
Association of Jungian Analysts (AJA) 1, 2
Astor, J. 5, 7–16, 23, 25, 44
Aveline, M. 120

Bachelard, G. 255
Baldwin, J.M. 65
Balter, L. and S. 61
Battye, N. 293
Beatrice 203, 204
Beebe, B. 64
Beebe, J. 200
Bell, C. 243
Belotti, E.G. 192, 196
Ben, case study 189–91, 192, 193
Benjamin, J. 63, 64
Berger, J. 220
Berman, M. 288, 289
Bettelheim, B. 209, 214, 215, 220
Binswanger, L.H. 61
Bion, W.R. 18, 24, 45, 58, 62, 67, 82, 124, 129, 148, 149, 237, 253, 259, 262, 263, 285
Bleuler, E. 292, 293
Bloch, E. 214
Bohr, N.H.D. 266, 291
Bollas, C. 74
Bowlby, E.J.M. 195, 220
Boyer, L.B. 61
Bratherton, W.J. 181, 183–97

Brenda, case study 174
Breuer, J. 292
British Association of Psychotherapists (BAP) 1
British Confederation of Psychotherapists 277
British Psychoanalytic Institute 58
Britten, C. 105, 119–28
Brown, G.N. 105, 119–28
Bruhl, L. 278
Bunster, J. 79, 80
Byng-Hall, J. 263

Capra, F. 292
Carette, J. 200
Caroline, case study 172, 173, 174
Charcot, J.M. 292
Clark, K. 248
Clark, M. 157, 170–9
Coleridge, S.T. 248
Colman, A. 238
Colman, W. 181, 198–207
Coltart, N. 107, 109, 116, 237
Connor, S. 287, 289
Cotter, J. 177
Covington, C. 193
Crowther, C. 209
Cwik, A.J. 154

Daniel 142
Dante 203
Darwin, C. 290
David, case study 176
Davidson, D. 147
Davies, M. 191
Descartes, R. 288
Dieckmann, H. 209, 214, 221, 227
Dietrich, Marlene 202
Dourley, J.P. 176